Gustav Adolf Zimmermann

The Theories of Darwin and Their Relation to Philosophy, Religion, and Morality

Outlook

Gustav Adolf Zimmermann

The Theories of Darwin and Their Relation to Philosophy, Religion, and Morality

1. Auflage | ISBN: 978-3-73261-748-7

Erscheinungsort: Paderborn, Deutschland

Erscheinungsjahr: 2018

Outlook Verlag GmbH, Paderborn.

Reproduction of the original.

THE THEORIES OF DARWIN.

H<small>ALL</small>, S<small>TUTTGART</small>, April 5, 1880.

We hereby authorize the Rev. Dr. G. A. Zimmermann to translate into English the book entitled

Die Darwin'schen Theorien und ihre Stellung zur Philosophie, Religion und Moral von Rudolf Schmid.

We declare that we know of no other translation of the said book and that Dr. Zimmermann's translation will be the only one authorized by us for the United States as well as for the British Empire and its Dominions.

(*The Author*) R<small>UDOLF</small> S<small>CHMID</small>.

(*The Publisher*) P<small>AUL</small> M<small>OSER</small>.

THE
THEORIES OF DARWIN

AND THEIR RELATION TO
PHILOSOPHY, RELIGION AND MORALITY.
By RUDOLF SCHMID,

President of the Theological Seminary at Schönthal, Würtemberg.

TRANSLATED FROM THE GERMAN

By G. A. ZIMMERMANN, P<small>H</small>.D.

W<small>ITH AN</small> I<small>NTRODUCTION BY</small>

THE DUKE OF ARGYLL

CHICAGO:
JANSEN McCLURG. & COMPANY
1883.

Copyright
By Jansen, McClurg & Co.
A.D. 1882.
R. R. DONNELLEY & SONS, PRINTERS.

AUTHOR'S PREFACE

The movement which received its impulse as well as its name from Darwin, seems to have recently passed its distinctest phase; but the more prominent points of opposition, religious, ethical, and scientific, which have been revealed through it, remain as sharply contrasted as before. The author of this book desires, in the first place, to be of service to such readers as feel the need of setting themselves right upon these questions, which touch the highest interests of mankind, but who lack time and opportunity to investigate independently a realm in which so many and so heterogeneous sciences come into mutual contact. The illogical and confused manner in which some noisy leaders confound these sciences and their problems and consequences, renders it still more difficult to arrive at a satisfactory result; and thus perhaps many readers will look with interest upon an investigation designed to simplify the different problems and the different attempts at their solution, and to treat them not only in their relations to each other, but also separately. But with this primary object, the author combines another: to render a service to some among the many who perceive the harmony between their scientific conviction and their religious need threatened or shaken by the results of science, and who are unwilling to lose this harmony, or, having lost it, desire to regain it. Those voices are indeed becoming louder, and more generally and willingly heard, which proclaim an irreconcilability between faith and knowledge, between the religious and the scientific views of the world; which declare that peace between the two can only be had at the price either of permitting the religious impulses of the heart to be stifled in favor of science, of satisfying the religious need of the mind with a nourishment which in the light of science proves to be an illusion, or, as sceptics in theory and eclectics in practice, of renouncing with resignation a logical connection and foundation to their former view of the world. The most striking proof of the extent to which these voices are heard, is the fact that it has been possible for a one-sided pessimism to become the fashionable system of philosophy in a Christian nation. The most effective means for opposing such discordant voices, and for making amends for the disagreements which they have occasioned, undoubtedly consists in the actual proof of the contrary of their theories, in the clear presentation of a standpoint from which not only the most unrestricted freedom of investigation and the most unreserved acknowledgment of its results shall be in perfect harmony with the undiminished care of our entire religious possession, but in which this peace is preserved and forever established by the very fact that one function of the mind directly requires the other, one possession directly guarantees the other. This is the standpoint of the author, and from it he has endeavored to treat all the questions which are to be taken into consideration. Should he, by his exposition of this standpoint, succeed in helping even a few readers in reaching the conviction of the actual harmony between the scientific, religious, and ethical acquisitions of mankind, or in confirming them anew in such conviction, he would find himself amply rewarded for this first extended venture before the public.

R. S.

AUTHOR'S PREFACE TO AMERICAN EDITION.

Six years have elapsed since I wrote the book which is now going forth in English dress. The great leader of the theories in question has passed away; the waves of thought he set in motion are assuming smoother shape; and I can only add to what I have already written, that not only have I had no occasion to retract any of the statements or views laid down in the book, but I perceive the religious as well as the scientific world growing more and more into accord with the views I have maintained, and which were at first so vehemently opposed.

I owe so much to the literary men of the English tongue on both sides of the Atlantic, that I shall be glad if, through the devoted labors of the translator, I am enabled to pay them a tribute of gratitude by aiding them in clearing the way for thought in these much disputed fields, or in reconciling in their minds the conflict between faith and science.

R. S.

Schönthal, Würtemberg, *September*, 1882.

INTRODUCTION TO AMERICAN EDITION,

BY THE DUKE OF ARGYLL.

It is well known that Mr. Darwin's theory on the Origin of Species has been accepted in Germany more widely, with more absolute faith, and with more vehement enthusiasm, than in the country of its birth. In Germany, more conspicuously than elsewhere, it has itself become the subject of developments as strange and as aberrant as any which it assumes in the history of Organic Life. The most extravagant conclusions have been drawn from it—invading every branch of human thought, in Science, in Philosophy, and in Religion. These conclusions have been preached, too, with a dogmatism as angry and as intolerant as any of the old theologies. It is the fate of every idea which is new and fruitful, that it is ridden to the death by excited novices. We can not be surprised if this fate has overtaken the idea that all existing animal forms have had their ancestry in other forms which exist no longer, and have been derived from these by ordinary generation through countless stages of descent. Although this is an idea which, whether true or not, is entirely subordinate to the larger idea of creation, it usurps in many minds the character of a substitute. This is natural enough. The theory, or at least the language, of Evolutionists, puts forward a visible order of phenomena as a complete and all-sufficient account of its own origin and cause. However unsatisfactory this may be to the higher faculties of the mind, it is eminently satisfactory to those other faculties which are lower in the scale. It dismisses as needless, or it postpones indefinitely, all thought of the agencies which are ultimate and unseen. Just as in the physical world, some trivial object which is very near us may shut out the whole of a wide horizon, so in the intellectual world, some coarse mechanical conception may shut out all the kingdom of Nature and the glory of it.

Two great subjects of investigation lie before us. The first is to ascertain how far the Theory of Evolution represents an universal fact, or only one very partial and fragmentary aspect of a great variety of facts connected with the origin and development of Organic Life. The second and by far the most important inquiry, is to estimate aright, or as nearly as we can, the relative place and importance of these facts in the Philosophy of Nature.

Subjects of investigation so rich and manifold as these may well attract all the most varied gifts of the human mind. This they have already done, and there is every indication that they will continue to do so for generations yet to be. Already an immense literature is devoted to them; and every fresh effort of observation and of reasoning seems to open out new and fruitful avenues of thought. The work which is here introduced to the English reader contains an excellent review of this literature, so far as it is represented in the English and German languages. Knowing the author personally, as I have done for many years, I recognize with pleasure in his work all the carefulness of inquiry, and all the conscientiousness of reasoning, which belong to a singularly candid and patient mind.

ARGYLL.

INVERARY CASTLE, SCOTLAND,

September, 1882.

NOTE BY THE TRANSLATOR.

The consideration which this work has received from the leaders of religious and philosophic thought in Germany, and, indeed, wherever it has been read in its original form, has led the translator to believe that an English version of it would be acceptable. Especially in America, where religious problems and religious thought are so intimately connected with the processes of scientific and philosophic investigation, and where the agitation of these problems is so peculiarly active and violent, it has seemed that a work marked by so much scholarship, profundity, and comprehensiveness and originality of treatment, must serve an important purpose to the cause of religious no less than of scientific truth. It may be explained here, that the author resided for some years in the family of the Duke of Argyll, and there breathed, to a certain extent, the scientific air of Darwinism in its very origin; and thus his familiarity with all the results of modern scientific research, added to his theological and philosophical acquirements, enable him, with a most admirable blending of the spirit of fairness and toleration with logical severity of treatment, to bring these different domains into their proper relation with each other and to establish between them that essential harmony in which consists the solution of these most profound and vital problems of man's welfare.

Of the translation it may properly be said that, while the aim has been to give the work the clearest possible form consistent with that strict fidelity to the original which is especially demanded by the character of its material, the translator has not hoped to make the work altogether "easy" reading. Peculiarities of the author's style have been, it is believed, largely preserved; and occasional difficulties of apprehension are no doubt to be expected, both from the method of treatment and from the profound and abstruse character of the topics treated. The translator will be well satisfied if it shall be found that he has succeeded in performing his task without adding unduly to the seeming obscurities of certain passages—obscurities which, however, will no doubt vanish before that degree of mental application without which such works may not be read at all intelligibly.

Acknowledgments are properly due and are gladly rendered to George C. Dawson, Esq., of Chicago, and to Mr. Francis F. Browne, editor of *The Dial*, for valuable assistance in revising and perfecting this version.

G. A. Z.

CHICAGO, *October*, 1882.

THE THEORIES OF DARWIN,

AND THEIR RELATION TO

PHILOSOPHY, RELIGION, AND MORALITY.

INTRODUCTION.

With the appearance of Darwin's "Origin of Species," on the 24th of November, 1859, a new impulse began in the intellectual movement of our generation. It is true, the whole theory advocated and inaugurated by Darwin is, in the first place, only one of the many links in the long chain of phenomena in the realm of the intellectual development of our century, all of which have the same character, and give their stamp to the entire mental work of the last decades. This stamp consists in the tendency of science, which has nearly become universal, not only to consider all phenomena, both of the physical and the mental life, in connection with their preceding conditions in space and time, but to trace them back more or less exclusively to these conditions, and to explain them exclusively by means of the same. What a Wilhelm von Humboldt, and, still more, a Jacob Grimm, prepared the way for in the realm of philology, a Lazar Geiger and a Steinthal, and (under direct influence of Darwin) a Schleicher and a Wilhelm Bleek further developed; what Julius Braun did in the realm of the history of art; what a Buckle and a Sir John Lubbock tried to do in the realm of the history of civilization; what a Max Müller did in the realm of the history of religion; what the Tübingen School began and its disciples carried out in the realm of the exegesis of the Bible; what a Strauss and a Renan, and in a certain sense also a Keim, did in the realm of christology; what, finally—without being so closely connected with individual names—was also done in the realm of the world's history: this, Darwin did in the realm of the history of the organic kingdoms, seconded by the geological principles of Sir Charles Lyell and by the investigations in biology and comparative anatomy of a number of scientists. From this point of view, the movement which was inaugurated by Darwin seems to us but the reflex of the universal spirit of the present time upon a particular realm; namely, that of natural science. But since, soon after the appearance of the before-mentioned work and long before the publication of Darwin's "Descent of Man," man also was included in the consequences of the evolution theory, and his existence was explained as a wholly natural development out of lower animal forms; since Darwin himself unreservedly adopted this theory of the descent of man from the animal world as an entirely natural consequence of his doctrine of the origin of species, the evolution question has gone far beyond the proportionately narrow and limited bounds of natural philosophy and of merely theoretical scientific interest—has surpassed in interest all the before-mentioned investigations, however lively this interest was and is to-day, and has stirred up the minds of all most thoroughly, not only in their scientific but also in their religious and ethical depths, some in acknowledgment and admiration, others in aversion and repugnance, and only a few in sober and unprejudiced judgment. While some see in Darwinism the flambeau which now lights mankind to entirely new paths of truth, and also to spiritual and moral perfection, others see in it only an unproved hypothesis, threatening to become the torch which might change the noblest and greatest acquirements of the culture of past centuries into a heap of ashes; while some date from it a new period of culture, others see in it a deep descent of the present from the scientific, religious, and moral height which mankind has ascended.

Under these circumstances, it has become an impossibility for religion and the moral interest as guardians of the highest and most sacred acquisitions of mankind, and still more for theology and ethics as the scientific representations of religion and morality, to remain idle spectators. It would certainly be more agreeable to them, and more profitable, if they could delay their judgment until the question became better cleared up. For the whole question presented by Darwin has not yet passed beyond the stage of problems and attempts at solution; and there is always something unsatisfactory in being compelled to deal with theories which in their fundamentals are still hypotheses. But since all tendencies of the present which are hostile to Christianity and to the theistic view of the world, from the most extreme materialism up to the most sublime monism (as pantheism and materialism of to-day have begun to call themselves), seemingly with the confidence of complete victory, take possession of Darwinism as the solid ground from which they hope to destroy all and every belief connected with faith in a living creator and master of the world, it has also become impossible for those to whom the religious and ethical acquisitions of mankind are a sacred sanctuary to take any longer a reserved and expectant position. Silence now would be looked upon only as an inglorious retreat; and thus nothing remains but openly to face the question: What position must religion and morality take in reference to the Darwinian theories?

In order to treat of the question with that objectivity which it requires, we have to begin with a synopsis of the theories themselves. In this representation we have to discriminate strictly between the merely scientific theories and the naturo-philosophical and metaphysical supplements and conclusions which have been brought into connection with them. For precisely in the mixing of the most different problems which are to be considered here, lies the main cause of the confused and superficial judgment which is so often heard upon these questions.

PART I.

THE THEORIES OF DARWIN.

BOOK I.

THE PURELY SCIENTIFIC THEORIES.

THE SCIENTIFIC PROBLEM.

The interesting problem which underlies Mr. Darwin's theories is the answer to the question: *How did the different species of organic beings on the earth originate?* We find ourselves in the midst of an endless variety of organic beings, animals and plants; we see ourselves, so far as regards the entire physical part of our being, in relationship with this organic world—especially with the organization and physical functions of the animal body. The organic individuals come and go. They originate by being begotten by and born of individuals of the same kind, or they spring up through the formation of germs and buds; and they produce in the same way new individuals, that resemble them in all essential characteristics. Like always begets like, so far as our observations go. But not only the individuals, but even the species to which they belong, must have originated at some definite period of time— and, indeed, as geology tells us, not all at once, but in a long series, which stretched through immeasurable epochs of the earth's history. Thus we come face to face with the question, already put, which we can now formulate more precisely: *How did the first individuals of each organic species come into existence?*

No human being ever has observed, nor ever could observe, the origination of a new species, because man, as it seems, did not appear on the earth until all the other organisms were in existence. For this reason, the scientists for a long time thought it unprofitable to occupy themselves with this question; and even in our time a great many of them declare the question to be absolutely insolvable, and every attempt at answering it to be an unjustifiable use of hypotheses. But the impulse toward investigation admits of no limitation so long as there is any probability of extending its field of action. Especially in the province of nature, so many things which could not be discovered by mere observation have been traced indirectly, and so many important and established facts have been added to our stores of knowledge, by first starting from hypothetical premises, that man has again and again endeavored to approximate an answer to the question of the origin of species by taking the indirect course of hypothesis and induction, whenever the direct way of observation did not lead to any result. Religion of course gives a solution to the problem by stating that the species have been originated by the creative act of God. It is wrong to say that this solution is opposed to the above-mentioned impulse toward investigation; for this solution suffices for religion, whether a natural progress in the origination of species be established or not. For, to the believer in religion, the whole universe, with all its objective phenomena and growth, is the work of God as well as the individuals of the already existing species; and a closer acquaintance with the manner of their origin is not only no disturbance to his ground of belief, but, on the contrary, an addition to his knowledge of the method of God's action. In every man of sound mind, the religious faith is not antagonistic or even indifferent to the scientific impulse toward investigation, but stands upon a most intimate footing with it. Hence the human intellect again and again makes the attempt to find an answer to the problem of the origin of species in a scientific way, and each endeavor of this kind necessarily ends with the dilemma that either the first individuals of a species, no matter whether it be the highest or the lowest, have been evolved out of inorganic matter, or they originated by descent from the most closely related species of their predecessors. The denial of the first part of our dilemma, and the affirmation of the second, is the "Theory of Descent."

But this theory of descent leads us at once into another dilemma. If the species originated by descent from the most closely related lower species, and under certain circumstances also from species of the same rank, and even by degeneration from the next higher, it must have occurred in one of two ways: either by leaps—called by naturalists "metamorphosis of germs" or "heterogenetic conception"—or by a succession of imperceptibly small alterations of the individuals from generation to generation. Each of these changes would have been no greater than the differences we observe to-day between the individuals of the very same species, but became in the course of time so massed and strengthened in one direction that new species have been evolved. This hypothesis is called the "Theory of Development," or "Evolution." We retain this name, although well aware of the fact that the authors do not agree in their use of the term "evolution." Professor Wigand, who adopts only the theory of a descent from one primordial cell to another, and who positively rejects the idea of a progress from one fully developed species to another, claims among other things that one value of his own theory is that he secures for the idea of evolution its full meaning. The expression still has a meaning for those who reject the real descent of the species or their primordial germs one from another, and acknowledge only the ideal bond of a common plan in their successive manifestations. But as soon as we examine more closely the literal and logical meaning of the word, we shall find it of most weight when we understand by it the before-mentioned gradual evolution in opposition to the theory of progress by leaps or new creations.

Moreover, it is well known that long before this no other term than evolution was used to designate the growth of a single organic individual from the primordial cell and egg to its fully developed form and vital function. Besides, we find ourselves also in harmony with most of the authors, so far as they have distinct conceptions of the different scientific problems, if we use the term "theory of evolution" for the gradual development of one species from another, in opposition to the hypothesis of a metamorphosis of germs, or even of a genealogy of primordial cells.

But each evolution theory leads again to new theories, as soon as it has to be proved in a scientific way. For it can claim a scientific worth only when sustained by earnest attempts to find and prove the productive power, agencies and laws of such an evolution of species. Those attempts can be made in various ways. As a philosophical question, many attempts at solution have been made, both in ancient and modern times; but being mainly in the realm of metaphysics, they do not come within the limits of our scientific essay. As a question for investigators of natural phenomena, only two attempts of sufficient importance to be mentioned have been made. The first one was made by Lamarck, who, taking the really different ideas of descent and evolution as one, made use of the hypothesis of transmutation; thus becoming the pioneer of Darwinism. The other attempt was made by Darwin in his theory of natural selection, or struggle, for existence, and is called the "Theory of Selection."

In defining our problem, therefore, we find ourselves under the influence of a scientific law of development. The simple problem which we started from has developed into a trinity of problems and attempts at solution. The simple question of the origin of species led us into the dilemma of a *generatio æquivoca*, or a descent; the hypothesis of a descent led to the dilemma of a heterogenetic conception, or an evolution; and the hypothesis of an evolution rendered necessary the attempt at explaining this evolution, and showed Darwin's method of explaining it by his selection theory. It will be well for the reader to keep distinctly in mind the difference between these problems and theories, in following our investigations, even if we cannot arrange our historical sketch according to the natural principle of division arising from these differences.

For it lies in the nature of the question itself, that these theories, in their historical progress, did not appear singly, but together. Those who inclined to the theory of a descent of species could claim for it the attention of scientific investigators only after having also made the attempt at conceiving this descent in a concrete way, and according to certain analogies of observation. The only analogy of the kind appeared in the sphere of individual development and individual differences on the one hand, and in that of closely related characters of allied species on the other; and thus led of itself to the evolution theory. As soon as the naturalists thought they had found the causes of such an evolution of the species, they naturally placed these causes in the foreground of their demonstrations, and erected upon them the structure of their entire theory; thus treating descent, evolution and selection as one single and indissolubly connected theory. But this manner of treating the question had also its dangers, which have already caused a great deal of confusion and misunderstanding, as well as much unprofitable controversy. Often friends and enemies of the theories placed that which was in favor of the theory of descent to the credit of the evolution or selection theory; and, on the other hand, that which seemed opposed to the selection theory was often held to be a weakening of the evolution and descent theory; and this was done, not only by amateurs, but often enough by the highest authorities also. In reality, however, it is quite conceivable that the idea of a descent may prove correct, and possibly the idea of an evolution of the species will have to be replaced by that of a heterogenetic generation, or by the theory that certain groups in the organic system are originated by heterogenetic generation, and others by evolution; and so the evolution theory must share with the theory of heterogenetic generation, or of a metamorphosis of germs. On the other hand, it is conceivable that even where the evolution theory is confirmed, the evolution can be accounted for wholly or partly by other reasons than those derived from the selection theory. And even this result of present investigations is not inconceivable: that the reasons for and against the different theories will be found to balance one another to such a degree that they will sooner or later lead science, in answering the question of the origin of species, to the old confession of Socrates—*"Ignoramus."*

We shall, therefore, have to arrange our historical sketch according to the historical order of the appearance of the theories, and treat the problems more or less as an undivided whole. But we shall keep in mind, during our historical sketch, not only the logical separation of the problems in question, in order not to lose clearness of judgment, but we shall also at the end of our review, if we consider the present condition of the problems, have to examine the same once more in detail, so far as regards the above mentioned separation.

CHAPTER I.

RISE OF THE DARWINIAN THEORIES.

§ 1. *Direct Predecessors.—Lamarck.*

The first man who gave direct expression to the idea of a successive generation of the species through transmutation, and who attempted to follow it up in a scientific way, was the French naturalist and philosopher, Jean Lamarck, born 1744. In the year 1801, and subsequently, he published his views, first in smaller essays and afterward more in detail in his *"Philosophie Zoologique,"* which appeared in 1809, and in the first volume of his *"Histoire Naturelle des Animaux sans Vertèbres,"* published in 1815. In these works Lamarck upholds fully the descent and evolution theory, and maintains that the simplest organisms are generated through a *generatio spontanea*, which is still taking place; but that all the more developed organisms, including man, are descended through a gradual change from other species. With this theory, he put himself in direct and conscious opposition to the old doctrine of the immutability of species and their characteristics, which had been ably maintained by Linnæus, and also made some attempts at explanation which approach very nearly the selection theory. A change in the physical conditions of life, especially the force of habit in the use or disuse of the organs, the inheritance of physical and psychical qualities thus attained, and the extension of the process of transmutation into extraordinarily long periods of time with very slight changes, are also, in his view, the probable causes of the variation and development of the species. He only lacks the idea of a natural selection in the struggle for existence, and the comparison of the processes in nature with the methodical selection of man in the breeding of domestic animals and plants, to identify his views with those of Darwin.

At first, Lamarck met only with violent opposition; but after a little while his views ceased to attract attention. The time had not yet come to make such an attempt at observing nature from the standpoint of evolution. The sciences which favor such a mode of observation, and even demand it—such as comparative anatomy and physiology and the history of the development of the different plants and animals—were only in their infancy, or were—like palæontology and the comparative geography of plants and animals—not yet in existence. The influence of Linnæus, whose views diametrically opposed those of Lamarck, predominated over all the investigations of natural science; Buffon, who favored the ideas of Lamarck, and loved to trace a unity in natural phenomena, was too instable in his investigations and views to arrive at a comprehensive principle; and even the eminent naturalist, Cuvier, of Montpellier, showed in his observation of nature a predilection for analysis rather than synthesis, and although his comprehensive mind inclined to generalize and explain, he placed himself in decided opposition to a theory which was founded only on a few decisive facts.

This last mentioned deficiency seems to have been the main cause of Lamarck's views soon being lost sight of. They nowhere found a support in facts; the force of habit played in them an exaggerated and unnatural *rôle*; the different illustrations of them—such as the long neck of the giraffe explained by the permanent and inherited habit of browsing on the branches of high trees, or the web on the toes of frogs, swimming-birds, etc., explained by the habit of swimming—were talked about and laughed at more as curiosities than as worthy of serious consideration.

Only twice after this did the question put by Lamarck attract wider attention from the learned world. The first time was when, in 1830, the bitter contest arose at the Academy of Paris, between Cuvier and Etienne Geoffrey St. Hilaire, the father of Isidor G. St. Hilaire. Geoffrey St. Hilaire had views similar to Lamarck's, but reached them from quite a different standpoint— from the observation of the analogy and homology of the organs; and accounted for the variation of species, not by the use or disuse of the organs, but on the one hand by the common original type of the organs, and on the other by the varied influence of the surroundings—the *monde ambiant*. Lamarck himself seems not to have been mentioned in this contest. The controversy turned much more on the question whether in observing nature we can proceed by synthesis and find in the analogies of the organisms the principles for explaining the real connection between the different organic forms, or whether the analytical process is the only correct one, and the synthetical should be discarded. The solution of it will probably be, that the one process must be supplemented by the other, as Goethe has already shown in his account of this controversy; but at that time it was decided in favor of the analytical principle, and the question was for the time dropped. It came up for a second time, but created little excitement, in 1844, when an anonymous work, "Vestiges of the Natural History of Creation," directed the attention and the interest of scientists again to Lamarck and his doctrine. But this interest also soon came to an end, until through Darwin's first publication the half-forgotten man again suddenly attained great honor.

Those who wish to form a closer acquaintance with the different advocates of the evolution theory before Darwin's appearance, will find them carefully arranged in the historical sketch which Darwin gives in the introduction to his work on "The Origin of Species"; and the most important extracts of Lamarck's *"Philosophie Zoologique"* are to be found in Oscar Schmidt's "Descent and Darwinism."[1]

§ *2. Indirect Preparations.*

While thus the ideas of Lamarck gradually fell into partial oblivion, yet contemporaneous with and following them arose several other series of thoughts, views, and investigations, which, although they only indirectly prepared for the revival of the evolution theory, yet exercised a deeper and more lasting influence on the minds of scientists. We refer to the ideas in regard to natural phenomena held during the first decades of our century; further, to the principles of comparative anatomy which, up to the present time, partly dependent and partly independent of natural philosophy, have been expressed, valued, and admired as leading thoughts; and, lastly, to the empiric results of comparative anatomical and biological investigations in palæontology and geology, as attained by the help of those very principles. And even physics and astronomy had to coöperate in preparing the way for the idea of evolution.

The philosophical ideas referred to, together with the points of view and results of comparative anatomy, led more and more decisively to the idea of an *original form*, or *type*, which retains its identity in all the modifications of form in plants and animals; and of a *ground-plan*, which is realized in the systems of the plant and animal world in higher and higher differentiations and in more and more developed modifications, diverging farther and farther from the prototype until it reaches its highest form, still reducible to the prototypes, in the most highly organized dicotyledons in plants, and in the animal world in the mammalia, and lastly in man.

Men like Cuvier and Geoffrey St. Hilaire, who otherwise stand diametrically opposed to each other, unite in these and kindred ideas. The naturalist Oken attains the same result, tinged with the views of Schelling; the poet Goethe, from an intuitive knowledge of nature, arrived at the same conclusion. The former, during a journey in the Hartz Mountains, at the sight of a bleached deer's skull, and the latter, upon picking up a sheep's skull in the Jewish cemetery at Venice, were struck by the same thought: the skull is only a modified vertebra. Oken founded upon this idea and kindred analogies his profound philosophy of the system of animals and plants which comes very near to the evolution theory, and in his cosmogony traces all organisms to a protoplasm in such a way as to bring him in this respect also very near to Darwinism. Goethe, in his metamorphosis of plants, develops ideas in which, in all seriousness, he makes a concrete application of his thought of a prototype to the leaf of a plant; and proved for zoölogy the fruitfulness of his idea of a type by his well known discovery of the mid-jaw bone in man. Although Oscar Schmidt seems to be decidedly right in supposing, in opposition to Ernst Häckel, that Goethe did not intend to have his idea of unity and development taken in a real but in an ideal sense, and hence could not be called a direct representative of the evolution theory, still he is all the more decidedly a predecessor of that theory in directing attention to the unity in plan and metamorphosis of plants and animals. Louis Agassiz, who, on the other hand, continued up to his death in opposition to the entire doctrine of descent, made the idea of *types* the principle of his whole classification, and said: "Man is the purpose toward which the whole animal creation tends from the first appearance of the first paleozoic fish." Richard Owen, who rejected the selection theory and favored that of descent, published, long before Darwin's appearance, some most interesting results of his anatomical and palæontological investigations from the point of view of the prototype and its modifications. "Man, from the beginning of organisms, was ideally present upon the earth," is a sentence which we quote from Owen's works.

In short, this ideal momentum in the observation of the organic kingdoms is not only the most beautiful blossom and the ripest fruit of the union between laborious and comprehensive detailed investigations and a generalizing philosophic penetration, but it was also a very efficient preparation of the mind for the evolution problem, so far as the summing up of the organisms under a type and plan is only the ideal reverse of its realistic reduction to a common pedigree.

We have yet to add the investigations in regard to the history of evolution of the single organisms, as well as those in comparative anatomy, which in former centuries were begun by scientists like Swammerdam and Boerhave and carried more nearly to completion by K. E. von Baer, Carus, and others. In reducing all the tissues of plants and animals to one cell, and tracing back also their individual developments to the first differentiation of the simplest cell, they followed out the unity of the plan of the organic kingdoms—which hitherto had been maintained only ideally and proclaimed as a philosophic postulate—farther and deeper into the sphere of empiric reality. We must mention, moreover, the great palæontological discoveries which, from the first foraminifera of the Cambrian formations up to the historical period of man, showed a great progressive scale in the appearance of the organisms and a very wide relationship between this scale and the natural systems of botany and zoölogy; and, finally, the principles of geology, which, under the leadership of Sir Charles Lyell, starting from the idea of an identity of the powers which were active in former times with those of the present, attempted to explain the most violent of the changes in the earth's crust in former times by causes active to-day. This often explains prodigious effects—such as the elevation and settling of entire mountains and continents—by the constant and related action of the slightest causes and most gradual steps; it opens the perspective into vast epochs of long and numerous geological periods; and sometimes, where scientists like Cuvier and Agassiz have supposed the most complete cataclysms and the most universal revolutions of the globe, there prove to have been only gradual changes with revolutions very partially and locally limited.

Finally, if we take into consideration the grand discoveries which strikingly illustrate the connection in extent and quality between the universe and all its agencies and powers—such as Robert von Mayer's discovery of the conservation of force and of the mechanical equivalent of heat, or the spectrum analysis and the information which it gives us by ever-increasing evidences of the identity of the cosmic and telluric substances—we may venture to say that the scientific and intellectual ground was well prepared for a theory which takes the origin of organisms into this common relationship of the essential unity and development of the universe.

Only one thing more remained to complete the hypothesis offered by Lamarck, of the *fact* of a development of species by a new and more satisfactory answer to the question as to the *manner* of their development. The task of answering in a more comprehensive and scientific way the question as to the manner of development has been undertaken by Darwin in his selection theory. Alfred Russell Wallace, who arrived at the same results contemporaneously with and independently of Darwin, has, with praiseworthy modesty, renounced his claim to priority of the discovery, as Darwin had been longer engaged in working out his theories and had begun to collect materials for proof.

CHAPTER II.

HISTORY OF THE DARWINIAN THEORIES.

§ 1. *Darwin.*

In order to explain the development of higher species from lower ones in a natural way, Darwin starts from two facts. The first fact is, that all individuals of the same species show, besides their specific similarity, individual differences: a fact which we call the *law of individual variability*. The other fact is, that each individual inclines to transmit to his offspring all his qualities —not only the characteristics of the species, but also those of the individual: a fact which we call the *law of heredity*.

To show how the whole basis of explanation of the evolution of one species from another is given in these two facts, Darwin calls attention to the rules according to which the often extraordinarily great varieties of domestic animals and cultivated plants are obtained and preserved; namely, the rules of *artificial breeding*. The breeder simply selects from a species those individuals having such individual qualities as he wishes to preserve and to increase, and refrains from breeding those individuals which do not possess the characteristics he wants or which possess them only in a small degree. He continues the same process with the next generation; and by the constant and effectual agency of the two before-mentioned laws, he will, after the lapse of a few generations, have breeded a variety in which the characteristics originally belonging only to a single individual have become common and permanent.

It is now important to consider whether nature, in *natural selection* (whence the name "Selection Theory") does not act unconsciously according to the same rules, and attain the same results, as man with his artificial and intentional selection; and, furthermore, whether she does not reach results which, according to that principle of natural selection, finally explain the origin of all, even of the highest and most complicated organisms, from one single original form or a few original and simplest forms. Darwin finds these questions answered in the affirmative; and arrives at this answer through the following conclusions.

The English political economist Malthus (1766-1834), in his "Essay on the Principles of Population," established a law in regard to the growth of the human race, which may be applied just as well to all the species of the entire organic world: that population tends to increase in a geometrical ratio, although the conditions of life for the individual remain the same or at most increase in an arithmetical ratio. The consequence is that if the species is to be preserved and the individuals of future generations are to continue to find sufficient food and other means for sustaining life, a great many individuals of each generation must perish very early, and even as germ and seed, and only a minority will be preserved and reproduced. This exuberant prodigality of life-germs, of which proportionately only a few are preserved and reproduced, takes place in the plant and animal world in a very marked degree. There a continual *struggle for existence* prevails; each individual has to get access to his conditions of life by wresting them from a whole series of other individuals of his own or other species; and now the question arises: which individuals will survive in this struggle? which will more probably be preserved and procreate offspring? Evidently, the answer is, those individuals which possess individual characteristics more favorable to the preservation of the individual than those possessed by other individuals. These individual characteristics are transmitted to the next generation. In this there will be again individuals that have in a still higher degree the characteristics thus transmitted and favorable for the preservation of the individual, or that add to these favorable characteristics new characteristics favorable in another direction to the survival of the individual in the struggle for existence. While these individuals, with more probability than the others, are thus preserved and reproduced, they transmit to their offspring not only the old favorable characteristics increased, but also those newly added. Among the favorable individual qualities, Darwin reckons the divergence of character, the perfection of organization, and the law of correlation; the latter, however, can not be explained by natural selection, since according to this law a variation in an organ brings about a corresponding variation in entirely different organs (*e.g.*, cats with white fur and blue eyes are also deaf).

This is *natural selection by means of the survival of the fittest in the struggle for existence*. Changes in the conditions and surroundings of life, and more or less perfect adaptation of the organisms to the new conditions of form, color, food and habit, are the main causes of those individual variations, the accumulation of which through many generations produces so great effects. If we only have behind us periods long enough to permit us to imagine each step in the development as an extremely small and hardly appreciable one, natural selection offers us not the exclusive but the main means of explaining the evolution of the whole animal and plant world out of one or a few simple organized original forms.

This is the outline of the selection theory, as given by Darwin in 1859, and still retained in all its essentials. It is true, in his work on the origin of man he added as supplemental the *sexual* to the common natural selection, and made it of special importance for the presentation of the *beautiful* in nature—for the production of beautiful forms, colors, and tones, and for the development of power and intelligence. And in the same work he said that there are many circumstances of structure which seem to be neither beneficial nor detrimental to the individual, and that to have overlooked this fact was one of his greatest mistakes in his former publications. But for the rest, he maintains the selection theory unchanged, with the single modification that it explains, if not the whole development of the species through descent, at least that which is of most importance in it.

That it was only one step in the course of reasoning to extend the selection theory to the descent of man, was seen by many as soon as Darwin's work on the origin of species was published and began to attract attention; although not a syllable upon this question was presented in this work. Various persons manifested their presentiment or perception according to their point of view—partly by the most violent opposition to the new doctrine, partly by scientific development or modification of their anthropogonic views, partly also by revelling in imagination in the consequences hostile to religious faith which they thought could be drawn from this doctrine. We remind the reader of the itinerant lectures of Karl Vogt about the ape-pedigree of man, and of the echo they found by assent or dissent in press and public; also of Huxley in England, Karl Snell, Schleiden, Reichenbach, and others; of the materialists,
L. Büchuer and Moleschott, and of the publications of Ernst Häckel. Finally, Darwin himself made us fully certain of the importance which from the

beginning he had attributed to his theory, by publishing his work on the "Descent of Man," in the year 1870.

In this work he explained the descent of man fully from the before-named principles of the descent, evolution, and selection theories, of which we have given all the essentials in the foregoing presentation. He carefully enumerates everything in the structure of the human body that reminds us of our relationship with the animals—especially those embryonic phenomena and rudimentary organs in man which are still to be found in use and in a more developed state in different animal species, and which led him to imagine our ancestors now with a tail, then with sharp ears, now living in the water, then being hermaphrodites. He reviews the spiritual qualities of man, and finds for them all analogous qualities in the animal world. He finds in his work on "Expression of the Emotions in Man and Animals," published in 1872, new confirmation of the genealogical relationship of both. He looks over the whole course of the zoölogical system and of palæontological discoveries, and searches for the points where the branches and twigs of the animal pedigree of man must have diverged. To begin with the lowest branches, he thinks the most important divergence took place where the series of vertebrates may have been developed out of the invertebrates. Here he adopts the investigations of A. Kowalewsky, and the deductions of Häckel founded upon them, concerning the larva of the ascidiæ, a genus of marine mollusca of the order tunicata, and sees in a cord, to be found in this larva, most decided relationship to the spine of the lancelet fish or amphioxus, the lowest of all the vertebrates, it being yet doubtful whether it belongs at all to the vertebrates. In the transition that once took place from one species of ascidian larva to a form similar to the lancelet fish, he sees the new branch diverging in the series of vertebrates. Out of the fish he concludes that the amphibia were developed, and out of those the reptilia, out of one of them the marsupialia, and from them the lemurs or half-apes, the representatives of which yet live in Madagascar and the southern part of Asia. From these there branched off on the one side the platyrrhini, or apes with a flat nose, on the new continent; on the other, the catarrhini, or apes with a narrow nose, on the old. Among the ancestor of the last, he searches for the common progenitors, from which again two branches started—on the one hand the ignoble branches of the catarrhine species of apes, always remaining lower in development, to which also belong the anthropomorphous apes, like the orang outang and gibbon in Asia, the gorilla and chimpanzee in Africa; on the other hand, that branch which represents the ascent of animals to man.

The refining agencies which finally raise the animal up to the man are essentially the same that on the lowest scales of the pedigree have caused the development of the lower organisms into the higher, namely: favorable individual variations, inheritance, acclimatization, survival of the fittest in the struggle for existence, natural, and especially, sexual selection. These are, if not the exclusive, still the main agencies which finally led the primate of the earthly creation upon the stage and furnished him with his superior faculties. But it is particularly by means of his social life, and of the forces which determine, transmit, increase and ennoble the various impulses and instincts promoting it, that man has become what he is. Through the need and faculty of reciprocal help, through sexual selection—which of course is a very essential factor of social life—there originated language, and reflection, and all the intellectual qualities; and through these again originated the moral qualities, which are most important in constituting the specific worth of man, and which were finally developed into self-consciousness and free moral responsibility.

But with the description of this attempt to explain more in detail these specific characteristics of man, we leave the ground of pure natural science and enter the region of philosophy, in which we have to take up the question again (in Book II, Ch. I) at the same point where we here leave it.

§ 2. *The Followers of Darwin.—Ernst Häckel.*

Darwin's theory soon found an enthusiastic corps of followers—on the continent, and especially in Germany, almost more than in his own country. The outlook into an entirely new explanation of the origin of man, and the probable use of this theory for attacks upon faith in a Creator and Master of the world, called wide-spread attention to it; and the theory opened to natural science itself entirely new impulses and paths, and promised the solution of many problems before which it had hitherto been compelled to stand in silence. To be sure, it threatened likewise to allure the mind from the slow but sure ways of solid study to the entertaining but insecure and aimless paths of imagination and hypothesis.

Among all the German followers of Darwin who adopted not only the idea of an origin of species through descent and evolution, but also the explanation of evolution by natural selection, and extended it so as to make the principle of selection of exclusive value, Ernst Häckel occupies the most prominent rank.

In his "General Morphology," published in 1866, and in his "Natural History of the Creation," the first edition of which appeared in 1868, and finally in his "Anthropogeny"[2] (why he does not say Anthropogony, we are nowhere informed), 1874, this scientist brought the new theory, which had been presented by Darwin in an almost bewildering flood of details, into connection and order, and, analyzing the powers active in natural selection, combined them into an entire system of laws. He at once drew the origin of man also into the course of reasoning on the new theory, and sustained the theory by the discovery of the *monera* and other low organisms of one cell, as well as by special investigations of the calcareous sponges. For these labors, he was rewarded by the warm and unreserved acknowledgment which Darwin made to him in his work upon the origin of man, which was published subsequently to the "Natural History of the Creation." There Darwin says: "If this work had appeared before my essay had been written, I should probably never have completed it. Almost all the conclusions at which I have arrived, I find confirmed by this naturalist, whose knowledge on many points is much fuller than mine." Häckel's labors rendered still greater service to the Darwinian theory by dividing the organic world into three kingdoms: the protista kingdom, the vegetable kingdom, and the animal kingdom,—a division which solves in a most simple way the difficulty that was felt more and more of securing for the lowest organisms a place among the animals or plants. He further aided the theory by leaving the choice open to adopt either a uniform or multiform pedigree of the organisms and their kingdoms and classes, and by treating each class under both points of view; and finally, by fascinating experiments to bring before us in detail the hypothetical pedigrees of all classes of organisms from the protista kingdom up to man.

We will try to reproduce briefly the pedigree which is of most interest—the hypothetical *pedigree of man*. Häckel divides it into twenty-two stages, eight of them belonging to the series of the invertebrates, and fourteen to that of the vertebrates. On this ladder of twenty-two rounds, he leads us from the lowest form of the living being, in slight and mostly plausible transitions, continually higher and higher, up to man; and makes our steps easy by mentioning at each stage, on the one hand the corresponding state in the embryonic development, on the other the still living creature through which, in his opinion, the former organisms of the corresponding round of the ladder are still represented, and which accordingly has been a creature that remained on its round, while other members of its family have been developed up to man and to many other genera and species.

He begins with the monera, the organisms of the lowest form, discovered by himself, which have not so much as the organic rank of a cell, but are only corpuscules of mucus, without kernel or external covering, called by him cytod, and arising from an organic carbon formation. The lowest and most formless moneron is the bathybius, discovered by Thomas Huxley, a network of recticular mucus, which in the greatest depths of the sea, as far down as 7,000 metres, covers stone fragments and other objects, but are also found in less depths, in the Mediterranean Sea, for instance. From the moneron he proceeds to the amœba—a simple cell, with a kernel, which still corresponds to the egg of man in its first state. The third stage is formed by the communities of amœbæ (synamœbæ), corresponding to the mulberry-yolk in the first development of the fecundated egg, and to some still living heaps of amœbæ. To the fourth stage he assigns the planæa, corresponding to the embryonic development of an albumen and the planula or ciliated larva. When these ciliated larvæ are developed, they contract themselves so as to form a cavity; and this fifth stage—especially important for his theory—he calls gastræa. In this form, he says, the progaster is already developed, and its wall is differentiated for the first time into an animal or dermal layer (ectoblast), and into a vegetative or intestinal layer (hypoblast). At the sixth stage, there branched off the prothelmis, or worms, with the first formations of a nervous system, the simplest organs of sense, the simplest organs for secretion (kidneys) and generation (sexual organs), represented to-day by the gliding worms or turbellaria; as the seventh stage, the soft worms, as he called them at first—the blood worms, or cœlomati, as he describes them in his "Anthropogeny"—a purely hypothetical stage, on which a true body-cavity and blood were formed; the eighth stage are the chorda-animals with the beginning of a spinal rod, corresponding to the larva of the ascidiæ. At the ninth stage, called the skull-less animals (acrania), and corresponding to the still living lancelet, we enter the series of the vertebrates. The importance of the eighth and ninth stages for the theory, we have already pointed out in our remarks upon Darwin, p. 43. The tenth stage is formed by those low fishes in which the spinal rod is differentiated into the skull—and the vertebral- column, called the single-nostriled animals (monorrhini), and represented by the cyclostoma of today (hag and lampreys). The eleventh stage is formed by the primæval fish or selachii (sharks); the twelfth by the mud fish, of which there still live the protopterus in Africa, the lepidosiren in the tributaries of the Amazon, and the ceratodus in the swamps of Southern Australia. On the thirteenth stage, there are the gilled amphibians (sozobranchia), proteus and axolotl; on the fourteenth, the tailed amphibians (sozura), newt and salamander; on the fifteenth, the purely hypothetical primæval amniota or protamnia (amnion is the name given to the chorion which surrounds the germ-water and embryo of the three higher classes of vertebrates) on the sixteenth, the primary mammals (promammalia), to which the present monotremes (ornithorhynchus and echidna) stand nearest; on the seventeenth, the pouched animals or marsupialia; on the eighteenth, the semi-apes or prosimiæ (loris and maki); on the nineteenth, the tailed apes, or menocerca (nose-apes and slender-apes, or semnopithecus); on the twentieth, the man- like apes (anthropoides) or tail-less catarrhini (gorilla, chimpanzee, orang outang and gibbon). And now we come to twenty-one—ape-like men or speechless primæval men (alali)—of whom we are reminded to-day by the deaf, and dumb, the cretins and the microcephali; and number twenty-two is *homo sapiens*, the man. The Australians and the Papuans are supposed to be the only remaining representatives of his first stage-development. In like manner, Häckel also gives us the stem-branches of all the types, classes and orders of the organisms, and forms from them a very acceptable hypothetical pedigree; or—if we prefer to suppose a polyphyletic rather than a monophyletic origin of species—hypothetical pedigrees of the whole organic world.

The perspicuity and clearness of Häckel's deductions, the extent of his knowledge, and the singleness of his aim, to which he makes them all subservient, lend to his works a great charm. But on the other hand we dare not conceal that, even on the ground of explanations belonging purely to natural history, the character of hypothesis is often lost in that of arbitrariness and of the undemonstrable. Even the unlearned in natural science often enough get this impression when reading his works, and will find it confirmed by scientists who not only contradict his assertions in many cases, but disclose plain errors in his drawings—errors, indeed, exclusively in favor of the unity-hypothesis; and in other cases they show that drawings which are given as pictures of the real, represent merely hypothetical opinions. There is especially evident in his works an extremely strong tendency to impress on his hypotheses the character of an established and proved fact, by giving them the alluring name of laws. Entire systems of laws of the selection theory are produced, and all imaginable assertions are also immediately called laws. For example, Huxley, in his anatomical investigations of apes and men, arrives at the conclusion that the differences between the highest and the lowest apes are greater than the differences between the highest apes and man. This purely anatomical comparison, Häckel calls repeatedly "Huxley's Law." We are well aware that the idea of law is capable of great extension in meaning, and in that respect we can refer to nothing more instructive than the well-meditated inquiry upon this idea in the "Reign of Law" of the Duke of Argyll (London, Strahan & Co.). But if we may venture to call purely anatomical comparisons of this nature *laws*, such a use of language destroys all logical reasoning; and this mistake appears again in Häckel's philosophic discussions, of which we shall have to speak hereafter. We shall have to refer also hereafter to an additional embellishment, which Häckel thinks himself obliged to give to his works—namely, that he makes on every occasion the strongest attacks upon faith in a personal God, a Creator and Lord of the world; that he traces all the motives of human action to self-interest; that he denies the liberty of man and the moral system of the world; that he makes consent to his view of things the criterion of the intellectual development of a man; and that he thinks to render a service to civilization by such a view of the world and of ethics.

In the consequent carrying out of the selection principle as the satisfactory key in explaining the origin of all species and also of man, Häckel is indeed, in spite of the approval of his works by the British master, more Darwinian than Darwin himself, who expressly refuses to give exclusive value to this theory of explanation. Hence there are among scientists only a few who go with him to this extent. In Germany, aside from the materialists, we only know of Seidlitz and Oskar Schmidt—who in the thirteenth volume of the "International Scientific Series" treats of "The Theory of Descent and Darwinism," and advocates not only the autocracy of the selection theory, but also all the monistic and atheistic consequences which are deduced from it. Perhaps Gustav Jäger, Schleiden, Bernhard Cotta—at least judging from their earlier publications—should be mentioned as followers of the pure selection theory; although they do not all draw from it the before-mentioned philosophic consequences. On the other hand, the number of those is very great who, although inspired by Darwin to adopt the idea of an origin of species through descent and evolution, yet have more or less modified, laid aside, or entirely refused the very doctrine which is especially new in Darwin's theory—the selection theory. In the following section we shall briefly give an account of them.

§ 3. *Modifications of the Theory—Moriz Wagner. Wigand.*

One of the most prominent objections to the selection theory, which strikes us at once from the standpoint of natural history, is the following: The varieties of a domesticated species, obtained by artificial breeding, are lost, and return to the original wild form of the species as soon as they are crossed long enough with other varieties or are left to themselves and to the crossing with individuals of the original form of their species; and hence we can not see how individual characteristics, even if favorable to the individual, will not be lost again by the crossing which is inevitable in a state of nature, with such individuals as do not possess those characteristics. Besides, it is an established fact, confirmed by all our observations stretching over thousands of years, that the characteristics of species are preserved in spite of all individual modifications, and that this preservation of the characteristics of species has its cause essentially in the free crossing of individuals.

This objection induced Moriz Wagner to take up again an idea already expressed by Leopold von Buch, and to complete the principle of a selection through natural breeding by another, and partly, indeed, to supplant it by the principle of *isolation by migration*. Isolated individuals, who, from any reason naturally to be accounted for, leave the mass of their fellows, can from the very consequence of this isolation transmit to their offspring common individual characteristics which are not destroyed again by the crossing with other individuals. They will especially fix and transmit these individual characteristics, when they are favorable to them for the conditions of existence in their new place of living, and these individual characteristics will so much the more be increased and developed in a direction favorable to the subsistence of the individuals in their new place of living, as there are more closely connected with this isolation variations in the conditions of existence, in climate, geographical surroundings, food, and so on. He very attractively applies this theory also to the explanation of the origin of man. According to his opinion, even the nearest animal progenitors of man were isolated, and the isolating power was the rise of the great mountains of the Old World, which took place previous to the glacial period. One pair, or perhaps a few pairs, of those progenitors were driven away from the luxurious climate of the torrid zone to the northern half of the globe, and found their return cut off by glaciers and high mountains; in place of a comfortable life on the trees, necessity urged them to gain support from conditions less favorable to existence, and necessity, this mother of so many virtues and achievements, finally made man what he is. In following out these ideas, Moriz Wagner has gradually and more and more decidedly given up the selection theory, and opposed it by sharp criticisms.

This *migration* or *isolation theory* also found a degree of favor, but subordinate in its nature. For it can not and will not pretend to solve the main problems. It only tries to explain how the individual variations, already in existence, might have been preserved and perhaps increased, and how new conditions of existence could have roused latent powers; but not how these variations and these powers originated. Just as little is the selection theory able to explain this; but it pretends to do it, and hence we can easily comprehend how during the last few years a constantly increasing number of voices, and more important ones, have been raised against the selection theory. This opposition came not only from those who—like Agassiz, Barrande, Emil Blanchard, Escher von der Linth, Göppert, Giebel, Sir Roderick Murchison, Pfaff, and others—directly reject each and every idea of descent on account of the difficulty in defending the selection theory; or who

—like Karl Ernst von Baer,[3] (the pioneer in the region of the history of individual development), like Oskar Fraas, Griesebach, Sandberger, and others—generally take a more reserved and neutral position, because of the uncertainty of the facts and the inaccessibility of the problems; but it comes especially from those scientists who are inclined to adopt an origin of species through descent and even through development, yet refuse to explain it by the selection principle, and look for the essential cause of the development in the organisms themselves, without claiming to have themselves found these causes. Among the most prominent advocates of this view, we may name the late Sir Charles Lyell, Mivart, and Richard Owen, in England; and in Germany, Alexander Braun, Ecker, Gegenbaur, Oswald Heer, W. His, Nägeli,

Rütimeyer, Schaaffhausen, Virchow, Karl Vogt, A. W. Volkmann, Weismann, Zittel, and here also Moriz Wagner, and among the philosophers, Eduard von Hartmann. Many of these men are but little aware of the difference between the two questions: whether, on the one hand, the adoption of the origin of species through descent does not of itself involve the idea of a gradual development of one species from another, almost unobservable in its single steps; or, on the other hand, whether a descent of species through heterogenetic generation in leaps and through a metamorphosis of the germs, could be imagined. They consider descent and evolution as identical; and this identification is explainable so long as we are not in a condition to come nearer to the eventual causes of the supposed variation of species. But men are not wanting who put these questions clearly and plainly, and separate them distinctly from one another. Among them we may mention K. E. von Baer, Ed. von Hartmann and Wigand; of the latter we will have occasion to speak more in detail hereafter. Among them we find also scientists who answer the question in the sense of a new-modeling of the species, of a heterogenetic generation, and of a metamorphosis of germs. To this class belong especially Oswald Heer—"Urwelt der Schweitz" ("Antediluvian World in Switzerland"), Zürich, 1865, p. 590-604; Kölliker—"Ueber die Darwin'sche Schöpfungstheorie," ("Darwin's Theory of Creation"), Leipzig, 1864; "Morphologie und Entwicklungeschichte des Pennatulidenstammes nebst allgemeinen Betrachtungen zur Descendenzlehre," ("Morphology and History of the Development of the Stem of the Pennatulidæ, together with General Remarks on the Descent Theory"), Frankfurt, 1872; and Heinrich Baumgärtner—"Natur und Gott" ("Nature and God"), Leipzig, Brockhaus, 1870. Heer has introduced into scientific language the term "new-modeling of the species," Kölliker that of a "heterogenetic generation," and Baumgärtner that of a "transmutation of the types through a metamorphosis of germs." Baer also is not averse to adopting the latter.

The botanist, Albert Wigand, of Marburg, takes a peculiar position. On one hand, the observation of the relationship of organic beings with one another leads him to adopt a common genealogy, a descent; on the other, the objections to adopting a descent of the species one from another appear to him insurmountable. In the first place, he sees all the species everywhere strictly limited—although in the second volume of his work, which appeared after the preceding lines were written, he again warns against a one-sided emphasizing of the invariability of species. In the second place, he sees so clearly, through the whole organic world, the differences, nay, the contrasts, of the species, in their building plan, in the numbers and conditions and positions of their parts, and in their mode of development, that it appears to him impossible to assume in the perfected organism a production of germs which in a course of generations, by a process even as gradual as possible, would grow into such an entirely new phenomenon as a new, even closely related, species would be. But if we adopt the theory of a heterogenetic generation, we explain by it the variety but not the similarity of species; for a heterogenetic generation would in the new species make everything different from the old one—a conclusion, the necessity of which it would be difficult to show. For these reasons, he refers the descent of the organic beings, not to the series of the species, with their individuals already specified and defined, but to the series of *primordial cells* living free in the water. The earliest primordial cells represented only the common character of the *whole organic world*, and out of them the primordial cells of the *animal* and those of the *vegetable kingdom* were produced by dividing the cells; so that the first ones embraced only the general and primitive characteristics of the whole animal, the last ones those of the whole vegetable kingdom. Out of these primordial cells of the two kingdoms, those of the *main types* proceeded—(for instance, the primordial cells of the radiated animals, the vertebrates, etc., the gymnosperms, the angiosperms, etc.); out of them those of the *classes*—(for instance, the mammalia, the dicotyledons); out of them those of the *orders*— (for instance, the beasts of prey, rosifloræ); out of them those of the *families* (canina, rosaceæ); out of them those of the *genus* (canis, rosa); and out of them those of the *species* (canis lupus, rosa canina). Only when the primordial cells of the species had been produced, were they developed into finished representatives of the species; and when once these primordial cells of the species had been developed into finished and full-grown individuals of the species, their transmission took place in the manner well known to us. Wigand published his criticism of the Darwinian Theories in his larger work, "Der Darwinismus und die Naturforschung Newtons und Cuviers," ("Darwinism and the Natural Science of Newton and Cuvier"), Braunschweig, Vieweg, Vol. I, 1874, Vol. II, 1876, and his own attempt at explanation in a smaller book, published at the same place in 1872: "Die Genealogie der Urzellen als Lösung des Descendenzproblems oder die Entstehung der Arten ohne natürliche Zuchtwahl" ("Genealogy of the Primordial Cells as a Solution of the Problem of Descent; or the Origin of Species without Natural Selection").

Whether this *genealogy of the primordial cells* found any followers, we do not know. None of the hypotheses thus far mentioned are so very far from having analogies in experience. The idea of a first development of the higher organisms out of their specific primordial cell, through all kinds of conditions of larvæ up to the finished form, demands of us the acceptance of monstrous improbabilities—(think, for example, of the first men, who, originating from a human primordial cell, grow in different metamorphoses of larvæ, first in the water and then on the land, until they appear as finished men). Moreover, the hypothesis, in claiming that a heterogenetic generation of one species from another must necessarily nullify all similarity between the organism of the child and that of the mother, is so little convincing, and shows—in the necessity of conceiving the universal type of organisms, the type of kingdoms, of main types, of classes, of orders, of families, of genera, and of species, as but individual existences which, in the form of cells and before the existence of the developed species, partly through many thousands of years, lead a real empiric and concrete life—such an abstract synthetical construction of nature, that we are not astonished that the theory of the genealogy of primordial cells stands almost alone. On the other hand, Wigand's larger critical work rendered great service in clearing up the problems. It is true, his judgment appears in many single cases not at all convincing, since he often enough fights his adversaries with sophisms and deduces from the views of Darwin and Häckel conclusions to which they certainly do not lead. But in the majority of cases, his work is full of real convincing power, and with the breadth of its philosophical view and with the sharpness of its definitions, as well as with its abundance of philosophic and especially botanical teachings and their ingenious application, it is directly destructive to the use of the selection theory as the principal key to the solution of the problems. Eduard Von Hartmann describes the work in his publication, "Wahrheit und Irrthum im Darwinismus," ("Truth and Error in Darwinism"), as a mile-stone which marks the limits where Darwinism as such passed the summit of its influence in Germany.

CHAPTER III.

PRESENT STATE OF THE DARWINIAN THEORIES.

§ 1. *The Theory of Descent.*

The historical retrospect of the Darwinian theories, from their purely scientific side, leads us of itself to a critical review of their present state. We can briefly indicate in advance the result to which it will lead us, viz.: that the descent theory has gained, the selection theory has lost ground, the theory of development oscillates between both; but that all three theories have not yet passed beyond the rank of hypotheses, although they have very unequal hypothetical value. We can best arrange our review by beginning with that theory which is the most common, and which perhaps may still have value when both the others find their value diminished or lost: *the theory of descent.* From that we proceed to the *theory of evolution*, and from this to that of *selection*.

The theory of descent is indeed at first sight exceedingly plausible, and will probably always be the *directive* for all future investigations as to the origin of species. The organic species show, besides the great variety of their characteristics and the unchangeable nature of these characteristics, many other qualities which are common to them; and these common characteristics are precisely those which are most essential. Moreover the higher the structure of the organisms which are differentiated, the more numerous and more valuable will become the evidences of similarity, and the greater also will be their distance from the inorganic and from the lowest organisms of their class, their type, or their kingdom. For instance, rose and apple-tree, elder and ash, wolf and dog, goat and sheep, ape and man, are not only a great deal farther removed from the mode of existence of inorganic bodies than the algæ, the monera, and other low organisms, but they have also, in spite of the great interval which separates them from one another and especially which separates man from every animal, much more numerous and important points of contact than, for instance, two families or genera of algæ or of mosses, of polyps or of infusoria, have among one another. Now our imagination refuses to accept the theory that the Creator, or nature, or whatever we wish to call the principle generating the species, in producing the new species, laid aside all those points of contact which are continually becoming more numerous and more important, and produced instead, by ever widening leaps, the new and higher species from the inorganic, which lies farther and farther from them. On the other hand, the theory appears to us all the more plausible, that every new species came into existence on that stage which is the most nearly related to it, and which was already in existence. If we add further, that the two old maxims of the natural scientists, *omne vivum ex ovo* and *omne ovum ex ovario*, have not been invalidated, in spite of all the searching for a *generatio æquivoca*, and that, even if the origination of the lowest organisms out of the inorganic could in future be proved, yet the truth of these maxims for all the higher organized individuals is established as a fact without exception. Moreover, if we take into consideration the fact that we can not at all imagine either the origin or the first development of a higher animal or a human organism without the protecting integument and the nourishing help of a mother's womb, we may venture to say that each and every attempt to render the origin of the first individuals of the higher species conceivable, leads of necessity to the descent theory. We have either to reject, once for all, such an attempt, as an unscientific playing with impossibilities, or to accept the idea of descent. It is certainly the lasting merit of Darwin, even if his whole structure of proofs should in the course of time show itself weak, that he not only had the courage (as others had before him), but also inspired scientists with the courage to trace the idea of a descent of species in a scientific way.

To be sure, so long as we have no other proof of the descent theory than the circumstance that we can imagine it, it will continue to be nothing more than an ingenious hypothesis. We have, therefore, to look to the realm of nature for more direct proofs; and we are there furnished with them. They are presented to us by geology in connection with the botanical and zoölogical systems, by geology in connection with vegetable and animal geography, by comparative anatomy, and by the history of the embryonic development of animals.

Geology finds in the strata of the crust of the globe a large number of extinct plants and animals of extraordinary variety; but all of them, however much they may differ from the organisms of to-day, are completely in harmony with the *botanical* and *zoölogical systems* in which we divide the still living organisms. Not only have by far the most of the now extinct genera and species their family and stem-companions, and many even their genera and species companions, in the living world, but also those genera whose nearer relations are now extinct—as, for instance, the club-moss-trees, the trilobites, the ammonites, the belemnites, the sauria, the nummulites,—show still a very perceptible relationship with living genera, and can be quite accurately included in the botanical and zoölogical systems; nay, they even fill up gaps in it. The anatomical, morphological, and, so far as we can judge, the physiological and biological relationship of the fossil with living organisms, is so great and comprehensive that in the present state of science a systematic botany or zoölogy, that should only treat of the fossils or of living organisms alone, would be imperfect. But the relationship of the fossil organisms with the natural systems of botany and zoölogy is apparent not only in this respect, but also in the fact that the single species during the long periods of time which are shown by geology to have elapsed, came into existence in a series, which again pretty closely corresponds to the natural system of the organic kingdoms; and that the fossil representatives of all classes and families, the nearer they come to the present world, appear the more nearly related to the living organisms, so that the fauna and flora of the ante-human time are lost in those of the human period by transitions gliding from the one to the other. For instance, in the Miocene formation of the tertiary epoch we find thirty per cent. of species still living to-day; in the Pliocene, even sixty to eighty per cent., and toward its end even about ninety-six per cent. of species which are identical with those now living.

A brief glance may still more closely illustrate this analogy between the geological series and the organic systems. Plants and animals seem to have appeared nearly at the same time, and at first in the form of the very lowest organisms. The earliest plants found by geology belong also to the lowest stage of the vegetable kingdom; they are the algæ. They are followed again by higher cryptogamous plants, especially ferns and club-mosses. Only at a later period flowering plants appear, among them being first the plants with naked seeds standing lower in the systems, as the cycad-trees and pine-forests; later, those with enclosed seeds, among them being again first the monocotyledons, last the dicotyledons,—all of them precisely corresponding to the botanical system. The same thing is true in the animal kingdom. If the eozoon Canadense, found in the laurentian slate of the Cambrian formation in North America, is really an organism and not an inorganic form, the earliest vestiges of animal life we can find are the rhizopodes or foraminifera; and these organisms belong to the lowest stage of life—to that stage which forms a kind of undeveloped intermediate member between the vegetable and animal kingdom, Häckel's kingdom of the protista. The next oldest animal organisms found in the Cambrian formation are the zoöphytes, and immediately above them the mollusca and the crustacea. In the following Silurian period we find corals, radiata, worms, mollusca, and crustacea, in great number, also all the main-types of the invertebrates; and in the highest Silurian strata there are also to be found representatives of the lowest class of vertebrates, of fish, but still of very low organization and little differentiated. That the five main-types of the invertebrates seem to have appeared quite contemporaneously, yet that the zoöphytes really appeared first, does not contradict the before-mentioned law of a progress in the appearance of the organisms from the lower to the higher. For in the zoölogical system also these main-types of the invertebrates do not stand one above the other, but by the side of each other: at most, the radiata, the worms, the mollusca, and the articulata, take their places above the zoöphytes. Only within the main-types, in the classes, orders, etc., do differences in rank take effect; and even here, not without exception. What difference in rank, for instance, is there between an oyster and a cuttle-fish? between a cochineal and a bee or ant? and yet the first two belong to one and the same type—the type of mollusca; and the last three to one and the same class—the class of insects. The vertebrates rank decidedly above the invertebrates; and in a manner wholly corresponding to this, the vertebrates also appear after the invertebrates. Just as decidedly as to their rank, the main classes of the vertebrates do not stand beside, but above one another: above the fish stand the amphibia, above them the reptiles, next the birds, and above them the mammalia. To this series of succession also the geological facts seem to correspond pretty closely; only long after the fish do the first amphibia and reptilia appear—although it can not yet be decided which of these two classes has left its earliest traces. If the interpretation of the gigantic foot-steps in the colored sandstone of North America, as belonging to the cursorial birds, is correct, the first appearance of birds falls in the time between the reptilia and mammalia; otherwise the first mammalia would have appeared before the first birds. For if we find the first real bones of birds only in the Jura and in the Chalk-formation, they are birds with tail-spines and with teeth in the beak—hence still related to the reptilia or the sauria. The first traces of mammalia to be found in the Upper Keuper formation, and in the Jura, belong to the order of opossums or marsupialia; *i.e.*, to that order which (excepting the echidna and the ornithorhynchus that, as so-called monotremeta, stand the very lowest in the class of the mammalia, but are very scarce) occupies the lowest stage among the multitude of mammalia. Only after them do the higher orders of mammalia appear; and last of all organisms, man.

If we follow more in detail the appearance of the single organisms, some remarkable modifications show themselves in the course of their appearance and growth. We have heretofore mentioned the possibility of the appearance of the mammalia before the bird. Another fact which deserves attention is, that frequently the lowest representatives of a class or an order do not at first appear where the highest representatives of the next lower class or order are in existence, but with lower representatives of a preceding class or order, viz.: such representatives of the same as are still less differentiated and unite in themselves comparatively still more generic and less specific characteristics —as for instance, the lowest and earliest amphibia, which do not appear at the same time and place with the most highly organized fishes, but with fishes of still lower organization. Moreover many groups of organisms show in earlier geological periods a richness of development from which they have now fallen far away. For instance, among the mammalia the pachydermata, among the reptilia the salamander and newt, among the articulata the cephalopoda, are at present remarkably reduced;—compare with the legions of ammonites and belemnites of the secondary period the small number of nautilus and cuttle-fish of the seas at the present day. A similar fortune was experienced by the ferns and club-mosses which formed whole forests in the carboniferous period. Other groups which once played a great *rôle*, are now wholly extinct; for instance, the trilobites of the primary, the sauria of the secondary, the nummulites of the tertiary periods. Now, all these modifications of geological progress would entirely correspond to the idea of a pedigree to which the descent theory traces back the whole abundance of forms of organisms. As soon as we seriously accept the idea of a pedigree, each of the two organic kingdoms would throughout form for its classes and species not only one single straight line of descent, but a tree, the branches of which are again ramified in a manifold way; a tree on which single branches—as perhaps that of the class of birds—may leave the main-stem or a main-branch, possibly being a branch destined to a higher development, and on that account held back in the process of development; a tree, finally, on which also branches and twigs can wholly or partly die off, as those of the extinct or reduced groups of organisms.

From the point where the geological formations approach the present time, *plant* and *animal geography* also assists *geology* in increasing the weight of the reasons for an origin of organisms through descent. With the tertiary period, the fauna and flora of the globe, which in former periods had a nearly uniform character all over the earth and showed no climatic differences, begin to separate according to climate, zones, and greater continents. This separation becomes distinctly evident in the middle tertiary formations, the Miocene, and much more distinctly in the higher tertiary formations, the Pliocene. The animals, especially the higher vertebrates, of the Pliocene formation on each continent or each larger group of islands, correspond very closely to the now living animals of the same geographical limit, with the exception of being generally of a much larger size. The Pliocene animal world of mammalia of the three old continents, for instance, corresponds exactly, through all its orders, to the present fauna of Europe, Asia and Africa; and that on an average it was built up more stupendously than that of to-day, we can see from the cave-bear and the mammoth. South America is the home of a peculiar order of mammalia—of the edentata, to which belong the sloth, the armadillo, and the like. All its predecessors are to be found also in the Pliocene strata of South America, and only there; and mostly in gigantic, but otherwise completely related, forms. New Zealand has no indigenous mammalia, but in their place great cursorial birds with but rudimentary wings. Exactly the same thing is found by geology in its tertiary and post-tertiary strata: nowhere a mammal, but gigantic birds with rudimentary wings, down to the dinornis, which probably died out in man's time. New Holland has merely marsupial and some monotrematous, but no placental, mammalia; even its tertiary strata give no placental mammalia, but marsupialia, in analogy with all living genera, herbivorous, and carnivorous. Indeed, the analogy goes so far that the same line which through the Indian Archipelago separates the present Australian animal and plant world from the Asiatic, forms also the separating line for the geological zones of the Pliocene epoch. All these are facts which render quite inevitable the idea of an origin of the higher organic species of to-day through descent.

But still, from another side, animal geography, though it does not yet speak for a common pedigree of the whole animal world, as the facts just mentioned also do not, still at least speaks for a descent of related, though at present separated, genera and species from common forefathers. The continents of the Old and New World are so constructed that toward the North Pole they approach one another very closely, and toward the South Pole they withdraw from one another. Without doubt there existed in the North, through long periods of time, a land-connection of America with Asia and with Europe. Now, both continents have their more or less characteristic animal world, and these characteristics are distributed over the two halves of the globe in the following extremely remarkable way: The fauna of the Old and the New World, in those groups of animal genera which live only in the warmer or tropic zones or only south of the equator, and have no associates of genera or families in the higher North, is in each hemisphere entirely characteristic, and differs in a marked way from the fauna of the other half of the globe. For instance, the rhinoceros, the hippopotamus, the giraffe, the antelope with undivided horns, the hedgehog, the mole proper, are only inhabitants of the Old World, whence also the horse originally came, the striped ones in Africa and the non-striped in Asia; on the other hand, the lemur, the ant-eater, the armadillo, and others, are limited to South America. The apes of the Old World have five molar teeth on each side of the jaw, narrow noses, tails usually short and never prehensile, and fleshy protuberances for sitting; the apes of the New World have six molar teeth, flat noses, and long prehensile tails. And on the contrary, where closely related species are found on both parts of the globe, they belong only to genera of which single species live or have lived in the far North; as, for instance, the rein-deer, still common to the Old and the New World in this very North which once formed a bridge between the two halves of the earth. The same is true in regard to cattle, the deer, the cat, the dog, the hare. Similar facts can also be shown of other animal classes. The farther the different species of these genera withdraw from the North Pole, the greater become the differences between the species on the one half of the globe and the analogous species of the other. Compare on this point K. E. von Baer's "Studien aus dem Gebiete der Naturwissenchaften, über Darwin's Lehre," ("Studies from the Realm of Natural Science upon Darwin's Teachings"), p. 356 f. If we add, further, the before mentioned fact, that those genera which are exclusively peculiar to one or the other continent, have their related predecessors in the tertiary strata of these continents, the hypothesis of a separate origin for each single species, without genealogical connection with the anatomically and physiologically related species, becomes neither more nor less than a scientific impossibility.

Moreover, there are several facts of *comparative anatomy* which have long been the joy of all zoölogists and have rewarded the toilsome labors of detailed investigations by a delightful view over the whole realm of the organic world, but which find a scientific explanation only in the descent theory. They are the *homology of the organs*, and to a certain degree also the so-called *rudimentary organs*. By homology of organs we mean the fact that within one and the same class-group of organisms all the organs, and especially the organs in their most solid constituents, in the skeleton, are built after one and the same fundamental plan, and therefore are even in their most widely separated modifications varied after this one and the same plan. This is especially true of the vertebræ and the limbs. This homology goes so far within one class, particularly within the class of mammalia, that, for instance, the hands and feet of man, the hands of the ape, the paws of the beast of prey, the hoof of the horse and of the ox, the paws of the mole, the fins of the seal and of the whale, the wing-membranes of the flying-squirrel, correspond to one another in their smallest parts and ossicles, and can all be registered with the same numbers and letters; *i.e.*, they are homologous to one another even to the minutest detail. The *ideal* plan and connection in the organisms, disclosed by these facts, and long ago acknowledged and admired, receives at the same time its simple *material* basis through the acceptance of a common descent.

A similar relation is observed in *rudimentary organs*.

Many of them, as the nipples of males, point, if not to a common descent from a lower form, at least to a common plan of the sexes. But when the embryo of the whale still has its teeth in the jaw, the grown up whale its hip-bones, when the eye of man still has its winking membrane, the ear and many portions of the skin their rudimentary muscles of motion, the end of the vertebral column its rudimentary tail, the intestinal canal its blind intestine; when sightless animals, living in the dark, still have their rudimentary eyes, blind worms their shoulder-blades; when in like manner the plants, especially in their parts of fecundation, show in great number such rudimentary organs as are entirely useless for the functions of life, but which are never misleading in determining their relationship with other plants:—how simply are all these facts explained by the descent theory, how not at all without it!

Finally, if we now mention the *history of the development of animals*, we shall have to postpone to the next section the consideration of the most essential facts furnished by this science; for the individual development of animals is a process which could speak not only for a descent of the species, but also for a descent of them through gradual development. But where, as in the present section, we treat the descent theory apart from the evolution theory, we have also to think of the possibility that the species or groups of species are not originated through gradual development, but nevertheless do originate through descent—namely, in leaps through metamorphosis of germs or a heterogenetic generation; and for such an idea we find confirmation in the observation of the history of development of animals, which we call *change of generation* or *metagenesis*.[4] By this is meant the following phenomenon: Certain animals, as the salpa and doliolum of the order of the tunicata, as well as certain mites and many tape-worms, produce offspring which are wholly dissimilar to the mother stock. These offspring have the capacity of reproducing themselves—if not by sexual means, as at the first generation, still by the formation of sprouts; and it is only the animals originated by the second generation (with many species, even those by the third) which return again to the form of the first generation. The plant-lice transmit themselves through six, seven, even ten generations by means of sprouts, until a generation appears which lays eggs. Now it is indeed true that the change of generation forms a circle in which the form of the last generation always returns to that of the first, and therefore leaves the species, as species, wholly unchanged. But it is nevertheless a process which shows that the natural law of an identity between generator and product, observed in other relations, is not without exception; and if we once have reason to suppose that the generation of new species took place in past periods of the globe, but has ceased in the present, such processes in the single period open to our direct observation—namely, the present (in which, however, according to our knowledge, the species remain constant)—are nevertheless hints worthy of notice. For they refer us to ways in which in those former times, when certainly new species did originate, this formation of species might possibly have taken place.

This consideration leads us to treat of the main objection raised to every descent theory: namely, that never yet has the origin of one species from another been observed, but that, on the contrary, *all species*—so far as our experience goes, stretching over thousands of years—*remain constant*. We will give no weight to the fact that the constancy of species seems by no means to be absolutely without exception; for on the whole, they certainly remain constant. The only example which goes to prove such an evolution of species as taking place to-day—viz: the natural history of sponges—seems not to have this bearing. The transitions of form, proven by O. Schmidt in the siliceous sponges and by Häckel in the chalk-sponges, seem to show, not the genetic coming forth of a new species out of another, and especially not the evolution of a higher species out of a lower, but rather the uncertainty of the idea of species in general and the worthlessness of the skeleton-forms, for this idea, in such low organizations as the sponges. But that objection already loses its chief force from the consideration that we have not only never observed the origin of one species from another, but never even the origin of a species itself; and that nevertheless all species have successively originated in time. If we, therefore, are not able to observe directly their origination, we have a right to make all possible attempts at approaching the knowledge of it in an indirect way. But we see this objection invalidated by still another fact. From all observations, it seems to be evident that those agencies which originated the species in general have ceased since man appeared. Now this fact is inconvenient for all those who, on metaphysical grounds, reject aim and purpose in the world and accept an aimless motion in the universe, a circle in which only identical powers are ever active to all eternity. From this standpoint, the scientists cannot, except by very artificial hypotheses, escape the conclusion that, if new species once originated through descent, new species ought still to originate through descent. In like manner, it is true, they are also obliged to accept the other conclusion: that if new species once originated through primitive generation, new species ought still to originate through primitive generation. On the other hand, those scientists who recognize aims in the world for which the world and each part of it is destined, and which are attained in the world through the processes of coming into existence, have to expect in advance that the organic kingdoms are also planned with reference to those aims. They naturally see the aim of the origin of species attained, where in the organic world beings appear who combine with the highest physical organization a self-conscious and responsible spiritual life, and who are capable of conceiving the ideal, even the idea of God. For, with the appearance of these beings, there enter upon the theatre of the world beings who go beyond the value of a purely physical organism and of a purely somato-psychical life, and in like manner represent again a higher order of beings; just as the first appearance of organic life on earth once introduced a new and higher stage of existence in contrast to the inorganic world. Scientists who take this standpoint can readily adopt the fact that we do not now observe the origination of new species; for it is in full harmony with their metaphysical doctrines, without the same being on that account essentially dependent upon the confirmation or rejection of the hypothesis of the present constancy of species. With this very fact, the maxim that if new species once originated through descent, new species must still originate through descent, has lost for them its truth, and therefore its power of demonstration. So we see even here, while in the midst of the discussion of a purely scientific problem, in what close correlation metaphysics and natural science stand, and moreover—since the metaphysical view is most closely connected with the religious—in what close relationship religion and natural science stand. At the same time we also see how little the metaphysical interest, and much more how little the religious interest, has reason to avoid the investigation of facts in nature.

§ 4. *The Theory of Evolution—Archæology, Ethnography, Philology.*

The evolution theory teaches that the species have developed themselves one from another in gradual transitions, each of which was as small as the individual differences still observed to-day among the individuals of the same species. It is not without support, especially in the *history of the development of plants and animals.*

Each organic being becomes what it is by means of organic development. Each plant, even the highest organized, begins in its seed-germ with a simple cell, and is differentiated in constant development up to the fully perfected individual. Each animal, even the most highly organized (man included), begins the course of its existence as an egg; and each egg has no greater value of form than that of a single cell. This egg-cell is differentiated, after fecundation, in gradual and imperceptible transitions, farther and farther, higher and higher, until the individual has reached its perfect organization. No organ, no function of the body, no power or function of the soul or of the mind, appears suddenly, but all in gradual development. Since we see all individuals thus originating by means of gradual development, the possibility lies very near that the different organic formations of all the organic kingdoms could also have been originated by the same means.

In still another direction does the history of the development of single plants and animals make this possibility plausible to us. In the animal world, and partly also in the plant world, the single individuals of higher species in their embryonic development pass through states of development, in the former stages of which not only the individuals of the most different species look confusingly similar to one another, but also the embryos in their organization remind us of the perfected state of much lower classes of beings. In order to give a clear idea of the first mentioned facts, Häckel, for instance, in his "Natural History of Creation" and in his "Anthropogeny," represents by engravings the embryos of different vertebrates and also of man; representations which—although, according to the judgment of competent scientists, unfortunately not exact, but modified, after the manner of stencil plates, in favor of greater similarity—yet make it quite clear that the similarity of the different embryos must be very great. We see, for instance, on one table the embryos of a fish, a salamander, a turtle, a fowl; on a second, those of a pig, an ox, a rabbit, a man; on a third, those of a turtle, a fowl, a man; and we find the similarity really great. Examples of the second fact—that individuals of higher classes or orders in former states of their embryonic development represent an organization which corresponds to the full-grown individuals of the lower classes—are: the tail of the human embryo, the gill-arches of the embryos of reptilia, of birds, of mammalia, and of man. Now Häckel here takes up again an idea first suggested by Fritz Müller, and derives from these observations the "biogenetic maxim," as he calls it: "The history of the germ is an epitome of the history of the descent; or, in other words, ontogeny (the history of the germs or the individuals) is a recapitulation of phylogeny (the history of the tribe); or, somewhat more explicitly: that the series of forms through which the individual organism passes during its progress from the egg-cell to its fully developed state, is a brief, compressed reproduction of the long series of forms through which the animal ancestors of that organism (or the ancestral forms of its species) have passed from the earliest periods of so-called organic creation down to the present time." In his latest publication, "Ziele und Wege der heutigen Entwicklungsgeschichte," ("Aims and Methods of the Present History of Evolution"), he admits into the formulation of his biogenetic maxim also the consideration of those phenomena in the ontogenetic development which are no recapitulation of the history of the stem, but originated by adapting the embryo to its surroundings. In the description and explanation of this theory, he uses a term which throws upon nature a peculiar reproach, never before made, namely: cenogeny, or history of falsifications, in contrast to palingeny, or history of abridgments. This amended formula now reads: The development of germs is an abridgment of the development of stems, and is the more complete according as the development of the abridgment is continued by inheritance, the less complete according as the development of the false is introduced by adaptation.

Now, we ask: Is this biogenetic maxim correct? and moreover, from the fact of the organic individuals originating through development, are we entitled to draw the conclusion that even the species must have originated through development? To this question we can no longer get an answer from the life-processes of living organisms; for we have already mentioned the fact that, according to the present state of our knowledge, we can no longer observe the origination of a new species. Moreover, the embryonic states of development show also, in all their similarity, even in the very first stages, and with especial distinctness in these first stages, many differences between the single species; and this is true especially of those species which, according to the followers of this so-called biogenetic maxim, should lie in the same stem-line,
—so that the direct scientific value of the embryological results to the palæontological investigation, or of the latter to the former, is so far very slight. Such a problem, however, as the one contained in that biogenetic maxim, which only gives to investigators the *direction* in which possibly an interesting and profitable path can be opened, does not at all deserve the name of a *"law."*
K. E. von Baer, the founder of the whole present science of the history of development, has certainly a most competent judgment of the correctness of this so-called biogenetic maxim; and he convincingly shows, in his essay on "Darwin's Doctrine," that the embryos never represent a former animalic form, but that their development follows the principle of representing first the common characteristics of the class, then those of the

order, etc., until finally the individual characteristics appear in the formation. Those who wish more information about embryology can find it in Heinrich Rathke's "Entwicklungsgeschichte der Wirbelthiere" ("History of the Development of Vertebrates"), edited by A. Kölliker, Leipzig, Engelmann, 1861; and those who wish to inform themselves as to the influence of the ontogenetic results of the solution of the phylogenetic problems, will find, besides the before-mentioned work of Wigand, rich and clearly elaborated material in the publication of Wilhelm His—"Unsere Körperform und das physiologische Problem ihrer Entstehung, Briefe an einen befreundeten Naturforscher" ("The Form of our Body and the Physiological Problem of its Origin; Letters to an Associate Scientist"), Leipzig, Vogel, 1875. The latter writer, although he advocates the descent theory, rejects the hasty assertions of Häckel with direct and convincing arguments.

Thus embryology, having from the simple fact of an origin of single plants and animals through descent at least confirmed the idea of the *possibility* of an origin also of species through development, forsakes us in the inquiry as to the *reality* of such a genealogy of development, and refers us to other sciences.

Such a science, from which we certainly are entitled to expect a decided answer, is *geology*. For if the evolution theory is right, those periods of the history of our globe in which new species originated—namely, the periods of geology—*must* show us also the *forms of transition* between the different species. And, indeed, geology gives us an answer; but it reads contradictorily: It says yes, and it says no.

Geology does show us forms of transition, and, indeed, most frequently in the lower classes of animals. Who that has once studied petrifactions, does not know the mass of forms of the terebratulæ, the belemnites, and the ammonites, in the Jura formation? Würtemberger has brought light into the perplexing division of species of the ammonites by simply showing their temporary and systematic transitions into one another. In the fresh water chalk formation of Steinheim, near Heidenheim, in Würtemberg, scientists have found, on the same place, in an uninterrupted series of strata, the snail valvata or paludina multiformis in all imaginable transitions—from the flat winding, showing the form of a chess-board, up to the sharp form of a tower. And it was not, as Hilgendorf thought, in a series which can be traced in the strata according to time, but, as Sandberger says, in quite a varied mixture, yet in all imaginable modifications. But even among the higher and the highest classes of animals, we can trace the transitions. The flying sauria, if not in their organs of flying, which remind us more of the bat, at least in head, neck, and toes, are closely connected with the birds—the oldest birds of the Jura and chalk formations, with their tail-spines similar to the reptilia and their teeth in the beak to the sauria. The tertiary formations especially show the primitive history of many vertebrates in very instructive forms of transitions—which, for instance, Rütimeyer, a scientist who is very cautious in his conclusions, very distinctly traced to the horse, to the ruminating animals, and lately also to the turtles. Still more in detail, W. Kowalewsky has lately shown us the primitive history of the horse, and Leidy and Marsh have further completed it by the addition of American forms, the former having at the same time described the forms which have led to the tapir.

But to such facts there are, on the other hand, experiences directly contradictory. Many lower and higher forms of animals and plants appear in the geological strata, so far as they have been explored, in a wholly independent way. We have mentioned, in the foregoing section, that the main types of the invertebrates appear somewhat contemporaneously and without any traceable intermediate form. The trilobites, a quite highly organized order of crustacea, appear in the strata of the silurian epoch almost suddenly, in very many and very distinctly marked species. The uncertainty of our knowledge shows itself most clearly when we ask for the geneologic relationship of the vertebrates. In Chap. II, § 1 and § 2 we have already referred to the value which Darwin, and more especially Häckel, lays on the relationship of the larva of the ascidia to the lancelet fish. Now the important testimony of K. E. von Baer, in his "Mémoires de l'Académie de St. Pétersbourg," Ser. vii, Vol. 19, No. 2, tells us that the nerve-ganglion of the ascidia lies on the side of the stomach, and on that account can not be homologous with the spine of the vertebrates, but that the cord in the larva of the ascidia is nothing more than a support for the tail in swimming, which afterwards disappears, as with many other larvæ. As to the course of reasoning in reaching these genealogical conclusions, he says: "The hypothesis is indeed flexible. According to common reasoning, that which shows itself early in the development is an inheritance of the first progenitors. Therefore the ascidæ ought to descend from the vertebrates, and not the reverse. But it was necessary to show the descent of the vertebrates from the lower forms. In order to respond to such a necessity, men sometimes reverse their conclusions. Although favorably disposed to the doctrine of the transmutation of the animalic forms, I want a complete proof before I can believe in a transformation of the vertebrate type into that of the mollusca." Moreover, the zoölogists Semper and Dohrn find in the embryonic development of the sharks, the scates, and other cartilaginous fishes, organs which would bring them rather into a nearer relationship with the ringed worms than with the crustacea. When, on the other hand, we look around in palæontology, the oldest fossil fishes remind us neither of the crustacea nor of the ringed worms, but of the crabs: a class of animals which lies entirely outside of Häckel's stem-line of vertebrates. Also the first appearance of mammalia does not show transitions. Thus far we have not found in the geological strata any vestiges of the half-apes, which, according to the hypothesis of the evolutionists, as a common stem-line for the lines of ape and man development, once played such an important *rôle*, and which have quite numerous representatives.

But the answer which geology gives to our questions as to the probable confirmation of the evolution theory, naturally becomes most interesting where the *origin of man* is treated of. Our attention is, therefore, especially directed to the most recent formations of the globe which show us the oldest remains of man. The most instructive are those parts of the skeleton which allow us to draw the most convincing conclusions as to the degree of mental development of an individual, namely: the parts of the skull. Although human bones seem to have been less easily preserved than those of animals, and are, comparatively speaking, very scarce, especially more so than prehistoric implements, still there are not wanting such remains, which go back far beyond historical time. The oldest known skull is the celebrated one of the Neander cave near Düsseldorf, with its large vault of the forehead, and its low height. Although Virchow finds on it evidences of rachitis in youth and of gout in old age, as well as of injuries, it nevertheless can not have been changed in its *fundamental form* by any sickness, even according to Virchow. This very skull now indisputably shows a still lower formation, which, although quite essentially different from the type of the ape, stands nearer to it than is the case with the skulls of men in later times. Of a later date, and of a correspondingly higher form, are the skull of Engis, of Cannstatt, the skulls of the Belgian caves (especially Chauvaux), of France, and of Gibraltar. According to the weighty authority of Schaaffhausen (note his opening address at the Wiesbaden Congress of the Anthropological Society, 1873), the skulls and the remaining parts of the skeleton show more indications of a lower formation the older they are. He especially calls attention to a certain bone of the roof of the skull—the *Os interparietale* or the so-called *Os Incæ*

—which has only recently been recognized as a characteristic of a lower formation of skulls, standing nearer to that of animals. As late as the summer of 1873, two human skeletons were found at Coblenz in a volcanic sand, of which Schaaffhausen says: "No less than eight anatomic marks of a lower formation, which probably have not heretofore been found together, indicate the great age of these remains." With all these traces of a difference between the former and the present state of the physical condition of man, the differences between the type of man and that of the animal are still great enough to leave wide open the possibility of the origin of man through some other means than that of gradual development. On the other hand, it is more or less in favor of the evolution idea, that so far such old remains of man have been found in places which certainly can not have been the cradle of mankind, and that those parts of the earth which we would naturally suppose to be the first dwelling place of the earliest human genera have been little or not at all investigated. And also the hypothesis of Häckel, that the cradle of mankind was a land between Africa and Asia, now sunk in the sea, and called Lemuria, can be neither proved nor denied. Such vague possibilities have indeed not the least scientific value.

In considering these contradictory results of geological investigation, we dare not overlook three points: First, our knowledge of the crust of the globe is still very fragmentary, and does not yet extend over the whole globe. Further, it lies in the nature of the case that the strata in mountain formations can only give a very incomplete picture of the whole variety of the real organic life which may have populated the earth and the sea. What a poor picture of the present plant and animal life would be offered, for instance, by the soil of our continents, the slime, sand, and pebbles of our coasts and of the bottoms of our lakes and seas, if we had to construct from them alone the fauna and flora of the present! A third, but purely hypothetical, consideration is rendered of importance particularly by Darwin and Häckel; namely, that the forms of transition without doubt existed for a shorter period than those forms whose organization has established itself in fully developed species.

Thus far we have directed our attention to inquiring how the organic individuals were originated—and have throughout observed a successive development; next, we have questioned geology—and here also have observed a progress in the appearance of the species, but have received at the same time contradictory answers to the question whether this progress presents itself as a gradual development of one species from another or as a sudden appearance. So the reasons for and against the evolution theory almost balance one another; and it is not improbable that the hypothesis of an origin of species through development will have to share its authority with the hypothesis of a descent of species through heterogenetic generation, as well as with the hypothesis of a primitive generation of lower organisms, still repeating itself at a later time. Thus for the origination of groups lying nearer together, we have the evolution theory; for the other groups, and especially for the origination of types where no transitions to other types can be traced, the theory of the heterogenetic or primitive generation recommends itself; and both theories thus far are of a purely hypothetical nature.

But there is still a third realm, which is just as open to our observation as the history of the development of organisms and as geology, and of which we can also ask, whether it does not open for us an indirect way to the knowledge of the origin of species, and especially of man—a knowledge which we can no longer approach in the direct way of observation. This realm is *natural history* and the *history of the development of the human race*. For mankind also is engaged in a process of development, and its present members do not stand on the same height. Now the question is, to what beginning can we trace backward the development of mankind, and to what succeeding stages of development from this present condition? And do we find in these earliest periods, and on these lowest stages, points that are connected with still earlier conditions and organizations, and especially points which could genealogically join together mankind and the animal kingdom? Three sciences, still young, favorite children of the present generation, participate in investigating this realm, namely, *archæology, comparative ethnology*, and *comparative philology*.

Archæology leads us back to far-off times. It is a fact that, chronologically speaking, man lived in the glacial period—according to French scientists, even before it; and that, palæontologically speaking, man and mammoth lived at the same time, and, according to a discovery made some thirty years ago at Denise in Middle France, probably even man and another older and defunct form of pachydermata, the elephas meridionalis, in North America man and the mastodon. The reader may compare the discoveries regarding the age of mankind, as they are described most recently by Sir Charles Lyell in his work upon this subject, in the publications of the Anthropological Congress at Brussels in the year 1873, and in those of the fourth General Assembly of the German Society for Anthropology, Ethnology and Primitive History, at Wiesbaden, in the year 1873.

Now, to be sure, from the oldest human *tools* and *utensils* that are found, we can expect still less than from the oldest human bones that they will throw direct light upon the answer to the question of the *origin* of man. For where man not only uses tools, but *manufactures* the same for use, a wide breach already exists between man and animal. Manufactured articles, therefore, can only throw some light on the history of the development of the already existing human race. And even this light is less clear than we perhaps expected in view of the first interesting prehistorical discoveries. It is true, all these discoveries show us an ascent from the simplest and roughest forms to the more perfect; from the split but unpolished stone to the polished, and from stone to bronze and iron. But a progress of the human races in manufacturing and using articles, from the simple and rough form to the more artificial, lies so much in the nature of the case, and is so taken for granted with every conception of the origin of man, even with that contradictory to Darwinism, that from this simplicity of the earliest tools we can not at all conclude that there was a condition of mankind lying near that of animals; and especially we can draw only general and uncertain conclusions as to that which makes man *man*, as to the spiritual and moral qualities of those prehistoric men. Moreover, in discoveries belonging to the very oldest, we come upon drawings and engravings from which we recognize the man of those primitive times as a creature whose life was not entirely taken up in the animalic struggle for existence, but was already adorned with those ideal pursuits and enjoyments which we are accustomed to ascribe to the height of civilization. Examine, for instance, the drawing of a mammoth on a mammoth tooth of Dordogne, which the French scientists Lartet and Christy have reprinted in their Reliquiæ Aquitanicæ (1868), and which Sir Charles Lyell has copied in his "Age of the Human Race." How much spirit and life in this primitive work of art! Or read what Fraas, in the "Journal of the German Society for Anthropology," March, 1874, reports about the picture of a grazing reindeer, engraved on a knife handle made of the horns of a reindeer, which was lately found in the cave of Thayngen near Schaffhausen, and which surpasses in beauty all rough drawings thus far found. The whole bearing of the animal— the muscles of the legs and the head, the form of the many-branched antlers, with the wide-spread eyes, the representation of the hair upon the body and under-jaw—all disclose a real artist among those savages.

This is also to be taken into consideration: that those men, whose traces we find, could possibly have been the descendants of more noble predecessors, driven off and degenerated, just as well as they could have been representatives of the whole former condition of culture of mankind. In England, where the questions of the first condition of culture of mankind are very warmly discussed, the Duke of Argyll particularly, in his "Primeval Man," advocates these views, and very forcibly calls attention to the fact that thus far the places of the discovery of the earliest traces of man undoubtedly lie very far from the original home of the human race; while Sir John Lubbock, in his "Origin of Civilization" and in his "Prehistoric Times," and also Tylor in his "Beginning of Culture" and in his "Early History of Mankind," take the opposite view of a progress of mankind from the most uncultivated beginnings.

Archæology, as a whole, seems to do no more than admit that its results can be incorporated into the theory of an origin of the human race through gradual development, *if* this theory can be shown to be correct in some other way, and that its results can just as well be brought into harmony with a contradictory theory.

Comparative ethnology gives us quite a similar result. It is true, there are races of mankind in the lowest grades of human existence. It is well known how Darwin, in his voyage on board the "Beagle," got one of his first vivid impressions of the possibility of an evolution of man from the animal world, by seeing the inhabitants of Tierra del Fuego; and it is remarkable that the arms, tools, and furniture, used by the lowest savages, are very similar to the earliest remains of civilized races found on earth. The conclusion lies extremely near, that the savages simply remained in earlier stages of human culture; and an ethnographic picture of mankind at present would in a similar way give an approximately correct view of its former development, as the natural zoölogical and botanical system of the present fauna and flora must give us at the same time the key to their pedigree; supposing the Darwinian theory to be correct.

If it were so, ethnology would be an altogether inestimable help for the exploration of the descent and development of the human race. For the extremely few and rare fossil remains of man—which, moreover, do not give us any answer to the most important questions in regard to the mental and moral quality of the primitive man—would be rendered complete by living examples of the kind, which remained at the old stages of development.

But much is still wanting, before the followers of an evolution theory dare to use ethnology directly as a primitive history of the development of mankind, prepared and preserved for them. Especially the before-mentioned objection of the Duke of Argyll—that the lowest savages of our time can just as well be depraved as be men who remained stationary in the process of development—has here increased weight. Moreover, even with the savages of to-day, a rude state of their tools and a low condition of their mental and moral life are not so nearly parallel as to allow unrestricted conclusions to be drawn. Finally, we still know too little about the state of culture of the savages; and the deeper and higher the intellectual and ethical possessions of mankind are, the presence of which among the savages is in question, the more uncertain is our knowledge.

This is especially true of the most important question in this connection—the question as to the existence or absence of an idea of God, and the different stages of development of religious ideas. While some assume as an established fact, that there are savage tribes without any idea of God or any religion, and even give the names of these tribes, especially of some from the interior of South America; while Sir John Lubbock systematically enumerates seven stages of religious development, from atheism to the connection of religious with moral conceptions, and lets each single race run through these stages in an identical series until it either remains on one of the seven stages or arrives at the highest: yet, on the contrary, other equally trustworthy scientists assert that there is not a single human race without some idea of religion and of a God—indeed, not a single race without a monotheistic presentiment—and that all heathenism, down to its most degenerate stages, consists not so much in a non-recognition of a God as in ignoring him. They call especial attention to the difficulty of getting acquainted with the ideas of a savage tribe without living with it through many years and being intimate with its language and customs, and especially without enjoying the unrestricted confidence of the tribe. Mutual misunderstandings, a suspicious reserve, evasive and untrue answers to questions, are entirely unavoidable without those conditions. At any rate, the fact deserves attention, that those who have been longest and most active among savages, and who enjoyed their confidence to the fullest extent, all reached this result: they found them not only not without religion, but also not without a presentiment of the monotheistic idea of God. Livingstone, for instance, expressed this idea decidedly of all the African tribes with which he became acquainted; and Jellinghaus gives the same evidence in regard to the Kols in South Asia.

The *anatomic* results of ethnology are more favorable to the descent theory, although they too lead no farther than to the conclusion that the skull-forms of the lowest tribes represent a lower stage of formation than those of the higher, and that these lower skull-forms are relatively nearer to the ape-form than the higher, but that they are still separated from it by a wide interval.

It appears, then, that even ethnology does not lead us essentially nearer the solution of the question than archæology and geological anthropology.

The relatively strongest support to the evolution theory is given by *comparative philology*; and since language is the most important and most decisive of all the distinctive characteristics which separate man and animal[5], this science deserves especial consideration.

In the realm of the natural sciences, the enormous progress of palæontology on the one hand and of systematic zoölogy and botany on the other took place step by step together, and thus prepared the way for Darwin's idea—which, from the rich material of analytical investigations, only tries to draw the simple synthesis, and to show at the same time in the zoölogical and botanical *system* a representation of the zoölogical and botanical *history of development*. In quite an analogous way, a process took place in the linguistic realm which in independent investigations prepared the way for Darwinism, and now, since Darwin's theory has sought acknowledgment in the realm of natural history, brings again Darwin's ideas to the support of philology.

Linguistic and ethnographic investigations, especially the linguistic works of the missionaries, long ago resulted in gathering rich material from the storehouse of the language of races now living, and the latest works in the realm of historical, etymological, and comparative philology had traced the branches and twigs of the better known languages to stems and roots lying far back. The result of the comparison soon became the same as in the realm of the organic world: what presented itself in the system of the living languages as a lower form, seemed to represent itself as the older and more original form also in the history of languages. Therefore, all the prominent linguistic investigators found themselves more and more urged to accept a theory which declares language, this entirely specific characteristic of man, to be subject to the same laws of development from the simpler and most simple forms as the world of the organic. Long ago so celebrated a man as Jacob Grimm, —"Ueber den Ursprung der Sprache" ("The Origin of Language"), Berlin, Dümmler—following the footsteps of Wilhelm von Humboldt, had established a theory, according to which language is "not created, but produced by the liberty of the human will;" and judging from many of his Darwinistic utterances concerning the origin and development of language, he had traced its development in such a way as to arrive at the conclusion that artless simplicity in the unfolding of the senses is the first period of its appearance.

The scientists divide all the languages of the earth into three great groups: first, the monosyllabic, isolating, radical, or asynthetic languages; second, the agglutinant, terminational, or polysynthetic languages; third, the inflectional languages. They are of the opinion that even the languages of highest rank—the inflectional—very probably took a starting-point from the asynthetic languages, and a course of development through the agglutinants, and that in like manner the agglutinants have behind them an asynthetic period. Thus they trace all the languages back to certain *roots*, which are more or less common to the different groups of languages.

To the question that now arises—*How did these roots originate?*—the linguists give us three different answers. The onomatopoetic theory, called by Max Müller the Wow-Wow Theory, traces them to imitations of the sound (W. Bleek, G. Curtius, Schleicher, Wedgewood, Farrar); the interjectional theory, called by Max Müller the Pooh-Pooh, or Pah-Pah Theory, traces them to expressions of the senses (Condillac); a third theory declares the roots to be phonetic types (Max Müller, Lazar Geiger, Heyse, Steinthal); while it is still an open question, whether the attempts at explanation of these types must here come to a standstill for the present, as Max Müller thinks, or whether, according to Lazar Geiger, we can trace the first root-expressions especially to impressions of light and color.

The reasons from which Max Müller, in his "Lectures on the Science of Languages" (Vol. I, Lect. IX), rejects the first two theories and proves the third, are quite convincing. Even if, in a purely hypothetical way, a language could be thought of *in abstracto*, the roots of which only consist in imitations of sounds or interjections, still in the *really existing* languages, so far as we can trace back and uncover their roots, the roots imitating sounds and the interjectional roots form only a small and entirely isolated minority, which neither shares in, nor is capable of development; they stand like "dead sticks in a live hedge." By far the greater number of roots, and all which are capable of development, express abstractions from visible objects, conditions and activities, and therefore presume a human intelligence, reflecting with self-consciousness, which formed and used the roots.

Now Max Müller sees, back of this period, still open to science, in which the root-elements of the human languages were fixed, a long period of exuberant and unhindered growth of the elements of language, in which the roots were separated from the multitude of nascent tones by elimination or natural selection in the struggle for existence. In this realm, which is no longer open to investigation, the naturalistic and the linguistic friends of the evolution theory are now in entire accord. Wilhelm Bleek, in his small, but very noteworthy essay, "Ueber den Ursprung der Sprache" ("Origin of Language"), Weimar, Böhlau, 1868, p. 11, uses this ingenious figure: what the animal world possesses analogous to language, takes about the same position as, in the art of printing, the block-print does in relation to printing with movable types. On page 12, he sees in the communication of the emotions among animals the sources from which under favorable conditions (in consequence of which the separation of language into articulated parts became possible) human language might have originated. This idea, which is closely joined to the interjectional theory, Darwin meets with a related idea, depending upon the onomatopoetical theory, when he says, in his "Descent of Man": "Since monkeys certainly understand much that is said to them by man, and when wild, utter signal-cries of danger to their fellows, may not some unusually wise ape-like animal have imitated the growl of a beast of prey, and thus told his fellow-monkeys the nature of the expected danger? This would have been a first step in the formation of language."

But philology, from the point where it goes farther back in search of the roots of language, leaves the safe ground of knowledge and commits itself to the fluctuating ocean of conjectures; and since also the scientific evolution theory has only a hypothetical value, the support of a hypothesis in the one science by a hypothesis in the other naturally adds no weight to its probability, either for the one or the other. Besides, we must not overlook the fact that the very point in the history of the development of languages on which the investigation, as it looks backwards, must at present pause—namely, the existence of linguistic roots—presumes a faculty of abstraction which can not be thought of without self-consciousness.

Therefore archæology, comparative ethnography, and comparative philology, show us quite clearly a *development*, but not an *origin* of mankind through development. Yet they do show an already existing development of mankind; for all three sciences lead back to starting-points, where mankind already existed with all the essential attributes of mankind, and leave us without answer to our questions as to the conditions lying still farther back. Their results we can without difficulty harmonize with a theory which supposes mankind to have originated by evolution, provided such a theory could be confirmed from another side; but they agree just as well with a contrary theory, which excludes the origin of mankind by gradual development.

Taking, thus, everything into consideration, we come to the conclusion that the evolution theory, like the descent theory, is so far only a hypothesis—and, indeed, a hypothesis which as such has a much more problematical character than the descent theory. For while in regard to the latter we had to say that we have either this explanation or none of the origin of the higher species, with the evolution theory there is not even room for this alternative. For even in case of its failure, a descent of one species from another through heterogenetic generation is certainly very possible. Besides, it is not only possible, but even probable, that both theories—that of heterogenetic generation and that of gradual development—may have to share with one another in the explanation of the origin of species; and even that, especially for the lowest species and for the beginnings of the main types, primitive generation also has its share in the establishment of the paternity.

The evolution theory could only pass beyond the rank of a hypothesis, if we should succeed in showing the impelling forces of such an origin of species through development. Such an attempt can be made in two ways—the metaphysical and the scientific-empirical. The first, the metaphysical, although it may be justified in its general principles, will always, from the point at which it attempts to approach the concrete questions as to the origin of single species, expose itself to the fate of being *a priori* rejected by science as unjustified, and of being *a posteriori* confuted by facts—a fate which it has richly and clearly experienced in the first half of our century. But the discussion of the metaphysical way does not belong to the present purely scientific part of our investigation; it will, however, be shortly taken up again in Book II. The other way, the scientific-empirical, will have to be looked upon as correct when it can show the impelling forces of development in such powers and laws as are either still active to-day or at least have their points of connection in powers and laws active to-day. Such an attempt is the selection theory. We have already in Chap. II, § 1 and 2, given an outline of this theory, and have only yet to discuss its present state of tenability.

§ 3. *The Theory of Selection.*

The selection theory also is not entirely without support in the realm of observed facts. How simply it explains the fixedness of the differences of closely related species arising from their geographical and climatical home! how simply the similarity of the color of many animals from the color of their abode, through which they have protection against persecution! how simply the so-called *mimicry*—*i.e.*, the similarity of certain species in form and color with form and color of entirely different species in the midst of which they live, a similarity which often gives them protection against persecution! The best known examples of this, in our regions, are the spinning caterpillars, which in a state of rest look strikingly like a twig of a tree or a shrub on which they live. In other regions there is a multitude of the most striking freaks of nature of this kind—for instance, butterflies and other insects, which at rest look like the leaves of plants under which they live; butterflies living among other butterflies which, by an offensive odor, are protected against persecution, and although they are themselves a favorite food for birds, carrying the form and color of that badly-smelling family of butterflies. We can also add the orchideæ, and their resemblance to bees, flies, butterflies, spiders, etc. A. R. Wallace and Darwin themselves recur often to these striking appearances.

But herewith we have mentioned nearly every support which the selection theory has on the ground of observed facts. More numerous and more weighty are the objections to it. First of all, we have to state that the selection theory no longer enjoys that protection which the descent and evolution theories can justly claim, against the main objection, mentioned in Chap. III, § 1, to all the ideas of descent, development and selection. That main objection is the permanence of species, observed through thousands of years; and the defense with which the descent and evolution theories successfully weaken it, is the statement of the fact that, since man appeared, no new species has originated, and that therefore the principle of the generation of species seems to have come to a stand-still. Now this fact is no longer in favor of the selection theory, but directly repugnant to it. For the selection theory expressly declares the origin of species through agencies that are all active still, and, therefore, if they really suffice to explain the origin of species, would not only have to generate new species, but also to develop *all* the existing species. All those circumstances which, according to the selection theory, have led to change of species, are just as active to-day as they are supposed to have been from the beginning of organic life; and the effect which we observe is not change but permanence of species. The individuals still have individual qualities; they still have the tendency to inherit, in addition to the qualities of the species, those of the individual; the individuals still change their abode, and therewith also their conditions of life; a natural selection still takes place in the struggle for existence; and what is the result? From an observation stretching over thousands of years, we find nowhere an effect of natural selection going farther than alterations in growth and color and purely external changes in form. All the dispositions of organisms and their reciprocal action aim not at increasing the individual differences, but at reducing them to the average character of the species. When the species change their abode or their conditions of life, they either perish or remain constant; at least, with the exception of the slight modifications before mentioned. Even those alterations which artificial breeding produces, have a tendency to return to the original species: as soon as cultivated plants and domestic animals are left to themselves, they run wild, *i.e.*, they reassume their original qualities. Even the bastard-formations either cease to be fertile, or, remaining fertile, finally return to one or the other stem-form of the originally crossed species. Nor can we oppose to these facts the consideration that the period of time during which mankind has observed the organisms is too short. For the permanence of very many species can be traced through thousands of years, and the shortness of the period of our observations is amply counterbalanced on the one hand by the multitude of species from all parts of the organic systems which come under our notice, on the other by the immense alterations in the conditions of existence to which man submits plants and animals. How great, for instance, are the alterations in the conditions of existence which tropical plants undergo in our hot-houses and gardens! And the only alteration they show is that they are stunted and only bear blossoms with difficulty and fruits with still greater difficulty.[6] Now, if the ever-active selection principle does not produce in thousands of years even minimum alterations which can be observed, science certainly is justified in doubting for the present the asserted effect of that principle.

Thus not only are the *facts* directly opposed to the autocracy of the selection principle; but *logic* is also none the less so. For, under the most favorable circumstances, selection would only explain the *preservation* and perhaps also the *increase* of useful qualities and organs, *if* the same are already in existence and have shown themselves useful to the individual; but would not explain their *origination*. This would rather most emphatically be left to *chance*. According to the strict selection theory, it would be *pure chance* that among the thousands and thousands of individual qualities of the individuals of a species, such qualities are always existing as offer advantages to the individual in his struggle for existence. And it would be a second series of chances, which from generation to generation would have to coincide with the first, that among the individual qualities advantageous to the individual and making it victorious in the struggle for existence, there should be found always just those qualities which develop the species and raise it to a higher rank and order in the zoölogical and botanical systems. But the total of improbabilities which would have to be overcome continually in this theatre of chance, would in the course of generations necessarily amount to infinity. Thus, in the very beginning, insuperable doubts arise as to how we can explain from two causes the world of organisms which is so richly, beautifully, and systematically arranged. The first of these causes is the inclination to individual alteration, inherited indeed in the organisms, but in itself absolutely indifferent, for the systematical idea in the framework of the organic systems and for the progressive element in the development. The other is the struggle for existence and natural selection, which approaches the organisms purely from without like individual variability, must as a whole appear a necessity, but in each single case in the concrete mixture of coinciding circumstances, would seem a work of chance for the individual which is to be changed.

Moreover, it is a demonstrable impossibility to explain the origin of just those organs and members in the structure of organisms which are systematically the most significant and functionally the most important, by means of natural selection. It is true that many of these organs and members, in their perfected state, offer to the organism an immense advantage over lower organisms; but if they had been originated through gradual development, they would have been in their first beginnings and earlier stages of development at least quite indifferent, often directly obstructive to the individual in its struggle for existence, and therefore would have been called into existence and developed by agencies which had an effect directly counteracting natural selection. How high, for instance, stand the vertebrates above the invertebrates! Yet how could the first deviation from the ganglionic system of the nerves of the invertebrates to the cerebro-spinal system of the vertebrates have occurred?— and, especially, how could the first deposit of the vertebral column have procured any benefit to the individual in the struggle for existence? We quote this objection from Karl Planck's "Wahrheit und Flachheit des Darwinismus," ("Truth and Platitude of Darwinism"), Nördlingen, Beck, 1872.

Still more striking is the insufficiency of the selection theory for the explanation of the origin of the organs of motion in the higher classes of vertebrates. A. W. Volkman says of it, in his instructive lecture, "Zur Entwickelung der Organismen," ("Development of the Organisms") Halle, Schmidt, 1875, p. 3 ff.: "Without doubt, animals with extremities will come from animals which lacked extremities. Now if the metamorphosis originated in the course of one generation, the animals with extremities would have an advantage over the rest, which ought to show itself in the natural selection; but if the development of an extremity needs 10,000 generations, the individual in which the process of the development begins produces 1/10000 of the extremity and the advantage, resulting therefrom is reduced to zero. For an organ can only be of advantage when it performs its functions; and on the first of the 10,000 stages of development the extremity can not perform its functions. Just think of the cetacea! Of the hind extremity, only its carrier, the pelvis, has been developed; and even this is only represented by the two hip-bones, hanging in the flesh. As to the python, the hind extremities are more complete, but they lie hidden under the skin, and therefore are of no use for local movement. Such examples show that in the history of the development of an organ thousands of years may pass, and numerous generations may arise and disappear, until it reaches that grade of perfection where it is of use to its owner. How therefore, can we look upon such an organ, when finally it is perfect, as a product of selection in the sense of Darwin?"

We find the scientific objections to the selection theory collected in detail in the before-mentioned works of Wigand, Blanchard, His, von Baer, and especially in Mivart's "Genesis of Species," (London, MacMillan, 1871); and it is a praiseworthy testimony of Darwin's love of truth, that lately he himself, the originator of the selection theory, willingly admits these weak points in his theory,[7] while Häckel and many of his followers in Germany still stoutly reject every doubt of the autocracy of the selection principle.

In summing up all we have said thus far about the theories of descent, of evolution, and of selection, we still find all three solutions of the scientific problems to be hypotheses, but hypotheses of very different value. The idea of descent has the most scientific ground; it will, as a permanent presupposition, govern all scientific investigations as to the origin of species, even if it does not exclude the idea of an often-repeated primitive generation of organisms—especially of those that stand still lower in development. More uncertain and less comprehensive is the position of the evolution theory; in all likelihood, the idea of an origin through development will have to share the sovereignty with the idea of origin by leaps through metamorphosis of germs. Still more unfavorable is the state of the selection theory. It possesses the merit of having started the whole question as to the origin of species; it may explain subordinary developments; natural selection may have coöperated as a regulator in the whole progress and the whole preservation of organic life. Ed. von Hartmann, in his essay, "Truth and Error of Darwinism," (Berlin, Duncker, 1875), on page 111, compares its functions with those of the bolt and coupling in a machine; but that the driving principle which called new species into existence lay or originated *in* the organisms, and did not approach them from without, seems to be confirmed more and more decidedly with every new step of exact investigation as well as of reflection.

BOOK II.

THE PHILOSOPHIC SUPPLEMENTS AND CONSEQUENCES OF THE DARWINIAN THEORIES.

THE PHILOSOPHIC PROBLEMS.

Although, in accordance with the requirements of the task before us, we have to restrict ourselves to giving the results of natural science only in their general outlines, still we believe that we have not overlooked any essential result which is of importance to the question of the origin of species and of man. We have now finished our scientific review; and the conclusion to which we see ourselves brought is that natural science, in its investigation of the origin of species, has arrived at nothing but problems which it is not able to solve. There is a very great probability of an origin of species, at least of the higher organized species, through descent; but whether through descent by means of gradual development or of metamorphosis of germs, or whether with one group of organisms it is in this way, with another in that, is not yet decided. The attempt to explain their entire origin exclusively by the selection theory, must be regarded as a failure; all indications rather show that, supposing the descent principle correct, the deciding agencies which formed new species did not approach the old species out of which the new ones originated from without, but that they originated or were already in existence within them. But what these agencies were, natural science is at present unable to state; and not only those scientists who reject every idea of a descent, but also those who are favorable to the ideas of descent and of evolution, rejecting only the selection theory, are at one in silent or open acknowledgment of this limit of our knowledge, be it permanent or temporary.

But now the question arises: does the search after these agencies henceforth remain the exclusive task of natural science, and have we therefore simply to wait and see whether it will succeed in finding them? or have we to look for the answer to these questions, which natural science can no longer give, in another science—namely, philosophy? The first question we will have to answer in the affirmative, the second in the negative. It is certainly understood that *metaphysical* principles must underlie all *physical* appearances; and the right to define these principles, so far as they can be known, is willingly conceded to philosophy by the scientists, with the exception of those of materialistic and naturalistic tendencies. This mutual re-approaching of philosophy and natural science is one of the most gratifying, and, to both, most fruitful evidences of the intellectual work of the present generation. But these metaphysical principles themselves become cognizable only when the physical effects, whose cause they are, become accessible to our knowledge; and every attempt to find them *a priori*, or only to extend them *a priori*, will always fail through the opposition of empirical facts; or even if this attempt accommodates itself to the existing state of knowledge at a given time, it will always be overcome by the progress of the empirical sciences. In the most favorable case, it can claim the value of a hypothesis which has to be put to the proof, whether it can be empirically confirmed and whether we can successfully operate with it in knowing the world of realities. But herewith it leaves the realm of pure philosophy, and makes the question of its right to exist dependent upon the decision of natural science.

Since the decline of the doctrines of nature held by Schelling, Steffens, and Hegel, there has come to our knowledge, from the domain of philosophy, but one earnest attempt to explain the origin and development of organisms down to the concrete differences between single types, classes, and even orders and families, from one single metaphysical principle; and this attempt has been made by an antagonist of the descent doctrine. K. Ch. Planck, in "Seele und Geist, oder Ursprung, Wesen und Thätigkeitsform der physischen und geistigen Organisation von den naturwissenschaftlichen Grundlagen aus allgemein fasslich entwickelt" ("Soul and Spirit, or Origin, Nature, and Form of Activity of Physical and Intellectual Organization, Clearly Developed from a Scientific Basis"), Leipzig, Fues, 1871, and in "Wahrheit und Flachheit des Darwinismus" ("Truth and Platitude of Darwinism"), Nördlingen, Beck, 1872, makes the "inner concentration" the moving principle of the whole development of the world. He thinks that what belongs to the organism and to the soul has originated and developed up to man and his spiritual nature thus: that the creating centrum of the earth produces individual centra on its periphery, which tend more and more to bring into view the principle of centralization, in its contrast to the purely peripheral form of existence, until it reaches its goal in man, with his centralizing spirit. We have no reason to reject the idea of a principle of concentration in the world and its parts; it is confirmed by observation, and shows itself fruitful in many respects. But in spite of the many ingenious and often suggestive ideas in the works of Planck, we have some doubt about a system which tries to explain the whole concrete abundance of the richness of formations and life-forms in the world, rising higher and higher up to spiritual existence and moral action, from the single idea of concentration, and makes this principle the mystical and mysteriously acting cause of a whole world and its contents. We doubt at the outset the success of this argument. We have especially the strongest objections to a philosophical system which submits all the contending physical theories of the present to the measure of that concentration principle, and from these purely metaphysical reasons takes side exclusively with the one or the other of the theories, or establishes new theories—from the theories of atoms and ether, of light and heat, down to geological questions as to whether universal revolutions of the world or a continual development took place. The solution of all these questions, in their full extent, we do not attribute to philosophy, but to natural science; although to a natural science which permits philosophy to define the ideas with which it operates and the general principles to which it comes. For this renunciation—which philosophy, however, can not at all escape—it will be the more richly rewarded in this, that it obtains the more certainly for its own work sure and sifted material. But all attempts which can not submit to this renunciation, give only an apparent right to that view which Albert Lange, in his "History of Materialism," defends, when he banishes speculative philosophy to the realm of imagination.

But in rejecting philosophy in the question of the causes of the development and organization of the organic kingdoms, we did not reach the end of the philosophic problems with which we are confronted. This whole question is itself only a segment of the problems before which we stand, and leads of necessity to other questions.

Already within the series of development of the organic world, so far as it is investigated by natural science, we have found and named a point (at the end of § 1, Chap. II, Book I), where the competency of pure natural science comes to an end, and the question arises whether another source of knowledge—*i.e.*, even philosophy—can not take up the investigation where natural science completes its task. This point was the *origin of self-consciousness* and of *free moral self-determination*; consequently, the origin of that which makes man *man*. Going still farther back on the temporal and ideal scale of organic beings, we arrive at another point, which natural science no longer can explain, and that is the *origin of sensation* and of *consciousness*. With the appearance of sensation and consciousness, the *animal world* came into existence. Moreover, the whole scientific question as to the origin and development of species, so far as we have hitherto treated it, started from initial points where the organic and life already existed; it, therefore, leads of necessity to the further question as to *the origin of the organic and of life itself*. D. F. Strauss, in his "Postscript as Preface," thus clearly and simply characterizes these still unfilled blanks in the evolution theory: "There are, as is well known, three points in the rising development of nature, to which the appearance of incomprehensibility especially adheres (to speak more categorically: which have not been explained thus far by anybody). The three questions are: How has the living sprung from that which is without life? the sentient (and conscious) being from that which is without sensation? that which possesses reason (self-consciousness and free will) from that which is without reason?—questions equally embarrassing to thought." But even the question as to the origin of the organic and of life can not be discussed without an investigation, leading us farther back to the question as to *the elements of the world* in general. The *doctrine of atoms*, and the *mechanical view of the world*, are the scientific evidences of the efforts in this direction.

So far as the attempts to solve these four questions start from the results of natural science and, from this starting-point of the known, try to solve the unknown, we will have to assign them in the encyclopædic classification of the sciences, to that department of philosophy which treats the doctrines of nature; and since our whole investigation starts from the Darwinian theories, and only tries to treat of what is properly connected with them, the attempts to solve these four questions offer themselves as the *naturo-philosophic supplements of the Darwinian-theories.*

After concluding our treatment of them, we shall have to speak of still another view, which presupposes all these attempts at solution to be wholly or nearly successful, and draws an inference from them which no longer belongs to the realm of natural science, but is a purely *metaphysical* hypothesis; it is the *abolition of the idea of design in nature*. In connection with this, finally, we shall have to discuss the name which this view has lately assumed, viz: "*Monism.*"

Whatever further questions may arise, belong either to the special subdivisions of natural science and philosophy, or to theological and ethical problems.

CHAPTER I.

THE NATURO-PHILOSOPHIC SUPPLEMENTS OF THE DARWINIAN THEORIES.

§ 1. *The Origin of Self-Consciousness and of Free Moral Self-Determination.*

If sensation, and its most developed form, consciousness, is a reflex of the material in something immaterial, which feels itself a unit in contrast to the material, and, where sensation rises into consciousness, is opposed as a unit to the material—self-consciousness again is the reflex of this sentient and conscious subject in a new and still higher immaterial unity; and this again makes this sentient and conscious subject, together with the sum of its feelings and ideas, its object, changing it from a sentient and conscious subject into a felt and presented object. Therefore it is clear, and will be the result of all thought upon these concepts, that as with sensation and consciousness, so also with self-consciousness, something new always comes into existence—a higher category of being, different from the merely material. The first is the form of being of the animal world; the latter that of mankind.

It is exactly the same with the first appearance of voluntary movement, and again with that of free moral self-determination. The reaction of the sentient subject upon his sensations is something qualitatively different from the purely mechanical and physical action and reaction of pure matter; although, in order to understand the possibility of a sensation as well as of a voluntary movement, we must admit that the physical qualities of matter must be such as to afford a basis and condition for sentient and reacting beings. That reaction is the reaction of something immaterial upon the material, even if it is entirely caused by the material and bound to the material. Now, with free moral self-determination a new subject comes into existence and activity in the individual, which makes that subject, reacting upon mere sensations and ideas, its object, and, as a new immaterial subjective unity, acts determiningly upon that subject which has just become object. This new subject, considered from the side of its receptivity, we call *self-consciousness*; from the side of its spontaneity, *free moral self-determination*. Whether we consider this freedom predetermined or not, does not at all alter the described fact and the qualitative difference between the form of human moral agency and that of purely animal spontaneity. For even those advocating determination must admit that the morally acting subject distinguishes itself from its object, and does not take its motives to action from the material and from the instinctive life which is bound to the sensual and dependent on it.

Now it is true that all these circumstances in organized individuals which serve self-consciousness and free moral self-determination as their condition, presupposition, and basis, all the dispositions of the soul and the manifestations of life found in the animal world, will be worthy of the closest attention even on this account: because they form the basis, the condition, and (if self-consciousness and freedom are once present) an essential part of the contents and object of self-consciousness and moral self-determination. But where the origin of man is discussed, the central point of the investigation is no longer the enumeration of those activities of the soul of man whose analogies we also find in the animal world, but rather in the answer to the question as to how that entirely new manifestation, self-consciousness and moral self-determination, came into existence or could have originated. This question is the more decidedly the central point of the investigation, since this new form, when once in existence, has for its object not only what already appears in the life of the soul of animals, but also receives a new object, which can only be an object of self-consciousness and of moral self-determination, and not of mere consciousness and instinctive life. These new objects are the ideas leading up to the conception of God and moral ideals.

Now this very question as to the origin of self-consciousness and of free moral self-determination is wholly misjudged as to its importance, and given remarkably little attention by those evolutionists who are well versed in the realm of natural science. The question as to the origin of self-consciousness is either entirely ignored—as if self-consciousness must originate wholly by itself, if only those first steps of an intellectual and social life which the animal world also shows, are once present and properly developed—or the solution is put aside with the most superficial analogies. The question regarding free moral self-determination, on the other hand, is either likewise ignored, and for the same reasons, or it is supposed that it must fail of itself, if only this self-determination is explained in a deterministic way.

It is true, Darwin devotes several chapters of his work, "Descent of Man," to a comparison of the intellectual powers of man with those of animals, and these chapters are full of the most interesting facts and comparisons; but although his work comprises two volumes, he devotes to the origin of self-consciousness, individuality, abstraction, general ideas, etc., only a single page, and justifies his brief treatment with the assertion that the attempt at discussing these higher faculties is useless, because hardly two authors agree in their definitions of these terms. What he says about self-consciousness is really contained in two sentences, namely: "But how can we feel sure that an old dog with an excellent memory and some power of imagination, as shown by his dreams, never reflects on his past pleasures or pains in the chase? This would be a form of self-consciousness." On the other hand, as Büchner has remarked in his "Lectures about Darwin's Theory": "How little can the hard-working wife of a degraded Australian savage, who hardly ever uses abstract words, and can not count above four, how little can such a woman exert her self-consciousness, or reflect on the nature of her own existence!" And in Darwin's *resumé* of his chapters on the intellectual powers of man and animals, he says, on page 126: "If it could be proved that certain high mental powers, such as the formation of general concepts, self-consciousness, etc., were absolutely peculiar to man, which seems extremely doubtful, it is not improbable that these qualities are merely the incidental results of other highly-advanced intellectual faculties: and these again mainly the result of the continued use of a perfect language."

If Darwin is thus not able to show us in the animal world a single real analogy which at all approaches self-consciousness, and, in order to supply this want, must have recourse to the purely hypothetical *possibility* that it is not certain whether an old hunting-dog does not reflect upon the past joys of the chase; if by the uncertainty of the expression that self-consciousness might be an "*accompanying*" result of other faculties, he nevertheless gives us to understand that he can not find the *sufficient* cause of the origin of self-consciousness in those other faculties; and, finally, if he closes the last mentioned quotation with a sentence which has for its premise the wholly illogical thought that language might have been able to reach "a high state of development" before the origin of self-consciousness and without its assistance: then, indeed, the result of all this certainly is that he has given no adequate consideration to the specific nature of self-consciousness. It is only under this supposition that it is possible for him to say: "Nevertheless, the difference in mind between man and the higher animals, great as it certainly is, is one of degree and not of quality." The authors may possibly not agree in the definitions of the idea of self-consciousness—we ourselves perhaps are only an additional example in confirmation of this fact—; but whatever the definition may be, the fact itself remains, that self-consciousness does not stand as one of the intellectual faculties beside the others and coördinate with them, but, as an entirely new form of being, introduces a qualitatively new and valuable factor into the subject. That which precedes the origin of self-consciousness—the purely conscious and not yet self-conscious life of the soul, as it shows itself with higher animals, especially with mammals—*may* have been the necessary condition and requirement for the origin of self-consciousness. It certainly *has* been so; and from this point of view, all these psychological studies of animals and psycho-physical investigations which are a favorite object of modern science, have a high value; but what has been called into existence by *means* of conditions is not on that account the *product* of those conditions. This very fact is one of the greatest mistakes of most of the modern evolution theories: that very often—and especially where they wish to draw metaphysical conclusions from their scientific results or hypotheses—they confound condition and basis with cause.

Now it appears to us that, in quite an analogous way, Darwin overlooks or contests the fact that with *free moral self-determination* something specifically new comes into existence. He certainly discusses the origin of the moral qualities of man more in detail than he does the origin of his intellectual qualities. He derives them, in their first beginnings, from the fixity, transmission and increase of the *social* impulses and instincts. These, being the basis of the whole moral development, and leading in their more mature form to love and to sympathy, originated by natural selection; and the other moral qualities, such as moral sense and conscience, progressed more by the effect of custom, by the power of reflection, instruction, and religion, than by natural selection. Higher and lower, common and special, permanent and transitory instincts come into collision with one another. The dissatisfaction of man when any of the lower, special, and transitory instincts have overcome the higher, common and permanent, and the resolution to act differently for the future, is *conscience*. Darwin considers that one a *moral being* who is capable of comparing with one another his past and future actions and motives, of approving some of them and of disapproving others; and the fact that man is the only creature who can with certainty be ranked as a moral being is, according to Darwin, the greatest of all differences between man and animals.

Here, again, the whole central point of the investigation as to the origin of man does not lie in the question of the origin of the instincts between which the moral subject, acting in moral self-determination, has to choose. For it is clear that the beginnings of these instincts are also present in the animal world. But the main question is, how did this faculty and necessity of choosing, this conscience and responsibility, this "moral sense," as Darwin calls it, originate? Now to this question we have a plain answer in the before- mentioned utterances of Darwin: It originated not as a *product* of the social instincts—it only has these instincts for its preceding condition, object and instrument; but it originated as a product of other agencies, which act upon these impulses and instincts, operate with them, choose between them; and as these other agencies Darwin mentions the high development of the intellectual powers. That this is his opinion, we can clearly see from an expression with which he introduces his essay on the origin of "moral sense": "The following proposition seems to me in a high degree probable—namely, that any animal whatever, endowed with well-marked social instincts, would inevitably acquire a moral sense or conscience, *as soon as its intellectual powers had become as well, or nearly as well developed, as in man.*" These intellectual powers which moral feeling and conscience require at their birth, are certainly, according to Darwin the power to distinguish oneself as subject from one's impulses and instincts, and to choose between them; *i.e.*, self- consciousness. We shall have to admit fully this intimate connection between moral self-determination and self-consciousness; but we must admit, at the same time, that moral self-determination—this new form of activity in which moral activity distinguishes itself from all *merely* instinctive activity—finds its sufficient explanation in the previous stage of the animal world as little as self-consciousness; and that moral self-determination has the condition and presupposition, but not the cause, of its existence in that which is also found in the previous stage of the animal world. The proof that the origin of moral self-determination finds its sufficient explanation in that which the previous stage of the animal world also has, would appear to have been given by Darwin only when he had succeeded in explaining the origin of self-consciousness from animal intelligence; but that he did not succeed in it, we think we have clearly shown. On the other hand, we willingly admit that the study of the social and all other instincts and impulses which are common to man and animals, and which in man form the object and instrument of his moral activity, has for us the highest interest, inasmuch as the only problem is to explain the conditions and prerequisites of moral self-determination—or, historically speaking, the conditions and prerequisites of the origin of morally acting beings. Furthermore we have to say here also that condition and prerequisite are not identical with cause, and it is precisely the *cause* of moral responsibility and of the origin of such morally responsible beings, which has not yet been discovered by the Darwinian theory.

The followers of Darwin enter still less into the discussion of the question as to the origin of self-consciousness and of moral self-determination. Häckel—who, in his "Natural History of Creation" and in his "Anthropogeny," expounds his whole evolution theory in all its antecedent conditions and consequences—has, indeed, much to say of the different faculties of the soul of man and animals. He traces these faculties in the case of man down to the lowest state of the most degraded races, and in the case of animals from the kermes up to the bee, from the lancelet-fish to the dog, ape, elephant and horse; and he also treats of the so-called *a priori* knowledge which "arose only by long-enduring transmission, by inheritance of acquired adaptations of the brain, out of originally empiric or experiential knowledge *a posteriori*," (Vol. II, 345). But we look in vain in his works for a treatment of the question as to the origin of the Ego—of self-consciousness. Nowhere does he enter into the analysis of the psychological ideas; he only compares the psychical utterances of different creatures, and thinks the whole problem solved when he says: "The mental differences between the most stupid placental animals (for instance, sloths and armadillos) and the most intelligent animals of the same group (for instance dogs and apes) are, at any rate, much more considerable than the differences in the intellectual life of dogs, apes, and men." Or: "If these brutish parasites are compared with the mentally active and sensitive ants, it will certainly be admitted that the psychical differences between the two are much greater than those between the highest and lowest mammals—between beaked animals, pouched animals and armadillos, on the one hand, and dogs, apes, men, on the other." The fact that in the human individual consciousness and self-consciousness are gradually developed, is to him a proof that in the organic kingdom also consciousness and self- consciousness came into existence gradually, and, indeed, hand-in-hand with the development of the nervous system; and with this result he thinks that he has relieved himself from the task of showing the "how" of the origin of self- consciousness. This becomes clearly evident from a remark about the origin of consciousness, in his "Anthropogeny," where he says that, if DuBois-Reymond had thought that consciousness is developed, he would no longer have held its origin to be a thing beyond the limits of human capacity. Häckel likewise seems to regard the question of the origin of moral self- determination as solved or rejected, if only freedom is denied—which, indeed, is repeatedly done by him.

A similar defect in the treatment of this question by evolutionists we find in the works of Oscar Schmidt, Gustav Jäger, and others. Even Emil DuBois-Reymond, who, in his celebrated and eloquent lecture on "The Limits of the Knowledge of Nature," given before the assembly of scientists at Leipzig, 1872, asserts so energetically that the origin of sensation and consciousness is inexplicable (see next section), seems to take the origin of self-consciousness for granted, and as needing no further explanation, if only consciousness is once present.

Since, then, the scientists leave us without a sufficient answer to the question respecting the origin of self-consciousness and of moral self-determination, we shall have to turn to the philosophers. Here, indeed, we find rich definitions and genetic analyses, but none that lead us any farther than to the information that consciousness is the necessary condition of self- consciousness; that animal instinct is the necessary antecedent condition of moral self-determination. Yet in the works of these very philosophers who are inclined to a mechanical and "monistic" view of the world, we find that they directly avoid the question as to the origin of self-consciousness and of moral self-determination. As soon as they are led near it, in the course of reasoning in their works, they suddenly turn aside again to the quite different questions of the connection between brain and soul, between physical and psychical, external and internal processes, etc. Evidently they feel that with this question they have arrived at the weak point of their system. That here is a weak point, we clearly see in the case of D. F. Strauss, a leading advocate of modern naturalism, and the greatest philosophic scholar of that school. It is true, in his "Postscript as Preface," as we saw before, he mentions the origin of self-consciousness as one of the points which need special explanation; but he seems to have made this acknowledgment more with the purpose of showing that DuBois-Reymond, in admitting the origin of self-consciousness to be explainable, has no longer any reason to contest the explicability of the origin of sensation and consciousness; for in his work on "The Old Faith and the New," he did not enter into that question at all. On the other hand, he makes in his last-mentioned work a remarkable confession. In answering the question—how do we determine our rule of life?—he comes to speak of the position of man in nature, traces a law of progress in nature, and says: "In this cumulative progression of life, man is also comprised, and, moreover, in such wise that the organic plasticity of our planet (provisionally, say some naturalists, but that we may fairly leave an open question) culminates in him. *As nature can not go higher, she would go inwards.* 'To be reflected within itself,' was a very good expression of Hegel's. Nature felt herself already in the animal, but she wished to know herself also." But still stronger is the following expression: "*In man, nature endeavored not merely to exalt, but to transcend herself.*" In § 1, Chap. II, we shall have to speak of this important acknowledgment of teleology in nature, which such an antagonist of teleology as Strauss makes in the above-quoted remarks about a progress in nature and a will of nature; but here we are more interested in the equally remarkable acknowledgment of the fact that man can not be explained from nature alone —that he is something which transcends nature. For that (according to Strauss) nature, in originating man, not only *intended* to transcend herself, but really did transcend herself and, that she succeeded in her intention, we can infer from the moral precept which Strauss gives: "Do not forget for a moment, that thou art human; not merely a natural production."

The result of our investigation, therefore, is that with self-consciousness and free moral self-determination something specifically new came into existence which had its antecedent condition in a previous state of existence, but has not yet found its sufficient explanation in this antecedent state.

§ 2. *The Origin of Sensation and of Consciousness.*

The limits of our knowledge show themselves still more clearly in the attempts to explain the origin of consciousness and its lowest form— sensation. Self-consciousness is without doubt ideally nearer to consciousness in this, that both are an immaterial activity; and yet we found no demonstrable bridge which leads from consciousness to self-consciousness. Still broader is the gulf between the material and the immaterial, between the unconscious and the conscious,—or, to describe the two realms with names which bring them nearest together, between that which is without sensation and that which has sensation: a gulf to bridge which philosophy also has vainly exerted its utmost efforts, as has been well known since the "supernatural assistance" of Descartes and the "preëstablished harmony" of Leibnitz. Wherein lies the real necessity that there should be sensation? How does the material become something that is felt? What is the demonstrable cause (not the condition, but the cause) of a sentient subject? To these questions, every science up to the present day lacks an answer. As is well known, DuBois-Reymond, in his previously-mentioned lecture upon "The Limits of our Knowledge of Nature," declares the origin of sensation and of consciousness to be one of two limits, beyond which we have not only to say "*ignoramus,*" but "*ignorabimus.*"

In abstracto, we might think of two attempts at bridging over this gulf: the first one is that we try to transform sensation itself into something material, and the other is that we attribute sensation also to that which, according to our observation, seems to be without sensation; namely, to matter and its elements, the atoms. Both of these attempts have been made—the former by D. F. Strauss in his "The Old Faith and the New," and by the English philosopher, Herbert Spencer, in his "First Principles of Philosophy;" the latter, first pointed out by Schopenhauer, was taken up and farther developed by Zöllner in his work, "Ueber die Natur der Kometen" ("Nature of the Comets"), Leipzig, Engelmann, 1872, and with special acuteness by an "Anonymus" in the work: "Das Unbewusste von Standpunkt der Physiologie und Descendenztheorie" ("The Unconscious from the Standpoint of Physiology and Descent Theory"), Berlin, Duncker, 1872.

Strauss says, in the previously-mentioned work: "If, under certain conditions, motion is transformed into heat, why may it not, under other conditions, be transformed into sensation?" And Herbert Spencer says, in his "First Principles of Philosophy," (page 217): "Various classes of facts thus unite to prove that the law of metamorphosis, which holds among the physical forces, holds equally between them and the mental forces. Those modes of the unknowable which we call motion, heat, light, chemical affinity, etc., are alike transformable into each other, and into those modes of the unknowable which we distinguish as sensation, emotion, thought: these, in their turns, being directly or indirectly retransformable into the original shapes."

But motion—even the finest material motion, that of ether, (which, in consequence of the very important discovery of the conservation of force and of the mechanical equivalent of heat, made by Robert von Mayer, at present is taken to be heat)—is so decidedly a material process, the sensation of motion is so decidedly a reflex of the material in something immaterial, that the assertion of a transformation of motion into sensation seems to us only to change the point of view, and not to explain the difference, but to efface it. And we think that the appeal of Strauss from his contemporaries, who do not understand him, to posterity, who would understand him better and esteem him, has but little prospect of being operative.

If that which has sensation and that which has it not, are to be brought genetically near one another, and hence the difference between the two at the point where the lowest sentient being has found its first existence, is to be made void or at least bridged over, then it is much more reasonable, and also in the line of Strauss's solution, to deny the difference between that which has sensation and that which has it not, and to do this in the sense in which we also declare that to be sentient which we have hitherto been accustomed to regard as without sensation; and we should likewise attribute sensation to the original elements of the world, be they called atoms or whatever one may wish. This is done by Zöllner and by the before mentioned "Anonymus." This conclusion is logical; it is even the only possible conclusion, if we once start from the axiom that the new, which comes into existence, must necessarily be explainable from agencies previously active, and known to or imagined by us through abstractions and hypotheses. Zöllner is certainly right when, in his work which appeared before the lecture of DuBois-Reymond, he puts the alternative, "either to renounce forever the conceivableness of the phenomena of sensation, or hypothetically to add to the common qualities of matter one more, which places the simplest and most elementary transactions of nature under a process of sensation, legitimately connected with it;" as also when he says (page 327): "We may regard the intensity of these sensations (of matter) as little and unimportant as we wish; but the hypothesis of their existence is, according to my conviction, a necessary condition, in order to comprehend the really existing phenomena of sensation in nature." Only we shall do well to choose the first alternative for the present, and, with DuBois-Reymond, answer the question as to the explanation of the origin of sensation with an "*ignoramus*"; indeed, we shall take a surer road with his "*ignorabimus*" than by a plunge into that bottomless ocean of hypotheses—in spite of the protest of Häckel, who (Anthrop., page XXI) sees that scientist who has the courage to admit the limits of our knowledge, on account of this "*ignorabimus*", walking in the army of the "black International", and "marshalled under the black flag of the hierarchy," together with "spiritual servitude and falsehood, want of reason and barbarism, superstition and retrogression", and fighting, "spiritual freedom and truth, reason and culture, evolution and progress." For a solution of the question which simply denies all sharply-marked differences in the world, and explains the new, which comes into existence with sensation, by the assertion that this new element is not new, but was already present, and that it exists everywhere, only we do not see it everywhere,— such a solution seems to us not to be the true way to interpret the problem of the sphinx. Even Ed. von Hartmann seems to infringe the impartiality of the true observer, when, in his "Philosophy of the Unconscious," he attributes sensation to plants. But when Zöllner says (p. 326): "*All the labors of natural beings* [and, as the connection indicates, of all, even of inorganic natural beings] *are determined by like and dislike;*" and when "Anonymus" attributes sensation to all atoms and to all complexities composed of them, even to stone, then all reasonable conception of natural things and processes certainly vanishes into thin air.

It will be remembered, however, that in treating the question of the origin of self-consciousness, although we were not able to solve the problem, nevertheless we had to ascribe high value to the investigation of all psychical processes on the low stage of sensation and consciousness, since they show us not the cause, but the condition and basis, of self-consciousness. Likewise, in the question as to the origin of sensation and of consciousness, although we are not able to solve it, we will willingly admit that we observe, even in that which has no sensation, qualities and processes which furnish the absolutely necessary condition and basis for sensation. For the same reason, we will also admit the manifold analogies of sensation which we observe in that which is without sensation. The whole system of symbols in nature which fills our treasury of words and penetrates, in a thousandfold way, our scientific and popular, our poetical and prosaic speech, our thoughts and feelings, bears witness to the fact that that which is without sensation is also a preparatory step to sensation, and feeling both active and passive springs from it. However, a preparatory step, as such, is not necessarily the cause; and the fact and the acknowledgment of a correlation is not on that account an explanation.

§ 3. *The Origin of Life.*

The third problem to be solved is the origin of life. As is well known, Darwin himself makes no attempt at explaining this problem, but is satisfied with the idea that life was infused into one or a few forms by the Creator ("Origin of Species," 6 ed., p. 429). His investigations and theories only begin where organic life, in its first and lowest forms, is already in existence.

But lately there have been made, in the realm of the organic, discoveries of beings which take the lowest conceivable round on the ladder of organisms, and which in their form and structure are so simple that from them to the inorganic there seems to be but a short step. We can no longer mention as belonging to the bridges which are said to lead from the organic world to the inorganic, the often-named *bathybius*, discovered by Huxley, and so strongly relied upon for the mechanical explanation of life—a slimy net-like growth, which covers the rocks in the great depths of the ocean. For after scientists like K. E. von Baer and others had already declared it probable that this bathybius is only a precipitate of organic relics, no less a person than the discoverer of the bathybius, in the "Annals of Natural History," 1875, and in the "Quarterly Journal of Microscopical Science," 1875, has suggested that the whole discovery is but gypsum, which was precipitated in a gelatinous condition. Likewise the utterances concerning the simplicity and lack of structure of the lowest organisms, are to be accepted only with great reservation; for most of these organisms show very differently and very distinctly stamped structures; of this fact, anyone may easily convince himself, who has had the opportunity of observing with the microscope low and lowest organisms, and to admire their striking and manifold forms. Nevertheless, there are monera whose structure seems to be nothing but a living clod without kernel and cover, and which in that respect represent the lowest conceivable form of organic being and life.

Now, relying on these discoveries, as well as upon the successful demonstration, by inorganic means, of organic acids in chemistry, and starting from the supposition that the first appearance of life must necessarily be explained by those agencies which are already active in the inorganic nature, many scientists have attempted the so-called *mechanical explanation of life*. This attempt has been made most logically and systematically by Häckel. He says that organic *matter*, organic *form*, and organic *motion*, in the lowest stages of the organic, which are almost the only ones to be taken into consideration when the problem of the origin of life is discussed, contain nothing at all which does not also pertain to the inorganic. In his opinion, organic *matter* is an albuminous carbon combination, of which we have to presuppose that, like all chemical combinations, under certain physical and chemical conditions it can also arise in the realm of the inorganic in a purely chemical and mechanical way. Organic *form* which, in its lowest stages, is so simple, like the moneron and the bathybius, and which stands still lower than a cell, is, moreover, something which there is no difficulty in explaining from inorganic matter. Finally, organic *motion* which alone is the last and lowest characteristic of the organic in its lowest stage—in which the process of life properly consists, and in which, therefore, we have to recognize the *punctum saliens* of the whole question—is only an increase and complication of the merely mechanical motion of the inorganic, likewise explainable by mechanical causes. This view Häckel expounds in the thirteenth and partly also in the first chapter of his "Natural History of Creation," and explains the origin of the first and most simple organic individuals either through what he calls *autogony* in an inorganic fluid, or through *plasmogony* in an organic fluid—a plasma or protoplasma. In fact, according to him, the only correct idea is that all matter is provided with a soul, that inorganic and organic nature is one, that all natural bodies known to us are equally animated, and that the contrast commonly drawn between the living and the dead world does not exist. This is but a repetition, in a more rhetorical way, of the same idea which "Anonymus" expressed in discussing the question as to the origin of sensation.

DuBois-Reymond—who, in his lecture at Leipzig, pronounced the origin of *sensation* and of *consciousness* a problem of natural science, never to be solved—is also of the opinion that the explanation of *life* from mere mechanism of atoms is very probable, and only a question of time. It is well known that the experimental attempts at originating the organic through chemistry are at present pursued with an eagerness that can have its stimulus only in the hope of success.

It is clear that the main point of the question does not lie in organic matter or in organic form, but in organic *motion*, for even the specific of the organic *form* originates only first through *organic motion of life*. If, therefore, life is to be explained from mechanical causes, it must also be shown that the merely mechanical motion of inorganic matter produces that motion which we know as organic motion, and *how* it produces it. The idea of "increase and complication of the inorganic, merely mechanical motion," with which Häckel throws a bridge from the living to the lifeless or from the organic to the inorganic, does not yet give us that proof; it seems rather to be one of those pompous phrases with which people hide their ignorance and make the uncritical multitude believe that the explanation is found: a manipulation against which, among others, Wigand, in his great work, repeatedly protests, as also does the Duke of Argyll in his lecture on "Anthropomorphism in Theology," having especially in his mind the deductions of Spencer. For we may review the whole known series of mechanical motions and their mechanical causes, and imagine their mechanical increase and their mechanical complication the largest possible; and still the life-motion of the organic will never result therefrom. If such a keen psychical and physiological investigator and thinker, and such an authority in the realm of the motions of atoms and molecules, as Gustav Theodor Fechner—"Einige Ideen zur Schöpfungs- und Entwicklungsgeschichte der Organismen" ("Some Ideas about the History of the Creation and Development of Organisms"), Leipzig, 1873, p. 1, f.—can find the whole lasting and effectual difference between the organic and inorganic in nothing else than in the way and manner of *motion*—namely, that the motion of the *organic* molecules is different from that of the *inorganic* molecules—and when he traces this difference with mathematical exactness, then an assertion which simply denies that difference, without attempting to show the identity of the two motions, to say nothing of proving this identity, is nothing more than a clear evidence that the mechanical theory has not yet succeeded in explaining the origin of life, and that those scientists who so haughtily look down upon the abuse of *"vital power,"* to the efficacy of which their antagonists began to resort when their knowledge came to an end, make exactly the same abuse with their *"mechanism."* That organic motion, even the organic motion of molecules, *once present*, comes into dependence on the well known laws of mechanism, we naturally will not deny; any more than that the human body, when serving the will of the mind, follows in its motions the laws of physiology and mechanism.

Preyer seems to make a mistake similar to that of those who efface sensation and motion, when, in an essay on the hypothesis of the origin of life, in the

"Deutsche Rundschau," Vol. I, 7, he even effaces the difference between life and sensation, and simply identifies life and motion. "Self-motion, called life, and inorganic movement of bodies by agencies outside of themselves, are but quantitatively, intensively, or gradually different forms of motion; not in their innermost being different.... Our will changes many kinds of motion into heat, makes cold metal to be red-hot simply by hammering.... Likewise inversely, as the law of the conservation of force must require, a part of the eternal heat of the metal can be now and forever transposed into the living motion of our soul." This whole manner of investigation and proof is one of those numerous unconscious logical fallacies which, introduced by Hegel, have gradually attained a certain title by possession. From the observation of a process, they abstract a characteristic, as general as possible,—as, for instance, from the observation of life the characteristic of motion; then they find that the process has the characteristic in common with still other processes—as, for instance, the self-motion of the living has the general characteristic of motion in common with the objective motion of the lifeless; and then they persuade themselves that the process which they try to explain is really explained by having found a quality of this process as comprehensive as possible. And in order to hide the falsity of the conclusion, they also give to the general idea, which they have found to be a characteristic of that process, the same name which the special process has,—as, for instance, they call motion life, no matter whether it is a motion of itself or a being moved, no matter whether it is performed from within or in consequence of an impulse from without; and then they say: "Behold, life is explained; life is nothing but motion." But it can be readily seen that life is also motion, and has therefore this characteristic in common with everything which is moved; but that the specific of that motion called life—namely, self-motion in consequence of an impulse renewing itself from within, and, as Fechner shows, self-motion in a rotatory direction of the molecules, precisely the same thing which in distinction from other motions we call life,—is not explained, but simply ignored.

There is still another bold hypothesis which we have to mention—namely, *that the organic germs were once thrown from other spheres upon the earth by ærolites*. Years ago this idea was declared by Helmholtz to be scientifically conceivable; then it was formally asserted and brought into general notice by Sir William Thompson, in his opening address before the annual assembly of the British Association at Edinburgh, in 1871, but rejected as formally and materially unscientific by Zöllner, in the preface to his work, "Nature of Comets," and again defended by Helmholtz in his preface to the second volume of a translation of Thompson and Tait's Theoretical Physics. However, this hypothesis also only defers the solution of the question, and, supposing its scientific possibility, leads either to the remoter question, how life did originate in those other spheres, or to the metaphysical assertion of the eternity of life and of the eternal continuity of the living in the world, and shows therewith very clearly the impossibility of its explanation.

This inexplicability would still exist, if what is quite improbable should happen, namely, that the experimental attempts at *artificially producing organic life* should be successful, and if thus the question as to the *generatio æquivoca*, which during the past decades so much alarmed the minds of scientists and theologians, should be experimentally solved and answered in the affirmative. For in view of the hopes of a possible explanation of life, which is expected to be the reward for the success of these attempts, Zöllner is fully right in saying: "That the scientists to-day set such an extremely high value on the inductive proof of the *generatio æquivoca*, is the most significant symptom of how little they have made themselves acquainted with the first principles of the theory of knowledge. For, suppose they should really succeed in observing the origin of organic germs under conditions entirely free from objection to any imaginable communication with the atmosphere, what could they answer to the assertion that the organic germs, in reference to their extension, are of the order of ether-atoms, and, with these, press through the intervals of the material molecules which form the sides of our apparatus?"

How little life is explained, at least according to the present state of our knowledge, also follows from the *insufficiency of all attempts* at *defining it*. The latest and most thorough attempt at such a definition of life, with which we are familiar, is that made by Herbert Spencer in his "First Principles", § 25, and in his "Principles of Biology," Vol. I, Part I, Chap. 4 and 5. Having made thorough investigations, he arrives at the general formula: "Life is the continuous adjustment of internal relations to external relations." To this definition we will not make the objection that it is nothing but a logical abstraction from the common quality of all processes and phenomena of life; for it certainly lies in the nature of a definition that it can be nothing else but that. Nevertheless, we will state that such a definition of life not only does not lead us any nearer to the comprehension of its processes, and especially of the richness and the organization of its forms and functions, but that it clearly shows us how little the origin of life is explained. For this very definition necessarily and obviously leads us to the questions: Whence do those internal relations originate, whence their adjustment to external relations, and whence the continuity of this adjustment? The answer to these questions this definition still owes us.

Therefore, not only self-consciousness and freedom, not only sensation and consciousness, but also life and the organic, remain a phenomenon which—at least, according to the present state of our knowledge and reasoning—enters into the realm of the world of phenomena as *something new* that can not be explained from the foregoing, although it presupposes the foregoing as the *condition*, not the cause, of its appearance; and no matter whether we have to think of the modality of its origin as a sudden or as a gradual one.

§ 4. *The Elements of the World, the Theory of Atoms, and the Mechanical View of the World.*

The investigating and thinking mind, when it attempts to explain the appearances and forms of that which exists, finds itself led further and further back, until it finally arrives at the last elements of the world and of matter. Whether we take the problem of life as solved or unsolved, the living has matter and its subordination to the efficiency of all its chemical and mechanical powers in common with the lifeless; and the organic, in its first beginnings, stands extraordinarily near to, and is grown on the ground of, the inorganic,— if not according to the category of cause and effect, still according to that of condition and consequence, of basis and structure. Therefore we stand at last before the question of the final elements of matter, which, indeed, constitutes organic as well as inorganic bodies.

The answer to this question is attempted by the theory of atoms: the doctrine which teaches that the whole material world is composed of simple particles which are no farther divisible, and from whose juxtaposition the chemical elements—and, in respect to their other forms of existence and combination, the whole world of bodies, with all their forms, states, and changes,—are composed.

This theory has not only the practical value that the physical (and especially the chemical) sciences can make and use their formulas most easily under the supposition of such simple primitive elements; but it also has the great theoretical merit that it has broken down the old barriers between *matter* and *force*, and has thus promoted considerably our method of regarding the world of material substances. Toward this result, scientists and philosophers—and, among the latter, the thinkers and investigators of both views of the world, the theistic and the pantheistic, the ideal and the materialistic,—have worked with equal merit, and have equally enjoyed its fruits, with perhaps the single exception of so pure a materialist as Ludwig Büchner, who, it seems, does not like to give up his old doctrine of force *and* matter as the two inseparable, equivalent, and equally eternal elements of the universe. That matter itself, even when looked upon from a purely physical standpoint, has an incorporeal principle; that the whole world of bodies, as such, has but a phenomenal character; that not force *and* matter are the two empirico-physical principles of the world, but that matter itself must be a product of elementary force active in the atoms; these doctrines have now be pretty nearly common property of natural science and philosophy. Investigators who like Wilhelm Wundt, rise from natural science to philosophy, or such as take their starting- point from philosophy—whether they be theists, like Lotze, I. H. Fichte, Ulrici, or occupy the ground of a pessimistic pantheism, as does Eduard von Hartmann,—all share this view and its fruits.

But in spite of all these preferences for the theory of atoms, we should not forget that it still has but hypothetical value—that it is but an idea of limits, which indicates, where the scientifically perceptible ceases, and that every attempt at moving this limit still farther on must either fail and lead into unsolvable contradictions, or, if successful, only leads to new difficulties and unsolved problems.

Already within that realm in which the theory of atoms is a supplemental hypothesis directly indispensable at present—*i.e.*, within their application in physical sciences—we meet suppositions which raise great doubts and difficulties. Such a scientific difficulty occurs when the atomism of the natural philosophers supposes a double complexity of atoms, material atoms and atoms of ether: complexities which both penetrate one another, and are supposed to follow partly totally different, partly the same, elementary laws of force. Material atoms are subordinate to the law of gravitation, while atoms of ether are not; and yet both act legitimately upon one another,—as, for instance, when heat passes into motion and motion into heat, which certainly presupposes a law of power acting in common for both. Another difficulty lies in the atomism of the chemists; and still another in the divergency of the aims at which the physical theory of atoms on the one hand and the chemical theory of atoms on the other seem to point. Chemistry is inclined to explain the difference of its numerous elements from the original difference of the atoms; and yet it is not at all certain that the elements of chemistry themselves are not composed of still more simple and less numerous primary elements. Many indications seem to point to such primary elements which are more simple in number and quality, and investigators even mention an element— hydrogen— in the direction of which we have to look for the way that will lead us to those primitive elements of matter. The divergency of aims, finally, consists in the fact that physical atomism prevailingly points to a conformity of the atoms of bodies; chemical atomism, on the contrary,—at least, according to its present state,—points to a dissimilarity among these.

The hypothetical and problematical nature of the theory of atoms strikes us still more clearly when we try to analyze it philosophically. First, we meet that antinomy which we always find where we try to pass beyond the limits of our empirical knowledge by means of conception. For, if the atoms still occupy space, we can not understand why they should not be further divisible, and if they do not occupy space, we can not understand how any sum of that which does not occupy space, can finally succeed in filling space. It is true, this very antinomy has led to the overcoming of that dualism of force and matter which so long enchained science, and the overcoming of which we greet as a progress of our theoretical knowledge of nature. We no longer look upon the atoms as material elements, but as centres of force. The antinomy has the further merit that, in the realm of the knowledge of nature, it brings to our consciousness the great advantage of a concrete perception and reasoning over purely logical abstractions. For Ulrici, in his "God and Nature," is right in calling our attention to the fact that we must think about the atoms, not in an *abstractly* logical and an *abstractly* mathematical way, but concretely; that we have to consider them, not as mere quantities, but as qualities; and that we can then easily arrive at the perception of something which occupies space, and which therefore, according to abstract conclusions of logic and mathematics, could still be thought of as divisible *in abstracto*, but which, even as a consequence of its *quality*, of its concrete natural form, is no longer divisible in reality. Nevertheless, in spite of all these remarkable attempts at overcoming the difficulties of the theory of atoms, that antinomy returns as often as we undertake to make that clearly perceptible which we have at last gained a partial conception of; and thus shows us, from this side also, that even with the theory of atoms we have arrived at the limit where not only our observation, but also the preciseness and certainty of our conceptions, ceases.

By the atomic theory, we do not gain anything for the ultimate explanation of the world and its contents, not even if its present hypothetical value should be changed into a complete demonstration. For the whole theory but removes the question as to the origin of things from their sensible appearance to the elements of that appearance, and leaves us standing just as helpless before the elements as before the appearances. For whence does the whole richness of the appearances in the world come? If the atoms are all alike, and their laws of force the simplest we can imagine, then their grouping into all the developments and formations of which we observe such an infinite and regularly arranged abundance, is not less unexplained than if we had not gone back to the theory of atoms at all. But if the atoms and their laws of force are different, the difficulty is not simplified, but doubled. For, first, the theory then owes us an answer to the questions wherein the difference of the atoms consists and whence it comes; and, second, the question we have to consider in supposing a uniformity of the atoms, is not disposed of or answered—the question, namely, as to the causes which bring these different atoms together to form precisely those complexities of atoms which we observe as the world of phenomena.

This insufficiency of the theory of atoms in explaining the world and its contents, is another proof to us that, however great the practical value of this theory may be for the operations of physics and chemistry, its theoretical value consists essentially in the fact that it formulates more accurately the perception of the limits of our exact knowledge. Even the idea of Lotze, that the atoms (in themselves different) are not really the final elements of matter, but consist of still more simple but likewise different elements, seems to us more a decoration than an extension of the limits at which our perception has arrived; we stand before a double door, but find both doors locked. We agree with DuBois-Reymond, when he declares, in his before-mentioned lecture, the impossibility of perceiving the last elements of the world, matter and force, to be the other limit of our knowledge of nature which, together with the impossibility of the explanation of the origin of sensation and consciousness, remains forever fixed.

Likewise, the peculiar modification which G. Th. Fechner gives to the theory of the last elements of the world, cannot escape the charge of leaving the problem of the world scientifically just as unsolved as before. Fechner not only finds, as we have already mentioned, the difference between the organic and the inorganic in the difference of the mutual motions, but he also finds that the character of organic motions is exactly the same as that which the bodies of the universe have among themselves in their motions. Thus he distinguishes the *cosmorganic* motion, which is performed in the whole of the universe, and the *molecular-organic* motion, which we observe in the single organisms of the earth; he makes God the personal, self-conscious soul of this cosmical organism; and, in using the law of the tendency to stability, with which he completes the Darwinian selection theory, asserts that the organic in the whole of the universe, as well as in the narrow sphere of single bodies on the earth, is the first thing from which the inorganic was separated and became gradually fixed. Thus, in his opinion, the problem which up to the present has occupied investigators,—namely, how did the organic originate from the inorganic?—would have to be reversed to, how did the inorganic originate from the organic?

Preyer would also reach a similar result with his above-mentioned theory of the identity of life and motion. For according to this theory, the living would be as old and common as motion, and the organic but the dregs of life.

We may, therefore, say that, without regard to the fact that neither pantheism nor theism will ever harmonize with Fechner's solution of this contrast which gives to God exactly the same position in the world as the soul has in the body, natural science will certainly treat with great reserve a cosmo-metaphysical system which so fully upsets all results of exact investigations into the history of origin and development, and has no other proof for itself than the identity, or at least the similarity, of the abstract formula according to which the molecular motions of organisms and the cosmical motions are performed. Although we thus have to deny to the proof of this identity or similarity the weight which Fechner gives to it, nevertheless it has still no small merit, since it throws new and clearer light upon the old thought, always attractive and yet so difficult to present,—of a macrocosmus and a microcosmus, which has been often enough treated with so much natural mysticism.

Thus, in our inquiry into the development of things, we have successively arrived at four points, each of which urged us to make the confession that here something new came into existence, which can not be explained from the preceding conditions of its being; these four points were: the origin of <u>self-consciousness</u>, the origin of sensation and consciousness, the origin of life, and finally the elements of the universe. Arrived at the last problem, we see the confession of our ignorance increased to the still more comprehensive confession that we are really not able *fully* to explain anything in the world. We are able to perceive a uniformity of law in the states and changes of things, and to abstract therefrom common laws of nature; we can observe single objects, and perceive their states and changes in their connection with one another and in their dependence on those laws. But we are not able to explain scientifically either the origin of these laws or the last physical causes of the qualities of things, which follow these laws.

We should reach the same result if we had not started from the objective world of the existing, as we were induced to do by our subject, but from theoretical investigations. Here also we should immediately find ourselves in a world of relations between subject and object, of a regularly arranged abundance of subjective and objective qualities, states and processes, of which the objective only come to our knowledge through the medium of the subjective, and of regularly arranged laws to which both the subjective and the objective are commonly subordinate. But why just these and no other qualities of the subject and of objects exist, why just these and no other laws reign, why just this and no other relation takes place between the perceiving subject and the perceived object, would remain unanswered as before.

Amidst a generation which is so fond of reveling in the thought of an extension of all the limits of our knowledge, and is inclined to proclaim as true that which it wishes and hopes, investigators are not wholly wanting who very decidedly express their consciousness of these limits of our knowledge, and at the same time combine it with the most logical scientific reasoning and investigation. Even when in detail they reach these limits from the most varying points of view, and draw them in different directions, they all agree in confirming the principle that it is one of the first and most indispensable conditions of successful investigation always to be conscious of the limits of its perception. Voices which remind mankind of these limits, are perhaps less popular, for man prefers to be reminded of the advances rather than of the limitations of his knowledge; but they are on that account the more worthy of our gratitude, for they keep us on the solid ground of the attainable from which alone sure progress in knowledge is possible. Among such philosophers we name Ulrici, and especially Lotze; among scientists, in the first place, two pioneers in their departments—namely, in the department of the mechanism of heat, Robert von Mayer—compare his "Bemerkungen über das mechanische Aequivalent der Wärme" ("Remarks on the Mechanical Equivalent of Heat"), and "Ueber nothwendige Consequenzen und Inconsequenzen der Wärmemechanik" ("Necessary Consequences and Inconsequences of the Mechanism of Heat"), Stuttgart, Cotta;—and in the realm of the development of organisms, K. E. von Baer—compare his "Reden und kleinere Aufsätze" ("Addresses and Essays"), 2 vols., St. Petersburg, 1864 and 1876. In this connection we have already mentioned the name of DuBois-Reymond. Otto Köstlin published two remarkable dissertations in this direction—"Ueber die Grenzen der Naturwissenschaft" ("Limits of Natural Science"), Tübingen, Fues, 2d ed., 1874, and "Ueber natürliche Entwicklung" ("Natural Development"), ib., 1875. In the latter he especially cautions against hastily confounding the laws of development of planets, development of the organic kingdom, and development of the individual organisms. Recently, Wigand, in the second volume of his work already frequently mentioned, attempts, with an extreme energy which does too little justice to the representation and investigation of the still unsolved problems, to formulate the limits of the knowable.

A contrary extreme, and of its kind a still more one-sided corrective of this too great stability, we have in those investigators who, by reason of the great progress which has been made in the realm of the theoretical knowledge of nature, allow themselves to be drawn on to the hope of still explaining all states and processes in the world—the spiritual and the ethic processes as well as the physical—from the pure mechanism of atoms; and who see in that which thus far has been mechanically explained, the only and the infallible way of explaining all that is still obscure. They call this view the *mechanical view of the world*; and, as "monism," put it in opposition to the "vitalistic, teleological, and dualistic view of the world." In order to obtain a correct view of this standpoint, we quote from Häckel's "Natural History of Creation", Vol. I, page 23, the following passage: "By the theory of descent we are for the first time enabled to conceive of the unity of nature in such a manner that a mechanico-causal explanation of even the most intricate organic phenomena, for example, the origin and structure of the organs of sense, is no more difficult (in a general way) than is the mechanical explanation of any physical process; as, for example, earthquakes, the courses of the wind, or the currents of the ocean. We thus arrive at the extremely important conviction that *all natural bodies* which are known to us are *equally animated*, that the distinction which has been made between animate and inanimate bodies does *not* exist. When a stone is thrown into the air, and falls to earth according to definite laws, or when in a solution of salt a crystal is formed, the phenomenon is neither more nor less a mechanical manifestation of life than the growth and flowering of plants, than the propagation of animals or the activity of their senses, than the perception or the formation of thought in man." Here crystallization, organic life, sensation, and formation of thought, are expressly put in one line of mechanism with the falling of a stone.

In the following section we will have occasion to discuss this view as a *view of the world*; but we believe that the presentation of this idea, and the exclusive vindication of it as a complete view of the world, needs just here, where we still stand on the ground of the philosophy of natural perception, some critical sifting.

In the realm of material nature, *mechanical* explanation and general explanation is directly identical; *i.e.*, a process of nature remains obscure so long and so far as its mechanism is not yet perceived, and in the same degree as its mechanism is perceived, the process also is explained. The uniformity of law in the occurrence of events according to the causal principle in the realm of material nature, can be approached by us in no other form than in that of mechanism, provided we understand by mechanism an activity according to law and which can be mathematically estimated as to size and number. So far, therefore, every scientific investigator in the knowledge of material nature takes his place on the standpoint of a mechanical view of the world.

But here we have gone to the full extent to which we are justified in taking a mechanical view of the world, and have fixed its limits in its own proper realm—the realm of the scientific perception of the material world; even if we do not join with Wigand in resigning scientific inquiry in that direction, and express the expectation that these limits are not fixed and not to be designated in advance, but will be moved farther and farther, and that not only in regard to the knowledge of the quantity of phenomena (which even Wigand, as a scientific investigator, naturally admits), but also in regard to their quality. In our researches hitherto we have often met such limits. We have found that in the realm of the material world such important phenomena and processes as life are at present not yet fully explained. By the mechanical view of the world, we have been led back to the last elements and to the most elementary forces of matter, but have been convinced that we are no longer able to find them with scientific certainty, and that consequently not a single quality of material existence is really explained and traced back to its last material causes, to say nothing of the transcendental causes which are entirely inaccessible to our exact scientific knowledge.

Now there is another realm of existence, just as large as and, according to its value, still larger than, that of the material world, which, not on account of its scientific inaccessibility, but in conformity with its own peculiar nature, entirely withdraws itself from the mechanical view. It is the realm of *psychical life*; and, still more decidedly and more evidently, the *realm of mind*. As far as our observations go, the law of causality reigns here also, and here also nothing takes place without a cause. But as here the *realm* in which the causal law reigns is no longer material nature, so even the *form* in which it is active is no longer that of mechanism. For we certainly cannot understand mechanical effect to be anything else than an effect of something material upon something material, whose uniformity of law can be exactly estimated mathematically as to size and number. Now if the application of mechanism to the psychical and spiritual realm does not express anything except the certainly quite insidious idea that here also causality reigns, it is nothing else but the substitution of another idea for the word mechanism—an idea which it never had in the entire use of language up to this time, and by the substitution of which the proof for a mechanism of the mind is not given, but surreptitiously obtained in a manner similar to the before-mentioned attempt of Preyer, surreptitiously to obtain the proof for the origin of life.

But if the mechanical explanation of the functions of the mind really means that they also consist in an effect of the material upon something material, and that this effect can be mathematically estimated as to size and number, it is an assertion which has first to be proven, but which cannot be proven and cannot be allowed even as an hypothesis, as a problem for investigation, because it contradicts our whole experience. And it contradicts not only the conclusions drawn from most natural appearances, which, as is well known, are deceitful and even tell us that the sun goes around the earth, but it contradicts the philosophical analysis just as much and even still more directly and decidedly than the direct impression—as became clear to us at the lowest point of contact between the material and the psychical, viz., at sensation, when we showed the impossibility of scientifically explaining the origin of sensation.

It is easy to see what facts made it altogether possible to produce such a materialistic psychology and to give it at the first superficial view a certain appearance of truth; but it will not be difficult to detect its want of truth. According to our whole experience, the human mind is bound to the body; its proper activity, its whole communication with the material and immaterial world outside of it, even its whole mutual intercourse with the minds of fellow-beings, is performed by means of bodily functions which, as such, are subordinate to mechanism. Therefore "physiological psychology" certainly belongs to the most interesting of the branches of science which at present enjoy special care, and works in this realm, like those of Wundt, are worthy of the greatest attention. Now if these points of contact once exist between the material and the psychical and spiritual processes, so that material functions causally influence psychical and spiritual ones, and psychical and spiritual functions similarly influence material ones, there must also exist between the laws of material processes and those of psychical and spiritual functions a relation which makes possible such a mutual effect, and we must be able to abstract from it the existence of a common higher law of which on the one side the material laws, and on the other the psychical and spiritual, are but partial laws. Precisely here lie the indications which appear to favor materialism in psychology. But it is only an appearance. For, from the acknowledgment and scientific investigation of a reciprocal action, to an identification of the two factors which act upon one another, is still an infinite step. If science is not even able to identify material motion and sensation, still less can it identify material motion and the spiritual and ethic activities. When this is done, it is done only in consequence of the same confounding of condition and cause which we had to expose on the occasion of the assertion of the possibility of explaining the origin of life or of sensation, and of consciousness or of self-consciousness. But we here also willingly admit that the realm in which causality reigns in the form of mechanism, aims at being the support, foundation, and instrument of another realm where causality still reigns, but mechanism ceases. How far investigation may still proceed in the direction of those interesting points and lines where both realms touch one another in causal reciprocal action, we do not know. We are hardly able to indicate the direction in which the investigation must proceed, and this direction seems to be assigned to it by the idea of *Auslösung*.[8] The idea of *Auslösung*, which plays such an important *rôle* in physics, seems to be still fruitful for the knowledge of psycho-physical life: bodily functions *lösen aus* spiritual ones, spiritual functions bodily ones. But so much the more clearly does this theory show the limits of mechanism: mechanism reigns in the world of bodies from the *Auslösungen* and to the *Auslösungen*, with which the mind induces the body to activity, and the body the mind; beyond these limits causality still reigns, but no longer mechanism.

Now if thus the mechanical view of the world has within its own most proper realm—the realm of material phenomena—its limits, even if they are capable of being moved farther; and if it is without any scientific acceptance in the realm of soul and mind: its usurpations reach the highest possible degree when it pretends to explain the last causes of things. For from its very nature it follows that it is only able to explain the reciprocal action of material things among themselves, when these things in their finalities, or the causes of their qualities and conditions, are already present, and the laws which they follow are already active. As to the origin of those qualities or their causes, and of these laws, this view leaves us entirely in the dark.

CHAPTER II.

METAPHYSICAL CONCLUSIONS DRAWN FROM THE DARWINIAN THEORIES.

§ 1. *Elimination of the Idea of Design in the World.—Monism.*

From this mechanical view of the world, quite a peculiar conclusion has been recently drawn—not by Darwin, who does not give any opinion at all about the mechanical view of the world, as such, or about its extension and influence, nor, indeed, by Darwinians, not even by all followers of a mechanical view of the world, but only by a part of them; namely, by those who have in a high degree attracted to themselves the attention of reading people. This conclusion is nothing less than the *elimination of the idea of design in nature*. This phenomenon demands our attention. Heretofore, the proof of plan, design, and end in nature, at large and in detail, was looked upon as the most beautiful blossom and fruit of a thoughtful contemplation of nature; it was the great and beautiful common property, in the enjoyment of which the direct, the scientific, and the religious contemplation of nature peacefully participated. Now this view is to be given up forever, in consequence of nothing else than Darwin's selection theory. With an energy— we may say with a passionateness and confidence of victory—such as we were accustomed to see only in the most advanced advocates of materialism,

Ludwig Büchner, D. F. Strauss, Häckel, Oskar Schmidt, Helmholtz, the editor of the "Ausland" and some of his associates, and our often-mentioned "Anonymus,"—in a common attack, assail every idea of a *conformity to an end* in nature, every idea of a goal toward which the development at large and individually strives; in a word, the whole category of *teleology*.[9]

In order to be just in our judgment, we shall have to let the advocates of this view speak for themselves;—the advocates of *Dysteleology*, as Häckel, who is so extremely productive in forming new exotic words, calls it; or of *Aposkopiology*, as Ebrard, in his "Apologetik" ("Apologetics"), correcting the etymology, somewhat pedantically calls it; or of *Teleophoby*, as it is called by K. E. von Baer, in humorous irony.

The anonymous author of the book called "The Unconscious from the Standpoint of Physiology and Descent Theory", asserts that, while the descent theory but puts the teleological principle in question by withdrawing the ground for a positive proof—an assertion which we certainly have to reject most decidedly (compare Part II, Book II, Chap. I, § 2-§ 6)—the selection theory directly rejects it. Natural selection, he says, solves the seemingly unsolvable problem of explaining the conformity to the end in view, as result, without taking it as an aiding principle. And Helmholtz says: "Darwin's theory shows how conformity to the end in the formation of organisms can also originate without any intermingling of an intelligence by the blind administration of a law of nature."

Häckel really revels in these ideas. He says (Nat. Hist. of Creat., Vol. I, p. 19): "These optimistic views [of the much-talked-of purposiveness of nature or of the much-talked-of beneficence of the Creator] have, unfortunately, as little real foundation as the favorite phrase, 'the moral order of the universe,' which is illustrated in an ironical way by the history of all nations.... If we contemplate the common life and the mutual relations between plants and animals (man included), we shall find everywhere, and at all times, the very opposite of that kindly and peaceful social life which the goodness of the Creator ought to have prepared for his creatures—we shall rather find everywhere a pitiless, most embittered *Struggle of All against All*. Nowhere in nature, no matter where we turn our eyes, does that idyllic peace, celebrated by the poets, exist; we find everywhere a struggle and a striving to annihilate neighbors and competitors. Passion and selfishness—conscious or unconscious—is everywhere the motive force of life.... Man in this respect certainly forms no exception to the rest of the animal world." And on page 33: "In the usual dualistic or teleological (vital) conception of the universe, organic nature is regarded as the purposely executed production of a Creator working according to a definite plan. Its adherents see in every individual

species of animal and plant an 'embodied creative thought,' the material expression of a *definite first cause* (causa finalis), acting for a set purpose. They must necessarily assume supernatural (not mechanical) processes of the origin of organisms.... On the other hand, the theory of development carried out by Darwin, must, if carried out logically, lead to the monistic or mechanical (causal) conception of the universe. In opposition to the dualistic or teleological conception of nature, our theory considers organic as well as inorganic bodies to be the necessary products of natural forces. It does not see in every individual species of animal and plant the embodied thought of a personal Creator, but the expression for the time being of a mechanical process of development of matter, the expression of a necessarily active cause, that is, of a mechanical cause (causa efficiens). Where teleological Dualism seeks the arbitrary thoughts of a capricious Creator in miracles of creation, causal Monism finds in the process of development the necessary effects of eternal immutable laws of nature." Häckel's "Anthropogeny" also is replete with attacks upon a teleological view of nature, which leave nothing wanting in distinctness and coarseness. On page 111, Vol. I, we read: "The rudimentary organs clearly prove that the mechanical, or monistic conception of the nature of organisms is alone correct, and that the prevailing teleological, or dualistic method of accounting for them is entirely false. The very ancient fable of the all-wise plan according to which 'the Creator's hand has ordained all things with wisdom and understanding,' the empty phrase about the purposive 'plan of structure' of organisms is in this way completely disproved. Stronger arguments can hardly be furnished against the customary teleology, or Doctrine of Design, than the fact that all more highly developed organisms possess such rudimentary organs." (Compare also Vol. II, p. 439: "The rudimentary organs are among the most overwhelming proofs against the prevailing teleological ideas of creation.") According to his opinion (Vol.
I. p. 245), comparative anatomy may no longer look for a "pre-arranged plan of construction by the Creator." Besides, he calls it an anthropocentric error to look upon man as a preconceived aim of creation and a true final purpose of terrestrial life; and on page 17, of Vol. II, he supports this judgment by comparing the relative shortness of the existence of mankind with the length of the preceding geological periods: "Since the awakening of the human consciousness, human vanity and human arrogance have delighted in regarding Man as the real main-purpose and end of all earthly life, and as the centre of terrestrial Nature, for whose use and service all the activities of the rest of creation were from the first defined or predestined by a 'wise providence.' How utterly baseless these presumptuous anthropocentric conceptions are, nothing could evince more strikingly than a comparison of the duration of the Anthropozoic or Quaternary Epoch with that of the preceding Epochs." And on page 234, Vol. II: "Hence it is that, in accordance

with the received teleological view, it has been customary to admire the so-called 'wisdom of the Creator' and the 'purposive contrivances of His Creation' especially in this matter. But on more mature consideration it will be observed that the Creator, according to this conception, does after all but play the part of an ingenious mechanic or of a skillful watchmaker; just, indeed, as all these cherished teleological conceptions of the Creator and His Creation are based on childish anthropomorphism.... But it is exactly on this point that the history of evolution proves most clearly that this received conception is radically false. The history of evolution convinces us that the highly purposive and admirably constituted sense organs, like all other organs, have developed *without premeditated aim.*"

Strauss, in his "The Old Faith and the New," gives to this idea its philosophic and universalistic finish. In § 67-§ 70, he eliminates not only the idea of design in individual cases, but also the idea of a design in the world as a whole; allows us to speak of design in the world only in a subjective sense, so far as we understand it to be what we think we perceive as the common final aim of the concert of the powers, active in the world; and finds, when in such a sense it is spoken of as design in the world, that the universe reaches its end in every instance. Only the parts develop themselves, driven by the mechanical laws of causality, and after having lived their period of life, sink back again into the universe, in order to make place for new developments and to prepare them in their turn.

For the view of the world which the antagonists of teleology construct out of this "mechanical" and "causal" view, they, as we have repeatedly seen, have invented the name "*monism.*" In contrast to all dualism in reasoning about the relation of body and soul, God and universe, time and eternity, and especially in contrast to the dualism with which the theistic view of the world is said to be loaded, monism claims that what was formerly divided into God and universe, force and matter, matter and spirit, body and soul, is but one; and it thus exhibits a reconciliation, a higher unity, of materialism and idealism, of pantheism and atheism, which unity in the scientific and the practical ethic realm has no antagonist to fight more energetically, and none which it is better able to fight successfully, than *dualism*, which the monistic view of the world, by a queer mistake as to the theistic position of God in nature, especially considers the whole theistic view of the world.

The scientific antagonists of teleology show such a scientific intolerance against their own associates, that one of the latest exhibitors of Darwinism, Oskar Schmidt, in his "Theory of Descent and Darwinism," bluntly classes one of the greatest and most deserving investigators in the realm of comparative anatomy and palæontology, Richard Owen, of London, with the

"'Halves' who, fearing the conclusions, with one word come to terms with the scientific conscience." And why?—because Owen still sees ends in nature, and by his inclination to the acceptance of a descent, does not allow himself to be prevented from giving adhesion to a teleological view of the world. And this invention of monism is proclaimed to the world in such a full consciousness of its great importance in the history of culture, that Häckel closes his "Nat. Hist. of Creat." with the following words: "Future centuries will celebrate our age, which was occupied with laying the foundations of the Doctrine of Descent, as the new era in which began a period of human development, rich in blessings,—a period which was characterized by the victory of free inquiry over the despotism of authority, and by the powerful ennobling influence of the Monistic Philosophy." At the end of the lecture, next to the last, in the same Vol. II, page 332, he pays the following compliment to the antagonists of monism: "The recognition of the theory of development and the Monistic Philosophy based upon it, forms the best criterion for the degree of man's mental development." In his "Generic Morphology," and in the first edition of his "Nat. Hist. of Creat.," he, in a geological scala, which closes with the human period, even divides the whole past, present, and future history of mankind into two halves: first part, dualistic period of culture; second part, monistic period of culture. Still, we will not omit to mention, with credit, that this anticipatory historiography has discreetly disappeared from the geological scala of the following editions of his "Natural History of Creation."

As to the further scientific consequences to which this anti-teleological monism leads, the advocates of it are in tolerable accord; although they are subject to the most incomprehensible illusions regarding the practical consequences of it, as we have seen in the above-quoted concluding words of Häckel's "Natural History of Creation." As to the scientific consequences, they express themselves plainly enough: the belief in a living Creator and Lord of the world no longer find any place; everything, even all the rich treasures of human life and history, become a result of blindly acting forces; the history of the world, ethics, and all spiritual sciences, are in the progress of perception dissolved into physiology, and physiology into chemistry, physics and mechanism. In his "Natural History of Creation," Vol. I, page 170, Häckel frankly calls the whole history of the world a physico-chemical process.

Whoever refers to a view of another person, is in duty bound to enter into that view, if possible objectively, even if he does not agree with it. The author of this book tries to comply with this obligation in all his representations, but must confess that in regard to the just described view of the world, he does not succeed in making it conceivable to himself in a manner to be justified even from a relatively scientific standpoint; a want for which, it is true, we have beforehand the explanatory cause in the quotation from Häckel's "Natural History of Creation," Vol. II, p. 332, given above.

Perhaps it appears relatively conceivable, when it is asserted that the observation of an order, a connection, a development, a plan, in the world, leads to the perception of such a quality of the laws, primitive elements, and forces of the world, that something like it *had to* result from them; but that it does not lead to the acknowledgment of a personal author of the world. We call such a view relatively conceivable, not because we agree with it—for we find a logic which, in contemplating the universe, starts from an intelligent author of the world, infinitely less surrounded by difficulties than one contrary to it— but because the acknowledgment or denial of a living God is in the last instance not the result of any scientific investigation or logical chain of reasoning, but the moral act of the morally and religiously inclined individual, and because, if the individual has once refused the strongest factor of faith in God,—namely, his self-testimony in the conscience,—it is no longer impossible for the individual to ignore his other testimonies as such, or to declare them deficient. Now we certainly can say that we see order and many results in the world, which are conformable to the object in view, and in consequence of this observation must admit that no imaginable quality of primitive beginnings, elements, and forces of the world had caused this result, but that this result must have already been in the plan. But there certainly are imaginable, *in abstracto*, infinitely many possibilities of other elements and primitive beginnings of the world,—perhaps of some whose result would have been but an eternal chaos, or of others whose result would have been but an eternal rigidness, or of still others whose result would also have been a certain order and variety of phenomena and processes, but less beautiful than that of the really existing world. Thus, then, this world now exists as a *special chance* of infinitely many chances; and who knows whether, in the course of thousands of millions of terrestrial years in the struggle for existence, it did not obtain its existence among infinitely many possibilities of worlds through a natural world-selection, and thus, by the result of its existence, fully legitimate its conformity to the end in view? With this deduction, we do not make, as it may seem, an awkward attempt at rendering the whole standpoint ridiculous by a wild phantasy; but we quote it from a celebrated and otherwise very meritorious book, namely the "Geschichte des Materialismus" ("History of Materialism"), by the too early deceased Friedrich Albert Lange. The reader will find it, in the second part, page 275, simply a little shorter and, as it seems to us, less clear, but as the only "correct teleology" which Lange professes. This whole view, like all world-theories and cosmogonies of pantheism, naturalism, or atheism, and even like the latest of Eduard von

Hartmann, is to us but a proof that the rejection of the reality of a living Creator and Lord of the world requires of its advocates mysteries and mysticisms of atheism compared to which the greatest difficulties of the Christian view of the world are but the merest trifles.

Therefore, if that first and second step in the rejection of the highest intelligence and omnipotence as the final cause of the world, are once made, it is easy for us to comprehend still other supports which this view of the world draws to itself. However large the number of things in the world for whose existence we can give a reason, or of which we can show that that, which preceded, aimed at their appearance, still the number of those to which we can not ascribe aim and design is just as large. There are even phenomena enough which in their main effects appear to us directly irrational; as, for instance, those which operate destructively,—all the tortures which animals inflict on one another, etc. Besides, we can also find imperfections in the degree of the conformity to the end in view in all those phenomena which appear to us as properly planned; for instance, the organic appears to us higher than the inorganic, and yet it is in its existence not only dependent on the inorganic, but is often destroyed prematurely by it. Of course, all these limits and barriers of our teleological perception are abundantly used by all antagonists of a teleological view of the world for the basis of their position. Furthermore, the way and manner in which man fixes his ends and reaches them, is essentially different from the way and manner in which nature acts. Man seeks to attain his ends with less expenditure of power and means, the more he acts conformably to the end in view; while nature, it often enough appears to us, when we have reason to imagine an effect of its processes also as the probable end of them, reaches this end only by an immense squandering of means—for instance, the preservation of organic species simply by the production of thousands of germs and eggs, most of which perish, and but very few of which are developed, and still less are transmitted. This is a difference to which Lange points, in order to reject a theory which recognizes a striving toward an end (Zielstrebigkeit) in nature, or at most to allow it a little place as the lowest form of teleology, and to reject every attempt to regard it as analogous to human striving toward an end, as *anthropomorphism*. Nature, he says, acts, as if a man, in order to shoot a hare, should in a large field discharge millions of guns in all possible directions; as if he, in order to get into a locked room, should buy ten thousand different keys and try them all; as if, in order to have a house, he should build up a town and leave the superfluous houses to wind and weather. Nobody should call such actions conformable to an end in view, and still less should we suppose behind this action any higher wisdom, hidden reasons, or superior sagacity. It is true, Wigand is right in replying to this, that when we observe such things in nature, we have to draw the conclusion that the very end supposed by the observing man—in this case, the preservation of the species—is not the only end, but that it has other ends besides; as, for instance, richness of life, inexhaustible abundance, preservation of other organisms, etc. Besides, this is but a single side of the comparison between the action of man and that of nature; and from this side action of man, conformable to an end in view, appears as a higher form of teleology, that of nature as a lower. But there are other sides of comparison, which just as clearly strike the eye; nature builds from within in full sovereignty of its process over matter and form. Man approaches his materials from without; nature works with never- erring certainty (Häckel's latest theory, that nature *falsifies* its laws and processes, can surely not be meant in earnest!); man often enough with error, false calculation, awkwardness, failure and capricious arbitrariness. In these directions, teleology of nature is infinitely superior to that of man.

We must be very careful in using anthropomorphism as a term of reproach. It may be used as a reproach in warning against careless reasoning and hasty comparison, but the idea of anthropomorphism is so extensible that it can be extended over all human reasoning and conception. Are not the reasons on account of which the so-called anthropomorphism is to be rejected, often enough just as anthropomorphistic as the ideas which are attacked? For instance, when the idea of the personality of God is attacked as an anthropomorphistic one, are not the reasons with which it is assailed exactly as anthropomorphistic as the conceptions which are to be assailed? Do we not derive all our reasoning, logic, our views, and in fact everything, at first from our human nature, and do we not in our most abstract reasoning always operate simply with the laws, as they inhere in our human nature? Is there even a single scientific description conceivable without its being full of anthropomorphisms? Even the works of Darwin which, according to the opinion of these opponents of anthropomorphism, destroy anthropomorphism and teleology, are the most striking proof in favor of it. The discovery of the general reign of the law of causality invalidates, as they say, the reign of the category of teleology; for the one category contradicts the other. Suppose it were so (we will, however, immediately see that the contrary is true) whence do we know that the category of causality has the preference over that of finality or teleology? The one, as well as the other, is anthropomorphistic, and is an undoubtedly necessary form of our human reasoning. We *believe* in their objective validity, because we cannot believe that the sum of existences and the relations between the perceiving subject and the perceived object aim at deceiving man; we do not want to be robbed of either the one or the other category; but if the question is as to the preference of the one category over the other (which we contest), who knows whether the category of finality has not more reasons for its superiority than causality? Compare, in reference to this whole question, also the clear analyses in the second volume of the work of Wigand, and the instructive lecture of the Duke of Argyll upon anthropomorphism in theology.

Nevertheless, all the points against teleology thus far quoted can be understood by us as attempts at rejecting the *necessity* of acknowledging a teleologically acting principle of the world—or, to express ourselves more clearly, of a living God—after having once rejected the deepest motive for this acknowledgment, namely: the self-testimony of God in the human conscience and mind. But it is one thing to declare that we are not obliged to accept a certain conclusion, and quite another to declare that we are obliged to accept directly the opposite of such a conclusion. It is one thing to declare that the phenomena in the world do not yet oblige us to suppose an author with a preconceived plan, and still another to declare that because I have found or still hope to find the causal connexion of phenomena conformable to the end in view, no author with a preconceived plan exists. This last assertion is one which the author of this work confesses not to understand, and in whose conclusion he cannot agree. Knowledge of the *origin* of something certainly does not exclude the question *wherefore* it exists, and does not even take its place, and when I have answered both questions satisfactorily, then I may and must justly ask whether both that for which something exists and that by which something exists, is intended or not, whether that which in the language of causality I call cause and effect, also belongs to the category of finality, according to which that very cause is at the same time called means, and that very effect also design. The one way of viewing postulates the other as its necessary completion; and the teleological point of view is so little an impediment for the causal, that we are much more fully convinced scientifically of the correctness of the teleological way of viewing, when first the causal chain of causes and effects lies plain before our perception without any wanting links.

We still have to mention two monstrosities which, as it seems to us, necessarily result from the rejection of teleology, although the opponents of teleology contest the fact.

The one is the reduction to *chance* of all single formations in the world. It is true, necessity reigns in laws and their effect; but if the degree and the sum of all qualities in the world are not based the one upon the other, if especially the single organizations originate by the way of natural selection, every coincidence of each single causal chain in the world with any other causal chain is something accidental for the one as well as for the other. Now, an explanation of that in the world which is conformable to the end in view, by chance, is a scientifically illogical idea. An accidental coincidence of many circumstances can in a single case produce something which is conformable to an end in view; but the probability that the formation conformable to the end in view is again nullified by the next throw of the dice of chance, is so great, and with every following throw grows so decidedly in geometrical progression, that this probability after a few terms becomes a certainty, and we can directly demonstrate mathematically that the world without a teleological plan would be and remain a chaos. As we have seen, even Lange finds himself obliged to admit this plan, with the exception that he makes this plan itself chance—special chance among infinitely many possibilities.

The other consequence of that elimination of the idea of design is that it forbids every difference between *higher* and *lower*, and changes everything into an indifferent and equivalent continual stream of coming and going. For the whole idea of higher and lower belongs to the category of teleology. If the new which originates is *but* a product of that which was already in existence, and if the latter does not aim at the production of the new, then the new is equivalent to the preceding; and it is but an illusion of man, preconceiving an end, when in the products of nature he discriminates between higher and lower. A beginning of the acknowledgment of this consequence is made, when Häckel, in his Anthropogeny, so violently attacks the idea that man is end and design of the terrestrial creation. But generally the antagonists of teleology are guilty of the inconsequence which, although from the principles of their system to be rejected, is indelibly impressed on our thinking mind and especially on our moral consciousness, that they still discriminate between higher and lower, and particularly that they willingly assign to the moral disposition and demand, and to the morally planned individual, the priority among existences. This fact is pronounced in a very striking way in the concessions of Strauss, which we have quoted on page 126, according to which nature, where it can no longer go beyond itself, wishes to go into itself, and in man has wished to go not only upwards but even beyond itself.

Therefore, not only theology, but also philosophy, and even natural science, in their most prominent advocates, have in a uniform chorus protested against this destruction of the idea of design. That it was unanimously done on the part of *theology*, is quite natural, and needs no further proofs. When we, nevertheless, mention expressly a single essay on these questions, it is done on account of the fact that in its energetic defense of the teleological point of view it is especially effective by frankly and impartially admitting the strongest positions of the opponent's standpoint—a thing which rarely happens on the part of theologians. It is the essay of Julius Köstlin "Ueber die Beweise für das Dasein Gottes" ("Proofs of the Existence of God"), in the "Theologische Studien und Kritiken," 1875, IV and 1876, I; especially 1876,

I, p. 42 ff. On the part of philosophy, we have to mention Ulrici, Fichte, Huber and Frohschammer, who have rejected the attack against teleology with inflexible criticism. Even Friedrich Vischer in the sixth part of his "Kritische Gänge" ("Critical Walks"), has forcibly maintained the right of teleology, especially of its highest revelation, the moral order of the world— in contrast to his friend D. F. Strauss, whose "The Old Faith and the New" he criticises; but it is true, in consequence of his pantheism, he reaches the wholly imaginary conclusion of supposing a moral order of the world without a regulator. And, to be able to make the systematized order and beauty of nature conceivable to himself without a Creator, to be able to make conceivable to himself a design in nature, an ideal, according to which nature works as an unconscious artist, he gives to philosophy the certainly unsolvable problem of finding the idea of timeless time, to which the "afterward" can just as well be a "beforehand"; he prefers to do this rather than to find the equally clear and deep solution of that teleological difficulty in the simple idea of a Creator, who, as such, also stands above time. One of the most remarkable philosophic testimonies for the right of teleology is the philosophic system of Eduard von Hartmann who, although he calls his absolute the unconscious, ascribes to it an unconscious intelligence and an unconscious will, and makes the observation and acknowledgment of designs and ends, which he sees in the whole realm of the world of phenomena, an essential part of his entire system. All attempts of this kind, as those of Vischer and Hartmann, fully and correctly to understand the language of facts on the one side and to reject on the other the necessary conclusion to which it leads—namely, the acknowledgment of a creative intelligence *above* the facts, and having an end in view—only increase in like manner as the above-quoted cosmogonic idea of Lange by the monstrosities of reasoning to which they lead, the power of demonstration for that which they undertake to contest. Natural scientists, finally, even Darwinians, have not only in *casual* utterances often spoken a weighty word in favor of teleology—as, for instance, those who, like Oswald Heer, Kölliker, Baumgärtner, believe in a metamorphosis of germs, but also men who are quite favorable to the idea of an origin of the species through descent—as, for instance, Richard Owen, at the end of his "Comparative Anatomy of the Vertebrates," separately published as "Derivative Hypothesis of Life and Species"; Alexander Braun, in his lecture "Ueber die Bedeutung der Entwicklung in der Naturgeschichte" ("On the Importance of Development in Nature"), Berlin, 1872; A. W. Volkmann "Ueber die Entwicklung der Organismen" ("On the Development of Organisms"), Halle, 1875; Schaaffhausen, in his opening address to the Wiesbaden Anthr. Versammlung, Braunschweig, 1874, and others; but they have also given to teleology entire treatises. Besides a more popular treatise of the astronomer Mädler in "Westermann's Monatshefte," October, 1872, there belong to them the frequently mentioned work of Wigand, and especially three essays of great importance from the pen of a man who in questions of development and its extent has among all contemporaries the first right to speak, namely, Karl Ernst von Baer. They are the essays on the conformity to the end in view in general, on the conformity to the end in view in organic bodies, and on Darwin's doctrine, published together with two other essays in the already mentioned "Studien aus dem Gebiete der Naturwissenschaften," (Reden und Kleinere Aufsätze, 2ter Theil), Petersburg, 1876. Nay, even the two founders of Darwinism, Darwin himself and A. R. Wallace, as we shall see in defining their position in reference to religion, express themselves decidedly teleologically; this is especially true of Wallace, and likewise of their active and able second, Huxley. Only a single utterance of Darwin in a later publication seems to take a sceptical position in regard to teleology; compare below Part Second, Book I, Chapt. III, § 1.

Finally, we have to say a word concerning the *name* which the anti- teleological view of the world gives to itself: the name "*monism.*" The view of the world which monism gives us, seems hardly comprehensible; and just as little does the name which it gives itself, seem justifiable.

If this name is to indicate only a maxim of *investigation*—the directive which scientific investigation has to take, in order to reach more general points of view—we could declare ourselves in full accord with it. All investigation strives after a unity of principle; this impulse is a scientific leading motive of our nature. Besides the absolute limits of our knowledge, there are still enough relative and provisory limits to it; and there also are enough low points of view, mistakes, and imperfections in science, to justify us when we expressly form and establish monism as a maxim of scientific investigation. All those theories and points of view need such a spur and corrective, which are hastily satisfied with a dualistic or a still farther expanded limit of our knowledge. Among them we rank in theology the antique heathenish dualism which separates God and the world in such a way that God is but the architect of the eternal matter, existing independently of God; and also the modern deistic dualism which considers only the elements, principles, and beginning of the world, as dependent on God, but not the entire course of their developments as a whole and in detail. In philosophy, taken in a narrower sense, we reckon with them the one-sided atomism which can no longer find the connecting link between the single elements of the world, or the one-sided assertion of realism or idealism, since at this time all views of the world which win acceptance from the present generation claim the praise of showing the reconciliation and higher unity of realism and idealism. In anthropology, there belongs to them such a treatment of psychology and physiology, that the one science does not trouble itself about the other, and the investigation does not seek or keep in mind that which is common to both, or that which is higher and superior to them; and in all natural sciences, every mode of investigation belongs to them, where the single science retains no sympathy with all other sciences and with the principles of all scientific investigation. In regard to these low points of view, mistakes, or imperfections, monism certainly is a correct and necessary maxim of investigation; but this maxim ought not to lead us so far that we—as very often happens from the *unity* or the possibility of grouping several forms of existence under general conceptions—make an *identity*, that we efface the differences instead of explaining them, and then think the effacement is an explanation; that we set forth the *assumed* form of unity as if one we had found, and in this manner falsify the method of knowing. For as certainly and as much as man is subject to the dangers of error and falsification, just so certainly and so little is nature subject to falsification.

But if the name "monism" is to designate a certain *view of the world*, it is for such a designation either too comprehensive and quite applicable to *all* views which have a right to the name of view of the world; or it is misleading, and not applicable to any. For the name, as if it were properly called henism, either expresses only the *unity* of the principle of the world, and designates a quality which is the characteristic of every view of the world, and which especially belongs to theism in a clearer and more perfect way than to any other standpoint; or the name is used to attest that the world *alone* exists, and that monism knows of but *one* existence,—namely, that of the world; while the contrary view of the world—that of theism, which in a manner wholly incompetent, and historically wholly unjustified, is called dualism—supposes *two* existences, God and the world. But then this name does not correctly represent either itself or theism. It does not correctly represent itself: for the so-called monism does not, indeed, suppose that that which *appears* in the world is the really existing, or that the processes which come into appearance have again their *final* cause only in the appearance, but it seeks the final causes of the phenomena in laws and principles which can no longer be observed by our senses, and of those it again seeks the common, highest, and very last principle, the perception of which it either, with Häckel, renounces or finds it, with other theories, now in atomism, and in attraction and repulsion, then in the law of causality. Thus it has not only a single existence and mode of existence, but it does exactly the same thing that theism does: it seeks the final principles of the world. And it does not correctly represent theism: for theism also does not know of two existences to which the idea of existing is applicable in fully the same way—namely, the world *and* God—- but in seeking a cause for the existence of the world, it finds it in God; the world, according to its view, only exists by the fact that it exists in and through God. So theism in this sense also contests with monism for the right of the name.

Therefore, when teleology allows the opponent's view of the world to appropriate the name monism exclusively to itself, it can do this only in the same sense as that in which, in order to avoid disputes, we are satisfied with many irrational names which have forced themselves upon us; as, for instance, we can perhaps call the clerical party in Bavaria the patriotic, because it calls itself so, or as we accept the title of the ultramontane paper "Germania," at Berlin, without conceding to the bearers of those names the care of patriotism and of the interests of the German empire in a higher degree than to parties and papers of a different standpoint. In fact, this linguistic arbitrariness does not particularly tend to clearness of conception and to the avoidance of obscure phrases.

PART II

The Position of the Darwinian Theories in Reference to Religion and Morality.

BOOK I.

HISTORICAL AND CRITICAL.

PLAN OF TREATMENT.

In discussing the conclusions which have been drawn by Darwinism in reference to religion and morality, it would seem appropriate to treat of the two realms together. For the grouping which we have to give to the different conclusions of Darwinian tendencies, in their position in reference to religion, is nearly the same which they also receive in their position in reference to ethical questions.

But, nevertheless, we prefer to separate the two questions; not only because in fact one author has laid more stress upon the religious realm, another more upon the ethical, but because in reality, and also in the solution which we shall try to give to the problems presented by them, both realms, although closely interwoven, and limited by one another, still are theoretically to be treated apart.

In order not to exceed too much the limits of our task, we must avoid going more into the details of the relations between religion and morality in general, than is absolutely necessary for the solution of our main problem. This restriction we can easily put on ourselves. For, first, every one who reflects at all on human life and action, and on his own religious and moral conduct, generally has a very correct, instinctive, and direct conception and perception as to the realm of the religious as well as of the moral—as to their mutual differences, as well as to their reciprocal relations—even if he has not yet tried to bring this conception into ideas and formulas; and, secondly, it will not be difficult to present a short formula as to the ideal relation between the religious and the moral, sufficient for the wants of science as well as for the practical needs of a more detailed investigation. The *religious* is the relation of our personality to God; the *moral*, the relation of it to the world, comprehensively taken, ourselves included. We purposely call it a relation of our personality, and not merely a relation of man, because in the religious the ethical moment of self-determination which is included in the idea of personality, is an essential factor; and because we gladly make it conspicuous, partly in opposition to the one-sidedness of Schleiermacher's feeling of absolute dependence, partly to prevent a contrary misunderstanding of our own view, as if we found the seat of religion in the activity of knowledge. For when, in our representation of the Darwinian conclusions and in our own investigation, we proceed as objectively as possible, and try to avoid all systematization which is unfruitful for our task, in discussing the Darwinian theories in reference to religion, we shall have to take chiefly into consideration their relation to religion in an objective sense, and chiefly also their relation to the contents of religion; but this would make it appear that we supposed religion in a subjective sense, religiousness, to be in the first place an activity and a possession of knowledge. Nothing lies farther from us than this thought; although religiousness certainly has and asks for solid, objectively true, and really possessed salvation, and however little we would overlook the word of the Lord: "And this is life eternal, that they might *know* thee, the only true God, and Jesus Christ, whom thou hast sent." (John xvii, 3.)

Those who wish to inform themselves in regard to the relation of religion and morality, will find the necessary information in Martensen's "Ethik" ("Ethics"), in Otto Pfleiderer's monograph, which partly assumes a contrary point of view, and in a thorough essay of Julius Köstlin (Theol. Studien und Kritiken, 1870, I), which appeared before the "Ethics" of Martensen.

In undertaking now to represent the conclusions which have been drawn from Darwinism, we treat of the religious realm as the higher, a realm demanding a sound morality prior to the moral realm; and we begin with those conclusions which take a hostile position in reference to religion, in order to proceed from them to the moderate and friendly relations.

A. THE DARWINIAN THEORIES AND RELIGION.

CHAPTER I.

MORE OR LESS NEGATIVE POSITION IN REFERENCE TO RELIGION.

§ 1. *Extreme Negation. L. Büchner and Consistent Materialism.*

The common point of beginning and attack of all those who take a negative position against religion, is the rejection of teleology. The most advanced of all materialists, Ludwig Büchner, in his self-criticism, which he gives in his "Natur und Wissenschaft" ("Nature and Science"), on page 465, openly declares, and quite correctly, that with the success or failure of the attacks upon teleology materialism itself stands or falls.

Now while many, as we shall immediately see, although opposed to a teleological view of the world, still are inclined to give a more or less lasting value to certain psychical processes which may be called by the name religion, Büchner, on the contrary, makes a direct attack upon everything which is thus called. He does not render it difficult for us to review his position. For, after having given it openly, but still with certain relative modifications, in different publications (especially in his book "Force and Matter," which appeared in 1855 in the first edition, and in 1872 in the twelfth) he gives it in cynical nakedness in the lectures with which he travelled through America and Germany in 1872-1874, and the contents of which he has made public in his pamphlet: "Der Gottesbegriff und dessen Bedeutung in der Gegenwart" ("The Idea of God, and its Importance at the Present Time"), Leipzig, 1874, Theo. Thomas. As is said in the preface, the design of the lecture is "to give a renewed impulse to the final and definitive elimination of an idea which, according to the opinion of the author, obstructs our whole spiritual, social, and political development, as no other idea does." He means the idea of God; not merely the theistic idea of a personal God, but the idea of God in general. For even the pantheistic idea of God, which he had formerly treated with a certain polite reserve, finds in his eyes even less favor than the theistic. He says: "If the absurdity is already great enough in theism, it is possibly still greater in pantheism, which moreover has always played a great *rôle* in philosophy;" and, "Christianity has but injured the spiritual and material progress of mankind." In agreement with Strauss, he sees the earliest origin of the idea of God only in ignorance and fear. "Every creating, preserving, or reigning principle in the world is done away with, and there remains as highest spiritual power present in the world only human reason. Atheism or philosophic monism alone leads to freedom, to reason, progress, acknowledgment of true humanity,—in short to humanism."

This materialistic opposition to everything which is called religion, is certainly independent of Darwinism, and originated before its time; but since Büchner himself sees in Darwinism but a grand confirmation of his view of the world, and believes that he has found in it that principle which, with urgent necessity, banishes teleology from the contemplation of nature— teleology, with the defeat or victory of which materialism stands or falls,—we are entitled and obliged to rank even this view of the world among the conclusions which in reference to religion have been drawn from the theories of Darwin. And, indeed, it is a most extreme conclusion, and simply puts itself in the category of negation to the contents of religion, as well as to religion in a subjective sense, to religious and pious conduct. It can be clearly seen how firmly a view of the world which makes war against religion and the idea of God its special life-task, is connected with all those destructive elements which lie in human nature, and especially in the social circumstances of the present, and which have their only and final ethical limit in the consciousness of God which, as a power never wholly to be effaced, lies in the depth of the soul of even those who wander farthest from a moral and spiritual life.

§ 2. Replacement of Religion through a Religious Worship of the Universe. Strauss, Oskar Schmidt, Häckel.

Strauss, in that testament of his scientific life and activity, "The Old Faith and the New," takes a somewhat different position in reference to religion. Even for him, the whole idea of God is abolished and replaced by the idea of the cosmos; but he makes this cosmos the object of religious worship, and has exactly the same feeling of absolute dependence in regard to it, which, according to Schleiermacher, constitutes the nature of religion. When Arthur Schopenhauer or Eduard von Hartmann bring forth their pessimistic accusations against the universe, his religious sensation reacts against it in the same manner as the organism against the prick of a needle. This pessimism, he says, acts upon reason as an absurdity, but upon sensation as blasphemy. "We demand the same piety for our cosmos that the devout of old demanded for his God. If wounded, our feeling for the cosmos simply reacts in a religious manner." While, therefore, Strauss, to the question, "Are we still Christians?" gives an emphatic "No," he answers the question, "Have we still a religion?" with "Yes or No, according to the spirit of the inquiry."

Among men of science who wrote about Darwinism, Oskar Schmidt, in his before-quoted publication, "The Doctrine of Descent and Darwinism," seems to take exactly the same position in reference to religion. At least, he unreservedly professes monism, rejects all teleological conceptions as imperfections, speaks of the caprice of a personal God, and sees the conception that the idea of God is immanent in human nature invalidated by the fact "that many millions in the most cultivated nations, and among them the most eminent and lucid thinkers, have not the consciousness of a personal God; those millions of whom the heroic Strauss became the spokesman."

Häckel, it is true, mentions Strauss only in the preface of the fourth edition of his "Natural History of Creation," but here he greets "The Old Faith and the New" as the confession which he also makes, and thus gives us an express right to place him in this class, although he calls his worship of the universe religion; it is, however, a classification which his whole position compelled us to give him. It is true, he speaks very warmly of his own religion, which is founded on the clear knowledge of nature and its inexhaustible abundance of manifestations, and which, as "simple religion of nature," will in the future act upon the course of development of mankind, ennobling and perfecting it in a far higher degree than the various ecclesiastic religions of the different nations, "resting on a blind belief in the vague secrets and mythical revelations of a sacerdotal caste." (Nat. Hist. of Cr., Vol. II, p. 369.) He also repeatedly speaks of "manifestations of nature," and even of a "divine Spirit which is everywhere active in nature." In that respect he seems to take in reference to religion, without regard to the historical form in which it appeared as Christian religion, a still more friendly and less problematic position than Strauss. Moreover, he demands for every individual the full right of forming his own religion; among the more highly developed species of men, he says, every independent and highly developed individual, every original person, has his own religion, his own God; and it would certainly, therefore, not be arrogant if he should also claim the right of forming his own conception of God, his own religion. But when we try to form a more complete idea of his position in reference to religion, we really do not find any essential difference between it and that of Strauss. According to repeated utterances, he can not imagine the personal Creator without caprice and arbitrariness; again and again he advocates monism with great warmth, and also identifies, in express words, God and the universe, God and nature. "Corresponding to our progressive perception of nature and our immovable conviction of the truth of the evolution theory, our religion can be only a *religion of nature.*" "In rejecting the dualistic conception of nature and the herewith connected amphitheistic conception of God, ... we certainly lose the hypothesis of a personal Creator; but we gain in its place the undoubtedly more worthy and more perfect conception of a divine Spirit which penetrates and fills the universe." Furthermore, the faith in a personal Creator is called a low dualistic conception of God, which corresponds to a low animal stage of development of the human organism. The more highly developed man of the present, he says, is capable of and intended for an infinitely nobler and sublimer monistic idea of God, to which belongs the future, and through which we attain a more sublime conception of the unity of God and nature. According to his Anthropogeny, the belief that the hand of a Creator has arranged all things with wisdom and intelligence is an ancient story and an empty phrase.

§ 3. *Pious Renunciation of the Knowability of God. Wilhelm Bleek, Albert Lange, Herbert Spencer.*

A more friendly position in reference to religion is taken by those who hold, not directly negative, but only decidedly sceptical views of the existence of God; who reduce the relative unsearchableness of God, which every religious standpoint admits, to an absolute unknowability; and who find the nature of religion either in a pious acknowledgment of this unknowability, or in a poetical substitute for the knowledge of God, *i.e.*, comprehending the unknowable in a figure. The most prominent advocates of this position are, on the side of exact investigation, Wilhelm Bleek; and on that of philosophy, Albert Lange in Germany and Herbert Spencer in England. Since all three use the Darwinian theories for their systems, they also belong to the ranks of our historico-critical essay.

Wilhelm Bleek, in the preface to his "Ursprung der Sprache" ("Origin of Language"), rejects all claims of a positively revealed religion to an objective truth—not in such a way as to substitute the universe in place of God, but so that he remains sceptical in reference to every attempt at forming an idea of God, demands a pious and modest confession of this non-understanding by man, and sees in this reverential modesty the certainly not very significant nature of his religion. In the preface he says that all worship originates in reverence for ancestors, and that even the doctrine of the atonement of modern theology has its origin there. The next step after reverence for ancestors was the worship of nature. But the grand turning-point at which the mythological mode of view gives way—in which mode of view he also reckons Christianity—is the giving up of the idea of the necessity of an atonement; for this whole idea is but anthropomorphism. It is when man has recognized the impossibility of a being, similar to man, as the final cause of all existences, and in reverential modesty has admitted his ignorance in reference to the nature of the origin of things, that he learns to understand how narrow a view he has of God when he thinks that he understands him.

On the side of philosophy, Albert Lange and Herbert Spencer reach similar results. Albert Lange, in his "History of Materialism," starting especially from premises of Kant, reaches the conclusion that the "thing *per se*," the "intelligible world," is absolutely hidden to us. What we perceive is but the world of appearances; and the fact that we perceive it, and perceive it as we do, is originally founded in the human organization. By virtue of this organization we are bound, in all our knowledge of the world of appearances, to the law of causality. Science does not get beyond this causal chain of finite and relative causes and effects; to the "thing *per se*" there is nowhere to be found a bridge, not even as Kant supposes, in the categoric imperative, nor in ideas. Inasmuch as science does not get beyond this chain, it is materialistic; inasmuch as it must nevertheless perceive the existence, or at least the possibility of the existence, of a "thing *per se*," even if it does not see any way to its perception, it is idealistic. But man also has ideal impulses, and he has to follow them just as much as the impulse of perception. By virtue of these ideal impulses, he makes in imagination a picture of the "thing *per se*" in the activity of philosophic speculation, art, and religion. Philosophic speculation is but imaginative conceptions. It has always a value in the history of culture, as a summing-up of the elements of culture and of the spiritual impulses and treasures of a certain time; but it errs as soon as it claims to be more than imaginative conceptions—namely, an adequate representation of the final cause of all things—for it lacks the necessary basis of experience. Art does not claim this, and therefore is not exposed to that danger of deception. Religion satisfies a need of the heart, to have a home of the spirit in the "thing *per se*"; but since the "thing *per se*" is not accessible for us, religion creates in mind that home, in order to rise above the common reality to it. Lange finds the highest realization of a perfect satisfaction of that impulse in the philosophic poems of Schiller. He sees the quintessence of religion expressly "in the elevation of minds above the real, and in the creation of a home of the spirit." Religion remains untouched in its full vital power, as long as it retains that as its quintessence; but it is exposed to all the dangers of a destructive criticism as soon as it seeks its quintessence in something else—for instance, in certain doctrines of God, the human soul, creation of the world, etc.

Herbert Spencer is in full accord with Lange in regard to the theory of an absolute indiscernibleness of the final cause of all things; but he reaches this result in a somewhat different way, and from his premises infers a different modification of the nature of religion. In his "First Principles" he appears to be a true scholar of the English and Scotch schools of philosophy, from which he takes his start in conscious and express opposition to the German modes of speculation, and begins with an empiric comparison of all actual contrasts existing in the world and in human life. He follows the axiom that a particle of truth lies at the basis of every error, and that each contrast becomes a contrast only by the fact that the two poles of the contrast have something in common. Now, in comparing with one another all contrasts between religion and science, and all forms of religiousness and irreligiousness, from fetishism up to monotheism, pantheism, and atheism, all imaginable cosmogonies, he finds, as the last truth common to all, and therefore alone absolutely certain, the *absolute indiscernibleness of the final cause of all things*. On page 44 he says, that religions diametrically opposed in their overt dogmas, are yet perfectly at one in the tacit conviction that there is a problem to be solved, that the existence of the world with all it contains is a mystery ever pressing for interpretation; and on page 45, that the omnipresence of something which passes comprehension, is that which remains unquestionable. And on page 46 he concludes: "If Religion and Science are to be reconciled, the basis of reconciliation must be this deepest, widest, and most certain of all facts—that the Power which the Universe manifests to us is utterly inscrutable." The acknowledgment of this fact is religiousness; the contrary of it is irreligiousness and anthropomorphistic arrogance, even if it appears in the name of religiousness. "Volumes might be written upon the impiety of the pious" (p. 110).

A comparison of the two philosophers is interesting.

In one direction, Lange does more justice to the religious need than Spencer does. While he sees in religion the metaphorical realization of the needs of the heart, of a "creation of a home of the spirit," he gives to the heart full play to satisfy its need, and to create and arrange for itself a spiritual home entirely according to its need. He especially acknowledges repeatedly the need of the heart for *atonement*, and vigorously defends this need and its satisfaction against Liberal Theologians (Reformtheologen), like Heinrich Lang; he also stands, as we see, in satisfactory contrast to Wilhelm Bleek. Without reserve, he admits into the hymn-book of his religion of the future hymns like that of Gerhard: "O Haupt voll Blut und Wunden" ("O Sacred Head, now wounded"). To be sure, all the concessions he makes to religion sink again to the value of a beautiful illusion, from the fact that for him they are but metaphorical approaches to the cause of all things, which after all still remains inaccessible. But nevertheless, in consequence of that idea of religion, religious life, and especially also religious service, has infinitely more room for rich development in Lange than in Spencer. For, according to the view of the latter, religiousness consists in nothing else but the perception and acknowledgment of this indiscernibleness of the final cause. All other things which may be still connected with religious life and reasoning, are but a misty veil. The acknowledgment of the indiscernibleness of the final cause of all things alone is the quintessence of religion. But such a religiousness, which expressly forbids imagining any quality or any state of the highest being, certainly would be, as Prof. Huxley correctly says in his "Lay Sermons," for the most part of the silent sort.

While thus Lange's conception of religion is superior to that of Spencer in admitting a richer development of religious life, a more various satisfaction of the religious need, in another direction Spencer is superior. He comes considerably nearer to a correct and full *conception of God* than Lange. His idea of the final cause of all things does not lie entirely in the conception that it is the absolute indiscernible; but Spencer is fully in earnest with the idea that this indiscernible is the real cause of the world and of all single existences in it. He accordingly forbids giving certain attributes to the absolute—not because it would be doubtful whether it has attributes or not, but because it stands *above* all these imaginable attributes as their real cause. Therefore he forbids, for instance, attributing personality, intelligence, will, to the highest being—not because it could also be impersonal, and in want of intelligence and will, but because it stands *above* all these attributes as their highest real cause, and because we can think of all these attributes only in human analogy, and therefore, when attributed to the highest being, can think of them only in rejectable anthropomorphism. He says, on page 109: "Those who espouse this position [personality of God], make the erroneous assumption that the choice is between personality and something lower than personality; whereas the choice is rather between personality and something higher. Is it not just possible that there is a mode of being as much transcending Intelligence and Will, as these transcend mechanical motion? It is true that we are totally unable to conceive any such higher mode of being. But this is not a reason for questioning its existence; it is rather the reverse.... The Ultimate Cause cannot in any respect be conceived by us because it is in every respect greater than can be conceived."

Thus we find in Lange a fuller and richer conception of the subject of religion; but this conception is in want of one thing—without which it is in want of everything—namely, of nothing less than of the objective reality. Spencer's religiousness has a much more meagre and less varied character: the acknowledgment and veneration of the indiscernible; but he nevertheless gives us with this content and object a *real* object, even an object of veneration, in which the abundance of all reality is hidden, with the only conception that the indiscernible does not let us look into its cornucopia, but only lets us judge of the abundance of its contents by the richness of that which it pours over us in the world of the relatively perceptible.

It will not be difficult to show the points at which each of these writers would have been able, had he so wished, to lead his conception of religion, the one to a real, the other to a full content.

Lange finds the last principle of perception which is accessible to us, in our *organization*. Now from our organization originate not only all modes of the perception of the empirical world, but just as well all our ideal impulses, especially the ethical. Which one of all those dispositions, impulses, and activities has the precedence, mainly depends upon the value which man places upon them. Now, when man attributes to the ideal and ethical a higher value than to the empirical, when in reflecting about himself he finds that even in the normal individual the empirical, sensual, and material is subordinate and subject to the ideal and especially to the ethical, then from the standpoint of Lange he is right, and obliged to estimate the truth of that ideal and ethical as higher than the truth of the empirical world, and to look at the whole empirical world only as being in the service of that ideal world. When, at the same time, we observe an inner harmony in our organization, this observation gives us the right and the duty of controlling the truth of our empirical perception by the truth of the results of our ideal and our ethical activity, and the latter again by the former. For if we do not wish to suppose that the human organization aims at a grand deception of mankind, we have, in spite of the superiority of the ideal and ethical activities, to establish the axiom that the empirical and the ideal and ethical cannot remain in lasting contradiction. Besides, if we should add to this that a religion like Christianity offers to man that which it gives to him on the ground of historical facts, then the reports of these facts will certainly be subject to historical criticism just as surely as all historical reports; but if they are confirmed, the ideal and ethical convincing power which lies in this religion, unites for us with the whole weight of the convincing power of the historical and empirical facts, although the reproduction and systematization of its contents is still deficient and capable of further development.

In Spencer's system, there are two points by which his own course of reasoning is able to bridge over the poverty of his conception of religion. The first point, given on pages 107-108 of his "First Principles," and also elsewhere in his works, is the acknowledgment that the final cause of all things is *higher* than all that we know, and is of such a nature that it really can be the real cause of everything, even the real cause of the spiritual and ethical. Thus he forbids us to think of qualities of the highest being, but he himself thinks of them; for this conception of the highest being as an *impersonal* is certainly something else and something much more valuable than the mere negation of personality. The other point which might be able to lead him out of the vacuum of his idea of God, lies in the method of his own investigation. When he seeks the truth by collecting what is common in all the contrasts, he also must seek and find something common between the highest cause of all things on one side and of the world as a whole and in detail on the other; and this something will consist of the necessity of the highest cause of all things being so qualified that *it is able* to bring into existence the world as a whole and in detail. If such ideas are also rejected as anthropomorphisms, then all reasoning and investigating is anthropomorphistic; and in that respect we refer to what we had to say above, when treating of teleology (p. 170 ff.). The same Duke of Argyll whom we there had occasion to quote, in an article in the "Contemporary Review" (May, 1871), upon "Variety as an Aim in Nature," has admirably shown that it is the mind of man from which we may draw conclusions as to the nature of the Creator, and that the picture which we thus get of him, can at the same time be seen true and yet dim, at the same time real and yet from a distance; for the human mind does not feel anything so much as its own limitations, and therefore can easily imagine each of his powers and talents as being present in the highest being in infinite perfection. If Spencer had made this comparison, and drawn the conclusions which follow from it for the nature of the final cause of all things, the indiscernibleness of God would for him be reduced to an unsearchableness, the unknowable be changed into an unsearchable, and we could willingly acknowledge the humble modesty in regard to the infinity of the deity, which his philosophy requires, as a factor of all true religiousness. But we have to present to him as an expression, not only of true religiousness, but also of true science, that passage of the Psalms: "He that planted the ear, shall he not hear? He that formed the eye, shall he not see?" (Psalm xciv, 9.)

§ 4. *Spinoza and Hegel in the Garb of Darwin: Carneri. Eduard von Hartmann.*

To the Austrian philosopher Carneri in his "Sittlichkeit und Darwinismus" ("Morality and Darwinism"), three books of Ethics, Vienna, Braumüller, 1871, we shall have to give a place of his own.

Inasmuch as religion and the beautiful are to him but a preliminary stage of truth which has to dissolve itself into philosophy—a philosophy which, inclined to monism, prefers to call itself pantheism—he takes a position in reference to religion similar to that toward materialism, namely: a negative position. But inasmuch as he still grants to religion in a subjective sense, to "religion in the form of piety," a lasting position and truth (religion, he says, has truth, but the positive God of religion has no reality, page 114), and inasmuch as he ascribes to it not only a transitory pedagogical value for the masses, which are not yet elevated to the height of philosophic reasoning, but a value also for the philosopher—namely, the value of religiousness and of piety—he rather belongs to the second and third of the before-mentioned groups.

Carneri, in his "Three Books of Ethics," gives us a whole philosophic encyclopedia. In thoughts sometimes rich, but without regularly arranged and quiet reasoning, and in full command and employment of modern terms which he uses sometimes like a genius, but often superficially and unjustly, he develops a view of the world which, although it appears in an independent way in all its fundamentals, as regards its contents takes its origin from Spinoza, and as regards form and dialectics from Hegel, but sometimes, it is true, sinks into weaknesses of which these philosophers would hardly have been guilty. So, for instance, when he simply identifies religious faith with conjecture, he takes a superficial view which he has in common with Häckel who, among other things, repeatedly says that faith begins where knowledge ceases. Dialectical motion is everything to him. In pursuing this dialectical motion, he gives us a multitude of outlooks into all imaginable realms of knowledge and life, but he always follows at the same time the formula of dialectical motion, and, where the difficulties of the real world are most invincibly opposed to this dialectics, knows, like his master, with almost chivalric ease, to mingle and confound abstract formalistic reasoning and thoughts naturally following from the given thought. Want of clearness in general makes the reading of this otherwise not unimportant book very difficult. On a Darwinian foundation in his conception of nature and its development, he puts a Hegelian structure into his conception of human spiritual life, but finally lets mankind, although it is the highest form of appearance in this development, sink back into death and destruction.

The God of this view of the world is the causal law; the conception of this causal law is the worship of the philosopher—a God, of course, so incapable of filling and quieting a mind longing for God—a worship so leathern that Carneri himself cannot get rid of the opinion that, with such religious ideas of reform, he will finally lose the last reader of his book. The aim of the development, also, does not promise to the mind any substitute for the rigidness of God, for the aim of the development is death—the death of the individual as well as of the universe. "He who has learned to get comfort in the deepest affliction from the absolute impartiality of the causal law, is on so good terms with death, whose inflexibility he comprehends, that without reluctance he gives to it the universe into the bargain." (p. 353.)

We give these glimpses into the dreary waste of the very latest advocate of pessimism which, as it seems, has fully and formally become the fashion, in order to show what monstrosities are demanded from thought, what revolting hardness from feeling, what nonentities of ethical striving, are offered as valuable wares, if man has once begun to break the bond between himself and his living Creator and Master. For this reason, not only the anti-teleological monists meet the fate of Nihilism, whether they appear in the plebeian roughness of Büchner or in the aristocratic gentility of Strauss, but also such a brilliant advocate of teleology as Eduard von Hartmann does not know of any other final end to offer to the world and mankind than nothingness, because he did not wish to be driven from his perception of ends in the world to the only conclusion to which it leads—namely: to the perception of an absolute intelligent and ethical personality that directs these ends. He prefers, rather, to suppose an unconsciously seeing substance of the world, which, after having once in the dark impulse of its unconscious will, made the mistake of creating a world, leads the same by the instinct of unconscious teleology in sad, melancholy, and yet relatively best development, until it is ripe to sink back into nothingness, and thereby to bring the absolute to rest.

Although we pity the individuals who came under the ban of such a pessimism, we nevertheless can be glad of the fact that the consequences of such a separation from God are at least exposed so clearly, and return from wandering through such barren steppes with renewed thankfulness to our Christian view of the world, with its divine plan and aim.

We have, next, however to review the representatives of theism and of the Christian view of the world—which review will show us that the song of triumph which monism began to raise before its expected victory, came very near disturbing the composure of persons here and there.

§ 5. *Re-echo of Negation on the Side of the Christian View of the World.*

In this condition of affairs, it certainly could not happen otherwise than that, even on the part of the theistic and positive Christian view of the world, some advocates were drawn into the contest who thought themselves obliged to see two irreconcilable antagonists in Darwinism and Christianity.

Science and religion had both been so much accustomed to see the origin of species, and especially the appearance of man on the stage of earth, hidden in impenetrable and unapproachable secrecy, that every attempt at clearing up this darkness very naturally appeared to both as an attack upon the creative activity of God. The mode of reasoning to which mankind, in its scientific as well as in its religious meditations, had accustomed itself for hundreds of years, was used to exclude from the idea of creation the conception of intervening agencies; and this was true not only in regard to the idea of the first creation of the universe, where the idea of intervening agencies naturally is left out, but also in regard to the idea of the creation of single beings. Moreover, mankind was so accustomed to see a contrast between origination and creation, that in the same degree in which man tried or was able to perceive the modalities of the origin of species, the divine causality, or at least the idea of creation, seemed to disappear; and for the word of the Bible, that God created creatures *each after its kind*, a place could no longer be found.

To this was added the fact that not only all materialism took possession of Darwinism as the irresistible battering-ram which, as they said, forever demolishes the whole fortress of theism and buries under its ruins all those who take refuge in this decaying castle, but that even *naturalists* let themselves be carried away without opposition by this anti-theistic current, and even submitted to be heralds and prophets of this new anti-theistic wisdom of monism. Let the reader think of Häckel's "Natural History of Creation" and "Anthropogeny," where he will find the most interesting reports from all realms of exact natural science, together with a wholly unsolved entanglement of descent, selection, and mechanical view of the world, and this mode of contemplation of the world, with eloquent and enthusiastic proclamation of monism and with unconcealed derision of the capricious arbitrariness of a personal Creator, all thrown together as one great entire system, formed at one stroke.

Is it, then, to be wondered at, that not only the uncritical among believers, but also those who thoughtfully examined the movements of the mind, believed in the loudly-proclaimed connection of Darwinism with the whole anti- Christian view of the world, and therefore protested immediately against everything which is called Darwinism? Can we reproach theologians for not immediately becoming scientists themselves, in order to form an independent judgment in the question, when even the most eminent scientists declared that amalgamation of the most heterogenetic as an inevitable consequence of Darwinism, and as much as possible diminished or concealed their want of harmony with a few other investigators who, although small in number, yet by their weight counterbalanced dozens of names of the second and third rank?

Thus we could read, in the journals of specialists, in pamphlets, in religious and political journals, even in local newspapers, a great many articles which were guilty of exactly the same confounding of the scientific and the religious, and again of the scientific and the philosophic, as those who had caused this confounding, and who, under the supposition of this solidarity of wholly distinct things, attacked and contested in the interest of religion, not only the anti-religious conclusions of Darwinian philosophers, but also Darwinism as a merely scientific theory, and rendered the contrast as strong as possible by adhering to that above censured, unmotived, indefensible, and one-sided conception of creation.

And although on the part of positive Christian theology there was a gradually increasing number of voices of those who in the idea of an origin of species through *descent* do not yet see an injury to the theistic and Christian conception of God and creation, still as a rule this concession was made only to the idea of descent, and not to that of selection and to that which is properly called Darwinism. As a rule, in most of the theological works which treat in general of the *Darwinian* questions, Darwinism and opposition to the Christian conception of God and creation were and are still taken as identical. For instance, Ebrard, in the first part of his "Apologetik" ("Apologetics"), Gütersloh, Bertelsmann, 1874, enumerates among the systems which are opposed to Christianity, in the same line with the doubtless anti-theistic and anti-Christian *aposkopiology* or negation of the idea of design, also the mechanistic system, or the negation of the organic vital force, and the Darwinian theory of descent. Besides, in reading his "Apologetics," we had earnestly wished, in the interest of science as well as of religion, that a theologian who writes a work which claims to be scientific and to advocate the Christian standpoint, had abstained from that coarse and disgusting contempt and derision of adversaries which we meet so often in his book, and which only causes friend and foe to take a position contrary to that which the author intended. Trümpelmann who, in an essay upon Darwinism, monistic philosophy, and Christianity (Jahrbücher für protestantische Theologie, 1876, I) gives a similar conception of the relation between Darwinism and religion, but defends his whole position with much more scientific acuteness and depth, has also not taken the tone which worthily treats an opposite opinion and its advocates.

CHAPTER II.

REFORM OF RELIGION, OR AT LEAST OF THE SCIENCE OF RELIGION, THROUGH DARWINISM.

§ 1. *Heinrich Lang, Friedrich Vischer, Gustav Jäger.*

In passing on to those who in Darwinism do not see a negation but a reformation of religion, or at least of theology, we first meet Heinrich Lang, the late spiritual leader of the "Reformtheologie" in Switzerland. He treats of "Die Religion im Zeitalter Darwins" ("Religion in the Age of Darwin") in Holtzendorff's and Oncken's "Deutsche Zeit- und Streitfragen," Jahrg. II, Heft 31, Berlin, Lüderitz, 1873.

With a very correct estimate of the lasting value of religion as well as of natural science, and with a warm apology for the religious realm, he regulates the boundaries of each by asking religion not to hinder modern knowledge of the world and nature, and by asking knowledge of nature to leave the realm of religion untouched in its self-certainty.

But when he, evidently still dependent on the old rationalistic supernaturalistic conception of miracle and providence, claims to find that as the result of modern knowledge of the world and nature a special providence is no longer conceivable, and no other hearing of prayer is possible than a subjective psychological one; that the processes in the world, in their entire final causal connection of causes and effects, nowhere leave a place for the freely acting hand of a divine Lord of the world, and that even a moral order of the world can only prove itself so far as guilt and punishment stand in a natural causal connection with one another: then his religiousness makes concessions to the modern view of the world which it is not at all obliged to make or justified in making, and forces upon religion a reform against the necessity and usefulness of which not only religious feeling and need, but also deeper and more consequent reflection on God and the world, just as strongly strives.

What remains to him as an independent realm for religion is nevertheless worthy of recognition. As faith of the human mind in a transcendental unity which manifests itself in the manifold and sensible, and carries through a moral order of the world—although one which, by the before-mentioned limitation of the natural connection of guilt and punishment, is very much reduced—religion gives to the mind warmth and worship; as confidence of the heart in an infinite possession in the anguish of the finite, it creates confidence in God, gratitude, devotion, energy, courage of life; as reverence for a holiness which stands unimpeachable above the fluctuating inclinations of our will, awakens the consciousness of guilt, and abolishes the guilt, it remains the basis of all moral action. Lang also sharply and correctly points out the insufficiency of Strauss's "The Old Faith and the New," as well as the conflict between his metaphysical naturalism which only leads to the struggle for existence, and his demand of self-submission to the universe, and of the moral and spiritual self-determination of man as of a being which goes beyond nature. Nevertheless we can not follow Lang in his ways of reform.

First—his conception of God is amazingly meagre, and of more than a Spencerian unapproachableness. God is to him, according to his "Dogmatics," nothing but the eternal, in itself perfect cause of all being, exempted from all changes of the world's process. When he gives the name of father to this primeval cause, as he does in his sermons and elsewhere, without being able to admit relation of mutual love of person to person, he only makes it glaringly evident how little his abstract metaphysics can satisfy religious need. Second—that which is claimed to be gained by this modern view of the world (namely, extension of the supremacy of religion to everything, even to the affairs of daily life), is not at all new, but is the effect of long-existing sound religiousness, and is the essence of all sound religious doctrine; and we therefore can not see how a view of the world, which, for instance, denies divine providence, and limits the hearing of prayer to its psychological effects, shall have greater force to leaven the whole daily life religiously, than our Christian faith in the Father without whose will no sparrow falls to the ground, and who says to his children: "Call upon me in the day of trouble: I will deliver thee, and thou shalt glorify me." Third—exactly that which Lang declares a purification of religion (namely, the before-mentioned elimination of divine providence and of all that which is connected therewith), appears to us not at all as a reform, but as an immense impoverishment and desolation of religion, which is so far from being required by natural science, that it turns out to be but a concession to the most superficial metaphysicians who, of course, have become very popular.

Friedrich Vischer is also to be ranked in this group. In the sixth part of his "Kritische Gänge" ("Critical Walks"), he speaks of Strauss' "The Old Faith and the New," and takes his determined position in reference to the religious question, quite essentially differing from Strauss. In regard to the aversion to miracles, he stands on the same ground with Strauss and Lang; in protesting against Strauss' elimination of the idea of design, and especially in demanding a moral order of the world, he is still more energetic than Lang. He particularly does not, like Lang, limit the moral order of the world to the simple empiric causal connection between human action and its consequences. But on the other hand, by his opposition to the idea of a personality of God, he again deviates more than Lang from the true meaning of Christian religiousness. On page 219 he says: "How, in spite of the infinite crossings of human action, is inner conformity to the end in view in general so established through that which we call chance, or rather by means of these crossings, that we can speak of a moral order of the world? Men, individuals as well as communities, follow their aims. Hereby there always results something quite different from that which they intended and wished. Sublime laws govern above us, between us, full of mystery in the midst of life; one of them in reference to guilt, punishment of guilt, is called nemesis. Faith in that meaning of the word, which we regard as a low one [he means the faith which has its dogmas beyond which the man of the most recent culture has passed, not knowing that he also carries around with him his dogmas, his "new faith"] is in need of a person who founds, carries out, and executes these laws. But the faith of the monists has no such need. Why not? That needs more sufficient demonstration."

Certainly it needs more sufficient demonstration. But this demonstration will never be possible, so long as we acknowledge the government of a moral order of the world. For this leads of necessity to faith in a living God, and this faith demands from our conception less pretensions than the faith in a kind of system of spiritual machinery by which chance and the wished-for are woven together, without this system proceeding from a highly spiritual and ethical intelligence. It nevertheless must be acknowledged that Vischer, from the standpoint of *ethical* need, vindicates the position and truth of religion, as he also beautifully and correctly defines its position in reference to morality, in saying that morality makes the demand, religion gives the strength to meet it.

From another side, Gustav Jäger makes a compromise between Darwinism and religion in his five lectures on "Die Darwinsche Theorie und ihre Stellung zu Moral und Religion" ("The Darwinian Theory and its Position in Reference to Morality and Religion"), Stuttgart, J. Hoffmann, 1869.

He makes still more valid concessions to religion and Christianity than Lang and Vischer; directly opposes materialistic monism; leaves to faith in a personal God, in the divinity of Christ, in individual immortality, in the answer to prayer beyond the psychological effect, in miracles, in short, to the full contents of Christian religiousness, their weight and truth; and in that respect we would have to rank him in the following group, if he did not by his manner of proving these concessions exclude himself from it, and rank himself in that group of which we treat in the present section.

According to his opinion, Darwinism gives to religion, if not new contents (although these contents are entirely subject to revision according to Darwinism), still a wholly new foundation, and, indeed, a foundation of subjective religiousness, as well as of the objective contents of religion, only from the standpoint of its practical usefulness in the struggle for existence. The faith in a personal God, in immortality, in redemption by the God-Man Jesus Christ, in the hearing of prayer, in help in danger even to the extent of miracles, strengthens man, gives to him a superiority to those who do not have that faith and who do not have the habit of prayer, and therefore is so far the best weapon in the struggle for existence; and herein lies the truth of religion, especially of the Christian religion, as the most successful weapon in the struggle for existence which takes place through the whole creation, from the lowest organisms up to the highest spiritual life of mankind.

We willingly admit that Christianity has certainly proved itself by far the strongest and most successful means of education to mankind, and that, if we must once express this experience in the Darwinian mode of speaking, we can express it as above. But with the attempt to make the *truth* of religion and the truth of its contents, even if only subjective, dependent only and solely upon the proof of its *usefulness*, nobody, either friend or foe, will be satisfied. The adversaries of religion and Christianity, perhaps with the exception of Büchner, will admit that Christianity has for some time been a quite useful weapon to mankind in the struggle for existence; but they will say that they are just about to replace it by a still more useful weapon; and the advocates of religion and Christianity likewise can not agree upon a mere grounding of their religion upon need which puts upon them every day the possibility of changing it for something still more useful. Both friend and foe will join in the conviction that objective truth is always the best guarantee for subjective success; and thus both will pass beyond the purely utilitarian apologetics or polemics to the questions as to the objective reality of the contents of Christian religiousness.

CHAPTER III.

PEACE BETWEEN RELIGION AND DARWINISM.

§ 1. *Darwin, Wallace, R. Owen, Asa Gray, Mivart, McCosh, Anderson, K. E. v. Baer, Alex. Braun, Braubach, etc.*

It still remains for us to take a glance at those who think religion and Darwinism, and Christianity and Darwinism, hold toward one another reciprocally amicable relations.

In the first place, we have to mention Darwin himself. In his earliest work, "Origin of Species," he repeatedly gives this opinion, as on page 421: "I see no good reason why the views given in this volume should shock the religious feelings of any one. It is satisfactory, as showing how transient such impressions are, to remember that the greatest discovery ever made by man, namely, the law of the attraction of gravity, was also attacked by Leibnitz 'as subversive of natural, and inferentially of revealed, religion.' A celebrated author and divine has written to me that he 'has gradually learned to see that it is just as noble a conception of the Deity to believe that He created a few original forms capable of self-development into other and needful forms, as to believe that He required a fresh act of creation to supply the voids caused by the action of His laws.'" On page 428, he speaks of the laws which God has impressed on matter; and at the end of his work, on page 429, he says: "There is grandeur in this view of life, with its several powers, having been originally breathed by the Creator into a few forms or into one." In his "Descent of Man," he also protests against the reproach that his views are irreligious, and says: "The birth both of the species and of the individual are equally parts of that grand sequence of events which our minds refuse to accept as the result of blind chance." In treating of the question as to the development of the moral instincts, he says: "If he [man] breaks through the fixed habits of his life, he will assuredly feel dissatisfaction. He must likewise avoid the reprobation of *the one* God or gods in whom, *according to his knowledge* or superstition, he may believe." And furthermore he remarks: "The question whether there exists a Creator and Ruler of the Universe, has been answered in the affirmative by some of the highest intellects that have ever existed."

It is true, all these expressions about religion are very general; but since in his works we do not find any utterance contrary to them and hostile to religion, we have a right to rank the celebrated originator of the whole agitation among those naturalists who are conscious of the limits of the realms of the natural and the religious, and are convinced of the possibility of a harmony between the two. For his casual utterances against a "creation" of single species always combine with the word creation the idea of that direct creation out of nothing, without intervening agencies, which is entirely correct for the idea of the first, origin of the universe, but which for the origin of the single formations within the universe is neither asked for by the religious view of the world, nor established by the Holy Scriptures, nor by a cautiously reasoning theology, although it very often controls the conceptions of naturalists as well as of theologians. Now, while Darwin rejects the idea of a sudden appearance of a new species out of nothing—or, as he once expressed himself in his "Origin of Species," the idea "that at innumerable periods in the earth's history certain elemental atoms have been commanded suddenly to flash into living tissues,"—and he is no doubt right in rejecting it,—still at the same time he does not deny the dependence of the successive origin of a new species on a divine author. But in calling that process creation and this one not, he gives the appearance of an opposition to the religious idea of creation—an appearance of which the greater part of the guilt is borne by those theologians who define the idea of the creation, even of a single form, in a manner which is only proper for the idea of the first origin of the universe.

It is true, we could rank Darwin still more readily among the scientists who are at peace with all the claims of religion, did he not in his "Descent of Man," when enumerating the "excellent naturalists and philosophers" who with him reduce the pedigree of man to lower forms, mention names of men who in their works firmly unite Darwinism and monistic naturalism or even materialism, and expressly protest against a separation of their naturo-historical results and their philosophic points of view. We mean Büchner and Häckel. The latter's "Natural History of Creation," he especially praises: "If this work had appeared before my essay had been written, I should probably never have completed it. Almost all the conclusions at which I have arrived I find confirmed by this naturalist," etc. The entire silence in regard to the anti-Christian results which these two authors derive from their naturo-historical premises, makes Darwin's own position in reference to religion again very uncertain. It seems that Darwin in his theology is not only inclined to theism, but, following the traditions of his countrymen of the last century, to a quite cool and superficial deism, and that he permits himself to be too much impressed by the anti-teleological deductions of many of his followers, and to be induced to separate in his later publications the Creator and his work more widely than he has done in the beginning. For while in his "Origin of the Species," and in his "Descent of Man" he nowhere contests a teleological view of nature, and rejects the idea of single creations only under the erroneous supposition that the idea of the creation of the single also excludes the action of intervening agencies, we find, on the other hand, in "The Expression of the Emotions in Man and Animals" a passage which, though in a reserved way, seems to give just as much support to the adversaries of teleology as to its advocates, if, indeed, not more. He says (page 338): "The belief that blushing was *specially* designed by the Creator is opposed to the general theory of evolution, which is now so largely accepted; but it forms no part of my duty here to argue on the general question. Those who believe in design will find it difficult to account for shyness being the most frequent and efficient of all the causes of blushing," etc. This inconsistency in his utterances has its origin in the fact that the strength of this naturalist does not seem to lie in logical philosophic thought.

A. R. Wallace, the independent and contemporaneous co-originator of the Darwinian theory, still more evidently and more decidedly expresses himself favorably as to the position of this theory in reference to religion. In his "Natural Selection," he says on page 368: "It does not seem an improbable conclusion that all force may be will-force; and thus, that the whole universe is not merely dependent on, but actually is, the WILL of higher intelligences or of one Supreme Intelligence."

He pronounces the belief that God created the new species in "continual interference" with the regular process of things, a lower conception, "a limitation of the Creator's power" (page 280), hence something which he makes objection to directly in the interest of religion. Moreover, he sees, especially in those stages which caused the physical development of man, and which became the material basis of his spiritual productions, moments of development which cannot be explained by natural selection or by a coincidence of material circumstances, but only by the preformation of the body after a certain design and for a certain purpose.

Richard Owen, the celebrated anatomist, and palæontologist of England, who, after having for a long time resisted the Darwinian theories, lately accepted the idea of development and rejected that of selection, takes a similar position. In the last part of his "Comparative Anatomy of Vertebrates," which was issued separately in 1863 under the title "Derivative Hypothesis of Life and Species," he sees in the causes which produced the new species only the servants of a predestinating intelligent will—for instance, the horse predestinated and prepared for man; and on page 90 of vol. V. of "Transactions of the Zoölogical Society," he says, "that natural evolution, through secondary causes, by means of slow physical and organic operations through long ages, is not the less clearly recognizable as the act of all- adaptive Mind, because we have abandoned the old error of supposing it the result of a primary, direct and sudden act of creational construction.... The succession of species by continuously operating law is not necessarily a 'blind operation.' Such law, however designed in the properties and successions of natural objects, intimates, nevertheless, a preconceived progress. Organisms may be evolved in orderly succession, stage after stage, towards a foreseen goal, and the broad features of the course may still show the unmistakable impress of Divine volition."

Professor Huxley, of London, the zealous and oft-mentioned advocate of the descent of man from the ape, says—what is so energetically contested by his warmest friends in Germany, by Büchner, Häckel, O. Schmidt, and others—that the teleological and the mechanical mode of viewing nature by no means exclude one another. He does this, of course, without going into any details of the religious question.

Asa Gray, an eminent and highly esteemed American botanist, who is particularly respected by Darwin, and is supported also by Sir Charles Lyell in "The Antiquity of Man," says in his essay on "Natural Selection not Incompatible with Natural Theology, a Free Examination of Darwin's Treatise" (London, Trübner, 1861), on page 29: "Agreeing that plants and animals were produced by Omnipotent *fiat* does not exclude the idea of natural order and what we call secondary causes. The record of the *fiat*—'Let the earth bring forth grass,' etc., 'the living creature,' etc.,—seems even to imply them, and leads to the conclusion that the different species were produced through natural agencies." And on page 38: "Darwin's hypothesis concerns the *order* and not the *cause*, the *how* and not the *why* of the phenomena, and so leaves the question of design just where it was before." And finally, in a passage which is adopted by Sir Charles Lyell (ib. page 505): "We may imagine that events and operations in general go on in virtue simply of forces communicated at the first, and without any subsequent interference, or we may hold that now and then, and only now and then, there is a direct interposition of the Deity; or, lastly, we may suppose that all the changes are carried on by the immediate orderly and constant, however infinitely diversified, action of the intelligent efficient Cause."

Mivart, an English Catholic, most decidedly advocates a reconcilability of Darwinian views, and especially of the evolution theory, as he establishes it with the full contents of Christian orthodoxy, in his remarkable book "On the Genesis of Species" (London and New York, Macmillan & Co., 2d. ed. 1871), in which we find a great many independent naturo-historical investigations. He assigns to the selection theory only a subordinate position, but on the other hand accepts an *evolution*, and, in close connection with R. Owen, explains it from inner and innate impulses of development of the organisms, which act now more slowly and gradually, now more by impulses; he places man as to his *physical* part entirely among the effects of the evolution principle, although, taking into consideration some utterances of Wallace, he thinks it possible, but not probable, that the creation and the preceding stage of his physical nature is also different from that of animals. But, on the other hand, in fully adopting the old scholastic creationism, he supposes a special creation of the *soul*, a separation of body and soul, which in this form is very contestable, and might better have been replaced by a separation of natural and rational or of physico-psychical and pneumatical parts of his being. With such a view of nature, he finds the fullest harmony between the evolution theory and religion, reconciles the plausible antagonism of creation and development by dividing the idea of creation into a primary creation (creation of the beginning out of nothing) and into a secondary creation (creation through intervening agencies, although that which is produced through them is still a creation and a work of the Creator), and declares his conviction that what is acting according to law in nature also stands under the causation and government of God like the first beginning of the universe—a postulate of our primary views without which the whole universe and our existence in it would harden into a cold mechanism without consolation or ideality.

Finally, at the assembly of the Evangelical Alliance in New York (October, 1873), there were heard many voices of eminent advocates of a theistic and Christian view of the world, which maintained the full consistency of an evolution theory with religion and Christianity. McCosh, for instance, as referee in the philosophic section as to the relation of the evolution theory and religion, said[10]: "I am not sure that religion is entitled to insist that every species of insects has been created by a special *fiat* of God, with no secondary agent employed." And still more plainly and more courageously, President Anderson, of the University of Rochester, in his very remarkable address, speaks about the unnecessary and unworthy fear of many Christian men, when they see the appearance of hypotheses with which science operates. At the end of his address, he says: "The evidence for the existence of a personal Creator cannot be affected by any considerations drawn from the mode, relative rapidity, or the nature of the proximate antecedents and consequences in the creative process."

From German sources, we can note fewer utterances of a friendly or at least neutral position between Darwinism and religion. For this fact there are many reasons. One may be, that on the continent in general there is a smaller number of those who, without being specialists in both realms, unite active religious interest and reasoning with a thorough study of those naturo- historical questions, while in Great Britain physico-theological studies have been for generations traditional and the object of interest for the majority of educated men. A second reason, indeed, is that some of the warmest scientific advocates of Darwinism at once attacked also theism and Christianity; hence with all those who did not have time and incitement enough to study the questions for themselves, they necessarily created the opinion that Darwinism really attacks even the fundamentals of religion, and their whole tendency had but a repelling influence even on scientists of deeper spiritual and ethical disposition and need. Finally, in Germany as well as on the whole continent, the number of those who do not care for religious questions in general, and who therefore interest themselves in the scientific questions brought up by Darwin, but do not trouble themselves farther for their position in reference to religion and Christianity, is unfortunately larger than in Great Britain.

Nevertheless, such friendly voices are not entirely wanting in our country. The botanist Alex Braun says, in his beautiful and significant lecture on the importance of development in natural history, p. 48: "Some said that the descent theory denies creation, and it is true, the Darwinians themselves caused this opinion by contrasting creation and development as irreconcilable ideas. But this contrast does not actually exist, for as soon as we look upon creation as a divine effect, not merely belonging to the past, or appearing in single abrupt movements, but connected and universally present in time, we can seek and find it nowhere else but in the natural history of development itself.... Theologians themselves, according to the Mosaic documents, acknowledge a *history* of creation; natural history, looked upon from its inner side, is nothing else but the farther carrying out of the history of creation."

Even K. E. von Baer, who expressly contests the idea of selection, thinks it only scientifically indefensible, but not anti-religious; an opinion also held by Wigand.

A similar friendly relation between Darwinism and religion is advocated by Braubach, in his publication, "Religion, Moral und Philosophie der Darwin'schen Artlehre nach ihrer Natur and ihrem Character als kleine Parallele menschlich-geistiger Entwicklung" ("Religion, Morality, and Philosophy of the Darwinian Doctrine of Species, as to its Nature and Character; a Small Parallel of Human Intellectual Development"), Neuwied, Hansen, 1869, a publication to which we pay special attention, since Darwin, in his "Descent of Man," twice paid it the honor of a quotation. It is true, the essay, through its peculiar dependence on an original and quite arbitrarily grouped scheme, gives the impression of something very singular, and is not very agreeably and easily read; but it shows such an energetic union of respect for science and its work and results, with adhesion to all the fundamentals of Christian truth, that it has to be mentioned as one of the rare voices which, even in regard to the realm of nature, pronounce the fullest harmony between religion and science. Braubach finds in the animal kingdom the *elements* of all the spiritual life of mankind, even of *religion* and *morality*; but everything is still wrapped in the lowest stage of sensuality. Nevertheless, he assigns to mankind, by its possession of the idea of *infinity*, something absolutely new, absolutely superior to the animal world, and sees the Darwinian ideas, even in the religious and moral possession of mankind, confirmed by the fact that they develop themselves on the way from the sensual stage to the rational exactly according to the principles of Darwin— namely, through transmission with individual variability in the struggle for existence, through selection of the fittest. With special earnestness, he pronounces the indissoluble unity of religion and morality, and says that religion, as it presents itself upon Darwinian grounds, is a moral religion.

We find here and there in periodicals many more voices which pronounce the conviction that, out of the present contest of minds, peace between religion and science will result.

B. THE DARWINIAN THEORIES AND MORALITY.

PRELIMINARY VIEW.

We can treat much more briefly of this portion of our task than of the position of the Darwinians in reference to the religious question, for the reason that the contrasts in the ethical realm are far less sharply drawn than in the religious realm, although in principle they are not less widely apart. For while there are a great many men who think that it belongs to good society and to the indispensable characteristics of high modern education to show either cold indifference or direct hostility in reference to religion and to the whole religious question; while a great many of the much-read works of *belle lettres* never tire of teaching the reading public that the religious question really no longer exists for the educated man, on the other hand, nobody, not even the extremest atheist and enemy of religion, wishes to renounce the reputation of having moral principles. Thus it happens that the positions taken by the Darwinians in reference to the ethical question are less varied than those taken by them in reference to the religious question. And we may also be brief for another reason, namely, that by reviewing the position of the Darwinians in reference to the religious question, we have essentially prepared the way for the principal questions which will have to be treated.

We shall group the utterances upon the relation of the Darwinian theories to morality as we did those in regard to the relation of Darwinism to religion; and shall first let the advocates of an irreconcilableness between the two speak, then those advocating a reformative influence of Darwinism upon morality, and finally those striving for neutrality and peace between the two. We shall have no occasion, except incidentally, to discriminate between the different fundamental principles and parts of ethics, but shall in the last part of our work treat of the question independently. In making subdivisions for them here, we should but cause infinite repetitions, unnecessarily complicate our review, and render it more difficult.

CHAPTER IV.

ANTAGONISM BETWEEN DARWINISM AND MORALITY.

§ 1. *Objections to Darwinism from an Ethical Standpoint.*

From what we said at the beginning of the preceding preliminary view, it is evident that we have to look for the advocates of an irreconcilableness between morality and Darwinism, not in the camp of the followers of the latter, but only in that of its adversaries. It is true, such advocates were never wanting. In pamphlets and journals, it has been often enough said that Darwinism cuts through the nerve of life, not only of religion, but also of morality.

It was demonstrated that in making man a mere product of nature, and degrading him to a being that is nothing else but a more highly developed animal, Darwinism takes from human personality its value, from the realms of morality its dignity, and from its demands their autonomy. In making the struggle for existence the principle of all development and, by extending it to the development and social relations of man, at the same time the human social principle, it puts in place of self-denial and love the principle of egoism and boorishness and the right of the stronger, gives full course to the unchaining of all animal passions, and coquettes with all the emotions which, flattering the animal part of man, aims at the subversion of all that exists and at the destruction of the ideal acquisitions of mankind. In tracing everything which constitutes the higher position and dignity of man back to his own work, and permitting it to be worked out of physical, spiritual, and ethical brutishness, in slow development and effort, closely related to the animal kingdom, it fosters and nourishes haughtiness in an intolerable way. And finally, in breaking off and denying the dependence of man upon God, and leading to mechanical determinism, it destroys the deepest and most effective motive to moral action—the tracing of the moral law to the authority of the divine Law-giver, and the consciousness of an individual moral responsibility.

It cannot be denied that many of the most zealous Darwinians gave too much cause for such a conception and representation of the ethical consequences of their system. In view of the fact that they applied the selection principle, with its most radical consequences, to the origin and development of mankind, and that they elevated the same to the ethical and social principle of mankind and did not permit the acceptance of any new and higher agencies in mankind except those already active in the animal and the organic world, and that they gladly treated this selection principle also in the social and ethical realm as a struggle for existence, it was simply an entirely logical conclusion that the advocates of the moral nobility of mankind reproached such a reproduced Darwinism with degrading the moral dignity of man and with replacing love by egoism. Besides, in view of the fact that they declared materialistic monism, even the most naked atheism, the only conclusion of Darwinism, and extended their mechanistic explanation of the world to a determinism in the highest degree mechanistic, and, carried to its utmost limit, to a denial of human freedom, it was not to be wondered at that those who recognize in theism the basis of all life worthy of man, and in the freedom of man one of the most precious pearls in the crown of his human dignity and of his creation in the image of God, complained of Darwinism's taking from morality its strongest motive and from moral action its responsibility. And, finally, in view of the fact that those who thus express themselves in their works showed but rarely, or not at all, some of the noblest fruits of moral education, such as respectful treatment of adversaries, humbleness and tact, they could not themselves reasonably complain that there was ascribed to their doctrine an influence detrimental to moral education. All this we find abundantly confirmed in the publications of Büchner and Häckel, and in many articles of the "Ausland."

But the question is, whether those Darwinians who drew these conclusions were by their scientific investigations obliged to draw them, or whether they did not rather reach their religious and ethical view of the world by quite other ways, and whether they did not in a wholly arbitrary and irresponsible manner make extensive use of Darwinism in this anti-religious and ethically objectional direction—a fact which we shall try to prove in the last part of our investigation.

Of course the Darwinians who spoke thus, did not intend to injure the moral principle, but only to purify and reform it; and therefore we shall have to speak of them in the following section.

CHAPTER V.

REFORM OF MORALITY THROUGH DARWINISM.

§ 1. *The Materialists and Monists. Darwin and the English Utilitarians. Gustav Jäger.*

Among those who ascribe to Darwinism a morally reforming influence, we have to mention in the first place the *materialists*. It is true that even before the appearance of Darwinism they established their own moral principle of naturalistic determinism and of the education of man only by science and enlightenment, in opposition to a morality which rests on the principle of the eternal value of the individual, of full moral responsibility, of the holiness of the moral law, and of a divine author of it; they stigmatized the ethical requirement of aiming at the eternal welfare of the soul as a lower stage of morality in comparison with their own, which carries in itself the reward of virtue; and they declared Christianity and humanity, Christian morality and the morality of humanity, two things irreconcilably opposed to one another. But in having taken possession of Darwinism as their monopoly, they have made it the basis of new attacks upon the present moral principle of Christendom; and therefore we have here to mention them with their moral system.

Büchner, in his lecture on "Gottesbegriff und dessen Bedeutung" ("The Idea of God and its Importance"), replaces the moral principle (which in his opinion is nothing innate but something acquired) by education, learning, freedom and well-being; says that only atheism or philosophic monism leads to freedom, reason, progress, acknowledgment of true humanity—to humanism; that this humanism seeks the motives of its morality not in the external relations to an extramundane God, but in itself and in the welfare of mankind; and that infidels often, even as a rule, have excelled by moral conduct, while Christianity has originated many more crimes than it has hindered, and it would no longer be possible to establish with real Christians a vital community as at present understood. He declares the utterance of Madame de Staël, that "to comprehend everything means to forgive everything," the truest word ever spoken; and concludes his lecture with the remarks that the more man renounces his faith and confides in his own power, his own reason, his own reflexion, the happier he will be and the more successful in his struggle for existence.

Strauss in "The Old Faith and the New," a publication which certainly has to be ranked here, for the reason that in it he founds on Darwinism his whole knowledge of the world, on the ground of which he wishes to arrange life, appears to be much more decent, and in the practical consequences much more conservative, than Büchner; but essentially stands upon quite the same ground. Häckel, Oskar Schmidt, and (as to his linguistic Darwinism) W. Bleek, group themselves around Strauss, partly with, partly without express reference to his deductions.

Strauss arrives at a peculiar inconsequence, but one well worthy of notice, when, in place of the struggle for existence which, according to the conclusions of those who also reduce morality to Darwinism, is still the *spiritus rector* of moral development in mankind, and yet cannot of itself possibly lead to the morally indispensable requirements and virtues of self- sacrifice and of mere subordination under the moral idea, he suddenly substitutes a going of man beyond mere nature, and herewith a moral principle, which can never be deduced from Darwinism alone, and which is directly opposed to monism and pankosmism, which is to be the basis of his ethics. The reader may compare the manner in which he metaphysically supports his moral principle when he says: "As nature cannot go higher, she would go inwards. Nature felt herself already in the animal, but she *wished to know herself also*.... In man, nature endeavored not merely to exalt, but *to transcend herself.*" Ulrici, the philosopher, in his reply to Strauss, has pointed out in sharp terms this inconsequence, as well as the other, that from the ground of a blind necessity which does not know anything of a higher and a lower, the difference of higher and lower, good and bad, rational and irrational, cannot at all be maintained; and that the requirement of a progress cannot at all be made, and its idea not at all be given. In this very perceptible inconsistency, Strauss calls that morality which he requires, "*the relation of man to the idea of his kind.*" To realize the latter in himself, is the summary of his duties toward himself; actually to recognize and promote the equality of the kind in all the others, is the summary of his duties towards others. He opposes the internal satisfaction which originates therein, to the "rough" idea of a reward of virtue and piety, coming from *without*, which, in order to connect both, is in need of a God. And he again reaches that inconsequence which from his metaphysical standpoint is entirely without motive, but as to itself only worthy to be recognized, when in another formula of his moral imperative he says: "Ever remember that thou art human, not *merely a natural production.*"

It is also this representation and realization of the *idea of the kind*, which those who combine with their Darwinism a negation of theism have mostly established before the appearance of the work of Strauss as the highest moral principle, and to which they are also led most naturally by Darwin's deduction of morality from the social instincts. Thus, Wilhelm Bleek, in the preface to his "Ursprung der Sprache" ("Origin of Language"), says (page XIII): "To aim at the inner and outer harmony of his genus in one or the other way, and to promote the correct relations of the different parts to one another in their reciprocal connections and in the greater parts of the whole organism (family, community, nation), are the highest visible designs of human existence, which must by themselves incite man to noble actions and to virtuous deeds. In the performance of this task lies the highest happiness which seems to be given to our species, a happiness accessible by everyone in his own way. Neither the fruit of eternal punishment nor the hope of an individual happiness, is really capable as a truly saving idea to elevate man to a higher existence; even if we take no account of the fact that each of these two fundamental dogmas of the vulgar dogmatism makes but refined egoism the lever of its ethics."

Häckel alone, in his "Natural History of Creation," with his utterances as to Christianity, morality, and the history of the world, again sinks down to the level of the coarseness of Büchner, and even below it. On page 19, vol. I, he entirely contests the reality of the moral order of the world, and continues: "If we contemplate the common life, and the mutual relations between plants and animals (man included), we shall find *everywhere* and *at all times*, the very opposite of that kindly and peaceful social life, which the goodness of the Creator ought to have prepared for his creatures—we shall rather find *everywhere* a pitiless, most embittered *struggle of all against all*. Nowhere in nature, no matter where we turn our eyes, does that idyllic peace, celebrated by the poets, exist; we find everywhere a *struggle* and a *striving to annihilate* neighbors and competitors. *Passion and selfishness, conscious or unconscious, is everywhere the motive force of life.* Man in this respect certainly forms no exception to the rest of the animal world." On page 237, vol. I, he professes the most extreme naturalistic determinism: "The will of the animal, *as well as that of man*, is never free. The widely spread dogma of the freedom of the will is, from a scientific point of view, altogether untenable." And on page 170, vol. I, he even says: "If, as we maintain, natural selection is the great active cause which has produced the whole wonderful variety of organic life on the earth, all the interesting phenomena of *human life* must also be explicable from the same cause. For man is after all only a most highly-developed vertebrate animal, and all aspects of human life have their parallels, or, more correctly, their lower stages of development, in the animal kingdom. The *whole history of nations*, or what is called *universal history, must therefore be explicable by means of natural selection,—must be a physico-chemical process*, depending upon the interaction of adaptation and inheritance in the struggle for life. And this is actually the case." That in his ethical naturalism he sees a real reform of morality, he expressly declares on the page next to the last of his "Natural History of Creation": "Just as this new monistic philosophy first opens up to us a true understanding of the real universe, so its application to practical human life must open up *a new road towards moral perfection*." (Vol. II, p. 367.)

In the low conception of morality and its principle, Häckel is perhaps seconded only by Seidlitz who says in his "Die Darwin'she Theorie" ("Darwin's Theory"), p. 198: "Rational and moral life consist in the satisfaction of all physical functions, in correct proportion and relation to one another. Man is immoral through excessive satisfaction of one function and through neglect of the others."

As in the religious question, so in the ethical, Carneri also takes a peculiar position. In reducing all the phenomena of existence, together with the whole spiritual life of mankind, to a close development of nature according to the causal law, in expressly grouping also the utterances of the will of man under this law of an absolute necessity, in fully adopting Darwin's doctrine as the wholly satisfactory key for the comprehension of the entire development of nature up to the history of mankind, in advocating an absolutely monistic determinism and a nearly exclusive dependence of the efficacy of moral principles on the theoretic cultivation of the mind, on reasoning and education, he, as before mentioned, stands on exactly the same ground with materialists and monists among whom he expressly ranks himself; in the inconsequence with which he makes concessions to the power of the idea and the ideal over man—concessions which could never be concluded from a mere immanent process of nature—he is closely related to Strauss. But it is peculiar that, although entirely dependent in his reasoning on that monistic view of the world, and that Darwinian view of nature, he defines his ethical developments and his reflections on the organizations of human life in a relative independence, which again separates him as moralist from these before-mentioned monists and materialists, and rather ranks him, as we have seen in Chap. I, § 4, in the line of the disciples of Spinoza and Hegel. From this it can also be explained, how it could happen that in criticisms and reviews of Darwinism and its literature the standpoint which he takes could find such different and diametrically opposed expositions. While, for instance, the "Beweis des Glaubens," in the March number of 1873, thinks that Carneri wishes to seek on Darwinian ground a new and better basis for morality than we had heretofore; while Häckel in the preface to the third edition of his "Natural History of Creation," page XXIX, mentions the publication of Carneri with the greatest praise, earnestly recommends all theologians and philosophers to read it, and greets it as the first successful attempt at applying fruitfully the monistic view of the world, as established by Darwinism, to the realm of practical philosophy and at showing that the immense progress of our knowledge of the world caused by the descent theory has only the most beneficial effect upon the further progressing development of mankind in practical life;—a criticism in the "Ausland" (8 April, 1872, No. 15), calls the same publication "an attempt at harmonizing Darwin's hypothesis with the current views of ethics, and at showing that those doctrines cannot be sustained which result as strictly logical conclusions from Darwin's theory, and which are opposed to the present views of morality."

In returning from this digression to Darwinism in its purest form, to Darwin himself, we have in the first place to resume the discussion entered upon as to the way and manner in which, according to Darwin, self-determination is originated. Love and sympathy, moral feeling (with this definition he seems to point at the consciousness of moral freedom of will and of responsibility), and conscience, are to him very important elements of morality; and in the moral disposition of man he sees the greatest of all differences between man and animal. He also willingly acknowledges the powerful impulse which morality has from religion, when he says ("Descent of Man," Vol. II, page 347): "With the more civilized races, the conviction of the existence of an all-seeing Deity has had a potent influence on the advance of morality." From these and all his other deductions, we see that Darwin in no way intends to modify the maxims of moral action; and if under the expression "reform of morality," with which we have headed the present chapter, we should understand but a reform of moral action itself, we should without hesitation have to rank Darwin with the next group, and not with that of which we now treat; just as in our review of the position of Darwinism in reference to the religious question, we had to rank him with those who take a neutral and peaceful position in reference to religion.

But if he does not touch upon morality in the maxims, he nevertheless comes forth in the *theory* of moral action, in the science of morality with reformatory claims,—namely, with the fact that reduces the whole moral life to those agencies which are already active in the preceding animalic stage. It is true, he makes, as we have seen, a distinction in the genetic derivation of morality.

He wholly reduces love and sympathy to social instincts which man has in common with the animal; and he lets the formal motives of moral action, sense of duty and conscience, originate through the high development of intelligence and other spiritual forces, and to be increased and transmitted by custom and inheritance, if those are present. But, on the other hand, development of intelligence is to him an exclusive product of the preceding stage on which it was developed, and thus, in his opinion, entire morality, notwithstanding that double derivation, certainly has purely and exclusively the natural basis as its origin. If that is once the standpoint to which man sees himself led, he has, in order to reason logically, but a double choice. He must either say that a development out of a natural basis can possibly be consistent with the appearance of a new and higher principle, or must give up the autonomy of the moral law, and leave the moral action of man, even in his maxims, to the unsteady flowing of development, or even of arbitrariness, and to the degree of education and intelligence of subjectivity. Neither the one nor the other is done by Darwin. It is true, on the one hand he shows that modesty, so often exhibited by him, of the investigator who does not wish to express any opinion on questions regarding which he has not yet attained a mature judgment; but on the other hand he also manifests the same aversion to going beyond purely naturo-historical speculations which, as we have seen in Part I, Book II, Chapter I, § 1, hindered him from obtaining a clear conception of the importance of the question as to the origin of self-consciousness and of moral self-determination, and the same want of sequence in reasoning, which, as we have found in Chap. III, prevented him from giving an affirmative or negative decision in such an important question, as whether a divine end is to be observed in the processes of the world.

In this naturalization of ethical principles, he is closely related to that peculiar moral-philosophic tendency in England, which long before Darwin's appearance, took its origin in John Stuart Mill, but which now, in the closest connection with Darwin's principles, has its main advocate in Herbert Spencer, and is commonly called the *utilitarian* tendency. We understand by this that conception of the moral motive which allows the moral good, however it may be ideally separated from the useful in the developed condition of mankind at the present time, in its origin to be developed at the outset from the same origin as the useful,—namely, from the sensation of like and dislike; a theory of utility which Sir John Lubbock still tried to complete and deepen by the theory of an inheritance of the sensation of authority. Activities which originally proved to be only useful, were inherited as traditional instinct by the offspring, and were thus freed from the sensation of the useful, and acted as *authority*; this is the origin of *duty*, according to the history of development. Inasmuch as this philosophic system aims at taking from ethics the absoluteness of its demands, and at drawing down these demands into the activities of originating and developing, it is also to be treated of in this place.

As in the religious question, so in the ethical, Gustav Jäger also stands nearer to a neutral relation between Darwinism and the hitherto valid principles. He puts the moral principles the same as the religious, into the balance of utility to man in his struggle for existence, and finds it thus easy and to be taken for granted, that the principles of morality, as they became the common property of mankind as influenced by Christianity, really prove themselves also the most serviceable to mankind. Social life is of more benefit to man than hermit life; this reflection leads him to the moral principle of charity. And as, according to Darwinism, rising development shows itself in an increasing differentiation and more richly organized physical development, so the organization of society according to the principle of the division of work is that form of social life which proves itself the most practical to man; and this reflection leads him to the full acknowledgment of the entire ethical organization of human life and its tasks.

But, as we saw, in treating of the religious question, that nobody, neither friend nor foe, could possibly be satisfied with the substitution of the category of utility for that of truth, we are compelled to say in reference to the ethical question, that a moral principle which, on such a foundation, has its basis and authority only in its utility, is really no authority, and loses its value with every individual who is unwilling to acknowledge its utility and thinks another ground of action may be more useful than the moral.

CHAPTER VI.

NEUTRALITY AND PEACE BETWEEN DARWINISM AND MORALITY.

§ 1. *Mivart, Alex. Braun, and Others.*

Evidently a real neutrality between the Darwinian theories of development and the hitherto valid and absolute authority of the moral principle is possible only, when we deny that the ethical demand is simply a natural process— although we may perceive its origin within the limits of a natural process— and when we fail to identify that demand with this process, and do not deduce it from the latter as its sufficient ground of explanation; but harmony between the two theories, in spite of all traces of Darwinism in the scientific parts of anthropology, is possible when we acknowledge the moral demand, if once present and valid, in its entire and, so to speak, its metaphysical independence in its full value, far exceeding all natural necessity.

It is shown by Mivart that such an absolute authority of the ethical demands, and such an independence of the whole science of morality, may be brought into accord with the scientific theories of development. In his book on "The Genesis of Species," he devotes a whole chapter to ethical questions. He discriminates, in the moral good, between the formal good (good with consciousness and will of the good) and the material good (good without consciousness and design), ascribes only the latter to the animal world in its moral features, and the former exclusively to mankind, and thus takes ground quite analogous to that held by him on the religious question, where he includes in the theory of development the physical part of man, but excludes the intellectual part, with the single qualification that in the religious question he unnecessarily renders his position more difficult by designating this intellectual or spiritual part by the term "soul."

German authorities, who see in Darwinism only a scientific question which can be solved by means of natural investigation, and who therefore, think the religious and ethical questions but little affected by it, have expressed themselves in regard to this neutral position toward morality still more rarely than as to its neutrality toward religion. The reason for this is probably that the independence of moral principles and the absoluteness of their authority entirely result from themselves, as soon as we have once admitted theism and left room in general for a freedom standing above natural causality—and perhaps it is due to the further fact that the realm of the moral is more palpably urged as a reality and necessity upon even the most indifferent mind than the realm of religion.

On the other hand, we find frequent utterances which *indirectly* refer to the ethical realm—for instance, expressions in reference to the ethical importance of an animal descent of man. Alex. Braun says: "Man *assents* to the idea of being appointed *lord* of the creatures, but then he may also acknowledge that he is not placed over his subjects as a stranger, but originated from the beings whose lord he wishes to be. It is not an unworthy idea, but rather an elevating one, that man constitutes the last and highest member in the ancient and infinitely rich development of organic nature on our planet, being connected by the most intimate bonds of relationship with the other members, as the latter are connected among themselves with one another: not a pernicious parasite on the tree of natural life, but the true son of the blissful mother Nature." In reducing descent, which he accepts, to a development from an *inner* force, and in ascribing to the Darwinian selection, with its struggle for existence, the value only of a regulator (he adopts this term of Wallace as a very striking one), Braun, in his concluding appeal to young students, calls especial attention to the ethical importance of a development proceeding from within, saying: "Life has its outer and its inner side; all its works and ways must follow mechanical laws, but its tasks and aims belong to a higher realm. We are permitted to take a glance into this realm through the all-embracing history of the development of nature, which leads up into our own inmost being, up to our highest end. Truly progressive development is the best wish for every youth," etc.

Inasmuch as that in which Alex. Braun finds a satisfaction for the fulfillment of the ethical tasks—namely, a deeper knowledge of man's connection with lower nature, and the pointing to the proper tasks of the development of mankind,—has thus far been the substance of all sound systems of morality, we did not mention these and similar utterances, of which we could gather many more from other writers, in the preceding part of our work—*i.e.*, in describing those who ascribe to Darwinism a reformatory influence upon morality; but we rank these utterances with those which predict from the descent theory neither injury to morality nor any especial enlightenment regarding it.

We have now reached the end of that part of our work which considers and treats of the views of others. To our regret, we have been compelled to restrict ourselves, in this review, to the countries of the English and German tongues; the former being the home of Darwin, the latter our own. We should have preferred to take into our review also the literature of France and Belgium, Holland and Italy; but we feared being able to give only an incomplete report. Besides, it is in Germany and Great Britain—and partly also in North America, related to both in language and origin—where the Darwinian agitation has taken deepest hold of the mind; and, in restricting our report to these countries, we are not likely to have omitted any view essential to the consideration of the present question. It is true that in the other countries named the Darwinian literature is also rich, and we are well aware of the incompleteness of our report in that respect. But we believe that we have not omitted any essential views and evidences, even if the names of many of their advocates have not been mentioned.

It still remains to us to investigate independently the position of the Darwinian theories, with their philosophic supplements, in reference to religion and morality: a task for which we hope to have essentially prepared the way through the preceding representations and investigations.

BOOK II.

ANALYTICAL.

PRELIMINARY VIEW.

In treating the *religious* question, we proceed from the supposition that religion is concerned not only in this subjective truth of religious impulse and sensation, but also in the objective truth and reality of its faith, although it attains these in a different way from natural science. A religion which should have the authorization of its existence only in psychology, and which was not allowed to ask whether the object of its faith also has objective reality, would stand on a weak basis, and its end would only be a question of time; for an impulse which can only be psychologically established, and to which no real objective necessity could correspond, must sooner or later either be proven a psychological error or be eliminated by progressing culture. On the other hand, if we find a reconcilableness or an irreconcilableness of Darwin's views with the objective substance of religion, the possible question as to its reconcilableness or irreconcilableness with subjective religiousness on the ground of those results wholly answers itself. In no way, not even in the most indirect, can we approve that method of book-keeping by which something can be true in regard to religion and false in regard to science, or vice-versa; on the contrary, we see in all attempts at healing in such a way the rupture which at present exists in the minds of so many, only a more emphatic avowal of that rupture.

In treating of the religious question as it affects the position of Darwinism in reference to the substance and the objective truth of the religious faith, without going into a detailed treatment of the question of the reconcilableness of a purely subjective religiousness with the Darwinian views, it will be of advantage to speak first of the position of the Darwinian theories in reference to the basis of all true and sound religion and religiousness—the *theistic view of the world*. In doing this, we shall discriminate the purely scientific theories of Darwin from the philosophic supplements and conclusions which have been given to and drawn from them, and shall have to consider each of them separately in connection with the theistic view of the world. If thereby we shall discover Darwinian views which can be brought into accord with a theistic view of the world, we shall also, in order to close our investigation, have to consider them with those parts of the theology of *positive Christianity* which can be affected by the Darwinian questions.

In treating the question of the relation of Darwinism to morality, our investigation can be somewhat abridged, because many of the principal questions which have to be considered have found their solution in what has been previously said, and partly also because they will present themselves in it different form.

The principal division in our discussion we shall most appropriately assign to ethics, and thus treat first of the position of Darwinism in reference to the moral principles, and then treat of this in reference to the concrete moral life. Where the question as to the position of Darwinism in reference to morality occurs, we shall no longer have to treat of it separately as to the different aspects of its problems—we should otherwise get lost in too many repetitions; but we shall only have to separate an ethical naturalism which supports itself upon Darwinian grounds, from pure Darwinism, and to treat of each in turn as to its position in reference to morality.

A. THE DARWINIAN THEORIES AND RELIGION.

CHAPTER I.

THE DARWINIAN THEORIES AND THE THEISTIC VIEW OF THE WORLD.

A. THE POSITION OF PURELY SCIENTIFIC DARWINISM IN REFERENCE TO THEISM.

§ 1. *Scientific Investigation and Theism. The Idea of Creation.*

At the very beginning of our investigation, we have to state that the absolute freedom of scientific investigation lies not only in the interest of natural science, but just as clearly in the direct interest of religion; and that every attempt at limiting the freedom of scientific investigation in a pretended religious interest, can only have its cause in the fullest misapprehension of that which the religious interest requires. For the religious view of the world consists in this: that it sees in the universe, with all its inhabitants and processes, the work of an almighty Creator and Ruler of the world; and therefore it cannot be unimportant to it, whether we also have a knowledge of this work, to a certain extent, whether we make use of the means which lead to the knowledge of the world, and whether we make progress in the knowledge, or not. The religious view of the world sees in every correction and enrichment of our scientific knowledge only a correction and enrichment of our knowledge of the way and manner of the divine creation and action; and every such correction and enrichment acts directly as an incitement to religiousness—although, fortunately for the universal destination of religion, the degree of our religiousness is not dependent upon the degree of our knowledge of nature. Therefore, the religious view of the world does not throw any barriers in the way of scientific investigation; it does not prescribe the route by which the latter is to reach its aim, and it does not forbid it any scientific auxiliary means, nor, indeed, any scientific auxiliary hypothesis, nor does it, so far as the communication of scientific knowledge is concerned, inquire after the religious or the irreligious standpoint of those who offer it such knowledge. In all these directions, it knows of but one requirement: that of exact and correct presentation; in a word, of but one requirement of *truth*. Real, well-founded, and certain results of natural science can never come into antagonism with religion; for precisely the same thing which in the language of natural science is called natural causal connection, is in that of religion called the way and manner of divine action and government. Where man has adopted any view, the proving of which, according to its nature, belongs to natural science, and natural science should show an error in such a view, he must simply give it up and surrender the erroneous opinion, that such a view is to form a constituent part of our religious perception. Just as decidedly, on the other hand, religion can ask of natural science that it should not use speculative views of religious character, the proving of which belongs to the science of religion, for the purpose of scientific generalizations, in case the science of religion should prove that such views are antagonistic to the nature and the principles of religion.

Those who, on religious grounds, look with suspicion upon scientific investigation, are frequently influenced by two erroneous notions, closely related to one another, without regard to the well-grounded aversion to the atheistic beauty with which so many scientific works are adorned. One of these errors is the notion that any object is remote from divine causality in the degree in which it has the cause of its origin in the natural connection, and that it would be easier for us to trace the origin of an object to the authorship of God, if we could not find any natural cause of its origin, than if we had knowledge of such a natural cause. The other error is the notion that the idea of "creation" excludes the idea of the action of secondary causes.

If the first mentioned opinion were correct, those certainly would be right who identify the progress of sciences with the progress of atheism; and ignorance would then be the most effective protection of piety. But this opinion is in direct conflict with all sound religious and scientific reasoning. It is in conflict with sound religious reasoning: for the religious view of the world sees in nature itself, with its whole association of causes and effects, a work of God; and as certainly as, according to the religious view of nature, a thousand years in the sight of God are but as yesterday when it is past, just so certainly is an object a work of God, whether its origin is due to milliards of *well-known* secondary causes, which all together are works of God—as well with reference to the laws which they obey as to the materials and forces in which these laws are active—or whether, when treating the question as to the immediate cause of its existence, we see ourselves led to an agency *unknown* to us. And that opinion is also in conflict with all sound scientific reasoning: for the fact that we do not have any knowledge of the immediate cause of a phenomenon, is by no means a proof that this immediate cause is the direct action of God who does not use any secondary causes; the phenomena may just as well have still more material or immaterial secondary causes, unknown to us. We will illustrate the error, referred to, by an example which will also reveal its relationship to the other error of which we shall have to speak immediately. It is certainly no evidence of an especially intensive piety, if we build the conviction that God is the Creator of man, among other things, on the obscurity in which for us the origin of mankind is wrapped. For from this obscurity no other conclusion can be drawn than increased proofs of the limitation of our knowledge; that piety which traces those phenomena whose natural causes we know, just as decidedly to the causality of God, is much more—we shall not say, intensive, but correctly guided—than that piety which traces back those whose natural causes are hidden to us. And, on the other hand, it is also no evidence of especial religious coolness or indifference, when we pursue with interest and the desire of success the attempts at bringing light into the history of the origin of mankind. He who does the latter can, according to his religious or irreligious standpoint, just as easily connect his interest with the hope of an enrichment of his knowledge of the ways and works of God, as with the hope of a confirmation in his atheistic view of the world. The reverence with which we stand before the action of God in those works whose existence is in a higher degree a mystery to us than the existence of others (for in reality everything is a mystery to us), is perhaps a little differently modified from the reverence with which we stand before the action of God in those of his works in the mode of whose origin we are permitted to get a deeper glance; but each is reverence, and we can get from both nutriment for our religious nature.

Those who favor the second error—namely, that the idea of creation excludes the idea of secondary causes—overlook the facts that the idea of the creation of the universe is essentially different from the idea of the creation of the single elements of the universe, as, for instance, of the earth, of the organisms, of man; that the idea of a creation without secondary causes can only be applied to the origin of the universe in its elements, forces, and laws, and that the first origin of the single elements in the world—as of the single planets, organisms, man—not only admits the action of secondary causes, but even requires and presupposes the action of conditions. For all single species of beings which have originated within the already existing world, have also certain elements, even the whole basis and condition of their existence, in common with that which was already before in existence; the planet has its elements in common with the elements of other planets, the organic has the same material substances as the inorganic, man has the elements and the organization of his body as well as a great part of his psychical activity in common with animals. Nothing urges us to suppose—and the analogy of all that we know even forbids us to suppose—that with the appearance of a new species of beings, the same matter and the same quality of matter which the last appearance has in common with the already existing, has each time been called anew into existence out of nothing. Only that which in the new species is really new, comes into existence anew with its first appearance. But we do not even know whether the proximate cause of this new does really come into existence for the first time, or whether it was not before in existence in a real, perhaps latent, condition, and is now set free for the first time. In the one case as in the other, we shall call the new, which comes into existence, a new creation. And if man thinks that the new only deserves the name of creation, when it occurs suddenly and at once, where before only other things were present, like a *deus ex machina*, certainly such an opinion is only a childlike conception, which becomes childish as soon as we scientifically reason about the process. It cannot be doubtful that religious minds which are not accustomed to scientific reasoning, have such a conception; whether theologians also favor it, we do not know, although it is possible. Certainly those scientists who intend to attack the faith in a living Creator and Lord of the world, take it as the wholly natural, even as the only possible, conception of a Creator and his creation; and of course it is to them a great and cheap pleasure to become victorious knights in such a puppet-show view of the conception of creation. But the source whence Christians derive their religious knowledge tells them precisely the contrary. The Holy Scripture, it is true, sees in the entire universe a work of God. But where it describes the creation of the single elements of the world, it describes at the same time their creation as the product of natural causes, brought about by natural conditions. The reader may see, for instance, the words: "And God said, Let the earth bring forth grass, the herb yielding seed, etc. And *the earth brought forth* grass and herb," etc. "And God said, Let *the earth bring forth the living creature*." Even the creation of man is thus related: "And the Lord God *formed* man of the dust of the ground." Certainly the forming presupposes a matter out of which man is formed. And, on the other hand, where the Bible speaks of single beings in the kingdoms long before created and perfected, of the individual man who is originated by generation and birth, of single plants and animals—in general, of single processes and phenomena in the world long before perfected, of wind and waves, of rain and flames, which altogether have their natural causes of origin—it speaks of them all precisely in the same way as when describing their first creation as works of God. The expressions "create, make, form, cause to appear," are applied to the single individuals of the kingdoms long before created, precisely in the same way as they are to the first origin of the first individuals of those kingdoms.

Thus, by the full freedom which religious interest gives to scientific investigation, we are well prepared to treat with entire impartiality the question as to the position of each of the Darwinian theories in reference to theism.

§ 2. *The Descent Theory and Theism.*

In the first part of our investigation, we found that the idea of the origin of the species, especially of the higher organized species, through descent from the next related lower ones, has a high degree of probability, although it is still not proven in a strictly scientific sense, and although especially the supposition of an often-separated primitive generation of single types is not excluded by that idea, and we can hardly suppose that the main types of the animal kingdom are developed out of one another. Now we are far from asking of *religion* to decide for itself in favor of the one or the other mode of conception, or to place its influence in the one or the other balance-scale of scientific investigations. It leaves the answering of these questions exclusively to natural science, knowing beforehand that it will be able to come to an understanding with the one as well as with the other result of its investigations. But we confess frankly that it is incomparably *easier* for us to bring the origin of the higher groups of organisms in accord with a theistic and teleological view of the world through descent than the origin of each single species of organisms through a primitive generation; and we reach this result especially by the attempt at teleologically perceiving the palæontological remains of organic life on earth. Theism and teleology see in the origin of things a striving towards a goal, a rising from the lower to the higher, a development—it is true a development really taken only in the ideal sense of an ideal connection, of a plan; or, as K. E. v. Baer, in 1834, in his lecture on the most common law of nature in all development, expresses himself, of a progressive victory of mind over matter. Such a plan and its realization we can much more easily conceive when, in the past genera which geological formations show us, a genealogical connection takes place between the preceding species and the now living species, than when each species perished and beside or after it the newly appearing species always originated out of the inorganic through primitive generation. In the first case, we see in the preceding a *real* preparation for the following, and also easily perceive, the apparent waste of enormous periods of time for the successive processes of creation. In the second case, the coming and going of genera in innumerable thousands of years, without any exterior connection, becomes an incomprehensible problem, and the striving towards an end according to a regular plan, which we observe in the development, of the organic kingdoms on earth, disappears completely in metaphysical darkness.

Precisely because so many advocates of a theistic view of the world have thought that for the sake of the theistic idea of creation they were obliged to suppose a primitive origin of all the organic species, and because, nevertheless, the fact is patent that in the course of the pre-historic thousands of years myriads of species came and perished, not to return again, they became liable to the reproach on the part of the adversaries of theism, that the Creator, as they supposed him, makes unsuccessful attempts, which he has to throw away, as the potter a defective vessel, until he finally succeeds in making something durable and useful; and this objection was and is still made, not only to these superficial theists and their unhappily-selected and indefensible position, but to the whole view of the world of theism itself and to the faith in God and the Creator in general.

For all these reasons, we can from the religious point of view but welcome the idea of a descent of species. Philologists have, if we are correctly informed, the canon that as a rule the more difficult text is the more correct one; but we doubt whether those should adopt this canon who try to read in the book of nature, whether with the eye of science or with that of religion—unless the faculty of reasoning is given to us in order to conceal the truth.

But, we have also to look for a manner of reconciling theism with all the different possibilities under which a descent is at all reasonable and conceivable. One of these possibilities is that of an entirely successive development of species out of one another by imperceptibly small transitions; and of this we shall soon speak. Another is the possibility of a descent by leaps, through a metamorphosis of germs or a heterogenetic generation. The real causes of such a heterogenetic generation, if it took place at all, have not yet been found; therefore we have to treat only of the abstract possibilities of its conceivableness. There are two such possibilities.

The birth of a new species took place in one of two ways: Either to those materials and forces which formed the germ of the new species, were added entirely new metaphysical agencies which did not exist before, and only the basis and the frame within which the new appeared, or that which the new species has in common with the old mother-species had the cause of its existence in the preceding. Likewise even the original productions of man are always composed of two factors—of the given pre-suppositions and conditions, and of the new which on their basis and within their frame comes into existence. Otherwise the causes of the new which was to originate already lay in all former stages, but were still latent and still hindered in their activity, and only at the time of the birth the new impulse came which set them free for their activity. This new impulse may very well belong to the causal connection of the universe, and be caused by something analogous to natural selection.

In the first case, which in its application to the origin of man is adopted by A. R. Wallace and Karl Snell, the reconciliation between descent and theism has not the least difficulty; for if the agency which in the new-appearing species produces that which is specifically new in it, came only into existence with the first formation of the germs of the new species in the mother-species, this new certainly cannot have its origin anywhere else than in the supermundane *prima causa* in the Creator and Lord of the world.

In the second case also, theism is in no way threatened. For if we have to refer the cause of a new phenomenon in the world so far back as even to the beginning and the first elements of all things, we nevertheless have to arrive at last at the cause of all causes; and this is the living God, the Creator and Lord of the world. Thus the new form of existence would anyhow have the cause of its existence in God; and the value, the importance, and the substance of its existence, would only commence from where it really made its appearance, and not from where its still latent causes existed. As little as we attribute to the just fecundated egg of man the value of man, although we know that under the right conditions the full man is to be developed out of it, just so little in accordance with that view would the differences of value within the created world be dissolved in a mass of atoms or potencies of a similar value. Neither should we have to fear that from such a theory cold deism would be substituted for our theism, full of life. For as certainly as theism does not exclude, but includes, all that is relative truth in deism, so certainly the supposition that the Creator had laid the latent causes of all following creatures in the first germs of the created, would also not exclude the idea of a constant and omnipotent presence of the Creator in the world. Undoubtedly it belongs to our most elementary conceptions of God, that we have to conceive his lofty position above time, not as an abstract distance from finite development, but, as an absolute domination over it; so that for God himself, who creates time and developments in time, there is no dependence on the temporal succession of created things, and it is quite the same to him whether he instantly calls a creature into existence, or whether he prepares it in a short space of time, or years, or in millions of years. In this idea we also find the only possible and simple solution of the before- mentioned problem of a timeless time which Fr. Vischer wishes to propose to philosophy.

§ 3. The Evolution Theory and Theism.

In speaking of an evolution theory, in distinction from the descent theory, we mean, as is evident from the first part of our work, that way and mode of constructing the doctrine of the descent of species which permit this descent to take place, not by the leaps of a metamorphosis of germs, but by transitions so imperceptably small that the difference of two generations which lie in the same line of descent, is never greater than those differences which always take place between parents and children of the same species—transitions so gradual that only the continuation of these individual changes in a single direction produces an increase and, finally and gradually, the new species. The treatment of the question as to what position this *evolution theory* takes regarding theism, is even more simple than answering the question as to the position of the descent idea in reference to theism.

For now we have no longer to discuss the different possibilities of a development, as heretofore we have discussed those of a descent, but only the idea of a gradual development or of an evolution in general. Of such possibilities, it is true, we find several. In the first place, we can look for the inciting principle of the development of species either in the interior of organisms, or we can see it approaching the latter from without. The only scientific system which has made any attempt at mentioning and elaborating the inciting principle of development is that of Darwin; a system that chooses the second of the alternatives just stated and sees the essential principle that makes the transmission of individuals a progress beyond one species, approaching the individuals from without. But while we shall have to treat of this specific Darwinian theory—the selection theory—still more in detail in the following section, we shall also there have to point, out everything that theism has to say in reference to a principle of development which approaches the organisms from without. Another possible explanation of the origin of species through development is to be found in the fact that we look for the inciting principle of development in the interior of organisms. This is done, so far as we know, by all those scientists who, although inclined to an evolution theory, are adversaries of the selection theory; but none of them claim to have found the inciting agencies of development. Thus, as in the preceding section, we are again referred only to the wholly abstract possibility of conceiving these inciting agencies either as coming into existence anew in the organism with each smallest individual modification which leads to a development of the species, or as being before present in the organisms, but still latent, and only coming into activity when they are set free. But the question whether theism could accept the one or the other possibility had to be treated of in the preceding section, and was there answered in the affirmative.

Thus it only remains to treat in general of the question as to the reconcilableness of the idea of the origin of species through evolution, through gradual development, *in general* with a theistic view of the world.

In the first place, we wish to render evident the fact which is so often overlooked by the friends of monism and still more by theistic adversaries of the idea of evolution, that the idea of a development of species, and also of man, does not offer to theistic reasoning any new or any other difficulties than those which have been long present, and which had found their solution in the religious consciousness long before any idea of evolution disturbed the mind. It is true, the question as to the origin of *mankind* is, to speak in the language of natural history, a still unsolved *problem*; and the supposition of its gradual development out of the animal kingdom is still an *hypothesis*—one of all those attempts at solving this problem which still wait for confirmation or refutation. But there is another quite analogous question whose position has long ceased to be a mere problem, and whose solution is no longer a mere hypothesis; namely, the question as to the origin of the perfect human or any other organic *individual*. To speak again in the language of natural history, this origin is no longer a problem—that is, without regard to the obscurity in which the existence and origin of every creature, as to its last causes, is always and will always be veiled for us. We know that the human, and, in general, every organic individual, becomes that which it is through *development*. It begins the course of its being with the existence of a single cell, the egg, and goes through all stages of this development by wholly gradual and imperceptible transitions, so that the precise moment cannot exactly be fixed when any organ, any physical or psychical function, comes into existence, until perfect man is *developed*. Man has this mode of coming into existence in common with all organized beings, down to the lowest organisms which stand above the value and rank of a single cell. At this place, and with the design of our present discussion in view, we ought not to render the importance of this fact obscure by a teleological comparison of the different eggs and germs with one another. If we look upon that which is to *come out* of the germs, and which certainly if prepared and present in the first vital functions of the germ, although we are not able to observe, prove, and estimate it by means of the microscope and the retort, then of course the difference in the value of the germs must be immense; and from this point of view we certainly look upon the germ of man differently than upon the germ of an oyster. But here the question is not as to the differences of value of organisms: no scientist who remains within the limits of his realm, will ever deny them; but we treat of the question whether such valuable objects come into existence suddenly or gradually—whether it is possible, or even a fact which repeats itself before our eyes, that a form of being of higher value comes forth from a form of being of a lower value in gradual development. And here it is an undisputed fact that all qualities of man, the physical as well as the spiritual, come into existence in such a gradual development that not in a single one of them can be fixed any moment of which it may be said: on the other side of this moment it did not exist, but on this side it did exist. All differentiations of his body, from the first differentiation of the egg-cell into a complexity of cells up to the last formation of his organs, take place in the same gliding development. All his psychical and spiritual functions and forces come into existence in this form of gradual development. Where, in the development of the human individual, is the moment in which consciousness, language, self-consciousness, memory, will, the perception of God, moral responsibility, the perception of the idea and the ideal, or whatever else we may mention, came into existence? Nowhere; all this, and all the rest, is developed in a gradual process. The only marked time in this development is the time of birth: it brings a great change into physical life, and is perhaps the beginning epoch of the spiritual development of man. But even the birth is not absolutely bound to a certain time; the child may be born too early, by weeks or even months, and its development nevertheless takes place; and even after birth, how slowly and gradually spiritual development begins and continues!

With this gradual process of individual development which we have long known, we have never found any difficulty in bringing two things into harmony. First, we always judged the value of the single qualities of man only in the proportion in which they were really present and came into existence, and in such a way that we entirely followed the flowing development of the individual. Therefore we looked upon the suckling, for instance, not at all as a morally responsible individual; upon the child of two years as more responsible, but to a far less degree than the child of school-age, and the latter again to a less degree than the man; and thus we have been long accustomed to reason, when looking upon all single qualities of man. Second, we did not find any difficulty in bringing into perfect harmony the idea of a gradual process of individual development and of the dependence of the latter on a complex totality of natural causes: with the idea of the absolute dependence on God, the Creator, of that which arose through development. Every religiously reasoning man has always looked upon himself as the child of his parents, gradually developed under the activity of complex natural causes, as well as the creature of God, that owes the existence of all its forces and parts of body and soul to God. Should it then, be so difficult, or is it only something new, to bring into harmony, when looking upon the entire species and genus, that which we were long ago able to bring into harmony when looking upon the individual—it being presupposed that the investigation leads us to a development of the entire species and genus similar to that of the individual development? Or have we here again to ask, as in § 1: is it more religious to make no attempt at removing the veil which covers the natural process of the origin of mankind, than to make it? It is true, the not knowing anything can, under certain circumstances, create and increase the sensation of reverence for the depth of divine power and wisdom; but a perception of the ways of God is also certainly able to create the same. On that account, we need not at all fear that by such an attempt and its eventual success we might get into the shallows of superficiality, to which nothing seems any longer to be hidden, only because it has no presentiment of the depths which are to be sounded. There will always remain enough of the mysterious and the uninvestigated, and each new step forward will only lead to new views, to new secrets, to new wonders.

But does not a development, like that which we here for the moment assume hypothetically, efface and destroy the specific value of man and mankind from still another side? Would not a *beginning* of mankind be really lost, in case that theory of evolution should gain authority? and would not there still lie between that which is decidedly called animal world and that which is decidedly called mankind an innumerable series of generations of beings which were neither animal nor man? We do not believe it. What makes man *man*, we can exactly point out: it is self-consciousness and moral self- determination. Now, in case development took place in the above sense, it may have passed ever so gradually; the epochs of preparation between that which we know as highest animal development and that which constitutes the substance of man, may have stretched over ever so many generations, and, if the friends of evolution desire it, we say over ever so many thousands of generations; yet that which makes man *man*—self-consciousness and moral self-determination—must have always come into actual reality in *individuals*. Those individuals in which self-consciousness came into existence and activity, for the first time, and with it the entire possibility of the world of ideas—the consciousness of moral responsibility, and with it also the entire dignity of moral self-determination—were the first men. The individuals which preceded the latter may have been ever so interesting and promising as objects of observation, if we imagine ourselves spectators of these once supposed processes; yet, they were not men.

§ 4. *The Selection Theory and Theism.*

The last scientific theory whose position in reference to theism we have to discuss, is the selection theory.

We have found but little reason for sympathizing with this theory. But since we believed that we were obliged to suspect it, not for religious but for scientific reasons, so the completeness of our investigation requires us to assume hypothetically that the selection principle really manifests itself as the only and exclusive principle of the origin of species, and to ask now what position it would in such a case take in reference to theism.

The only answer we are able to give is decidedly favorable to theism.

It is true, development would in such a case approach the organisms merely from without. For the principle lying within the organisms, which would then be the indispensable condition of all development, would be first the principle in itself, wholly without plan or end, of individual variability; second, the principle of inheritance which for itself and without that first principle is indeed no principle of development, but the contrary. The causes from which the single individuals vary in such or such a way, would then be the outer conditions of life and adaptation to them: *i.e.*, something coming from without. And the causes from which one individual, varying in such or such a way, is preserved in the struggle for existence, and another, varying differently, perishes, would be approaching the individuals also from without; hence they are a larger or smaller useful variation for the existence of the individual.

Now if, through these influencing causes of development, approaching the most simple organisms from without, a rising line of higher and higher organized beings comes finally into existence (a line in which sensation and consciousness, finally self-consciousness and free-will, appear) we again reach the teleological dilemma: all this has either happened by chance, or it has not. No man who claims to treat this question earnestly and in a manner worthy of respect, will assert that it happened by chance, but by necessity. But with this word the materialist only hides or avoids the necessity of supposing a plan and end in place of chance, as we have convinced ourselves in Part I, Book II, Chap. II, § 1. The only exception in this case is, that the bearer and agent of this plan would not be the single organism (as is easily possible when we accept a descent theory which is more independent from the selection theory), but the collection of all forces and conditions, acting upon the organism from without. And for the question, whence this plan and its realization comes, we had again but the one answer: from a highest intelligence and omnipotence, from the personal God of theism. The *locus* of creation and the *locus* of providence would now, as ever, retain their value in the theological system, with the sole exception that most of that which so far belonged to the *locus* of creation would now belong, in a higher degree than in the hitherto naturo-historical view, to the *locus* of providence and of the government of the world. When looked upon from the theocentric point of view, the new forms which we had to suppose as called into existence only by selection, would remain products of divine creation: the "God said, and it was so," would retain its undiminished importance; but looked upon from the cosmic point of view, they would present themselves as products of the divine providence and government of the world, still more exclusively than in every principal of explanation which finds the causes of development in the organisms themselves or in an immaterial cause acting upon the organisms from within. The first as well as the second point of view is in full harmony with the religious view of things.

We do not conceal that on the ground of all other analogies we sympathize more with those who look for the determining influences of the origin of new species rather within than without nature, and who, while looking at that which the higher species have in common with the lower, do not forget or neglect the new, the original, which they possess. But we are indeed neither obliged nor entitled, in the name of religion, to take beforehand in the realm of scientific investigation the side of the one or the other direction of investigation, or even of the one or the other result of investigation, before it is arrived at. Let us unreservedly allow scientists free investigation in their realm, so long as they do not meddle with ethical or religious principles, and quietly await their results. These results, when once reached, may correspond ever so closely with our present view and our speculative expectations, or in both relations be ever so surprising and new; the one case as well as the other has already happened: at any rate they will not affect our religious principles, but only enrich our perception of the way and manner of divine activity in the world, and thereby give new food and refreshment, to our religious life.

A. THE DARWINISTIC PHILOSOPHEMES IN THEIR POSITION REGARDING THEISM.

§ 5. *The Naturo-Philosophic Supplements of Darwinism and Theism.*

We still have to discuss the position of theism in reference to the *philosophic* problems to which a Darwinistic view of nature sees itself led, and in the first place its position in reference to the naturo-philosophic theories with which the descent idea tries to complete itself.

In the first part of our book, we have found that not a single one of the naturo-philosophic problems before which the descent idea places us, is really solved: neither the origin of self-consciousness and of moral self- determination, nor the origin of consciousness and of sensation, nor the origin of life; and even the theory of atoms, although it is quite important and indispensable for the natural philosopher and chemist according to the present state of his knowledge and investigation, has not yet been able to divest itself of its hypothetical character. Religion might, therefore, refuse to define its position in reference to theories which are still of a quite problematic and hypothetical nature. But by giving such a refusal, religion would not act in its own interest. The reproach is often made that it has an open or hidden aversion to the freedom of scientific investigation—a reproach which, it is true, is often enough provoked by its own advocates; often the assertion is made by advocates of free investigation, that free science has led, or can lead at any moment, to results which shake or even destroy theism and with it the objective and scientifically established truth of a religious view of the world. The consequence of this assertion is exactly, as before-mentioned, that minds whose religious possession is to them an inviolable sanctuary, and who lack time and occasion, inclination and ability, to examine scientifically these asserted results of science, really suspect free science and contest the right of its existence. Another consequence of this state of war between religion and science is the fact that so many minds in both camps fall into a servile dependence upon battle-cries: they confound freedom of investigation with license; science with apathy or hostility to faith; faith with lack of scientific perception, blind unreasoning belief, etc. Such a state of affairs does not, indeed, serve the interests of peace and truth; only a correct treatment of philosophy as well as of religion can lead to them.

Such a way of peace and truth from the side of religion and its scientific treatment is entered upon, when religion sets itself right, not only with all real, but also with all *conceivable, possible* results of the other sciences, not only of the exact, but also of the philosophic sciences. If it finds, in such an investigation, that such conceivable results are reconcilable with the theistic view of the world which is the basis of religion, it has already shown its relationship to the freedom of investigation. But if it finds anywhere a possible result which is in conflict with its theistic view of the world, it is obliged to examine the mutual grounds of dissent, as to the degree of their truth and their power of demonstration; and in case its own position is the stronger, better founded, and more convincing, to prove this fact. If it does this, it again acts according to the principle of free investigation—with the single difference that in such a case it not only makes this allowance to the opponent, but also uses this principle for itself in its own realm and especially in the border land between itself and its opponent; but at the same time it shows in this case (what, indeed, so many are inclined to deny), that religion also has its science, and that theology itself is this science, and has the same rights as the sciences which are built up in the realm of material things or of abstract reasoning.

We therefore assume hypothetically, that the origin of self-consciousness and of moral self-determination is fully explained by consciousness; the origin of consciousness and sensation by that which has no sensation; the origin of the living and organic by the lifeless and inorganic; and that atomism also is scientifically established and proven: how, then, would such a theory of the world and theism stand in respect to each other? By this assumption, we think we should simply stand again at the point, the basis of which we had to discuss in Part I, Book II, Chap. II, § 1, when treating of teleology. We should always see something new, something harmoniously arranged: a process of objects of value, continually rising higher and higher, coming forth out of one another in direct causal connection; and should have a choice of one of two ways of explaining this process. We should either have to be satisfied with this final causal connection, and perceive in this process itself its highest and last cause, in doing which we should be obliged again to deny order and plan in this process, to reject the category of lower and higher and the acknowledgment of a striving towards an end in these developments, and after having climbed to that Faust-height of investigation and knowledge, to throw ourselves in spiritual suicide back into the night and barbarism of chaos, or of a rigid mechanism to which all development, all life, all spiritual and ethical tasks, are but appearance; or we should have to treat the idea of development seriously and recognize a plan and a striving towards an end in this world-process, and should then find ourselves referred to a higher intelligence and a creative will as the highest and last cause which appoints the end and conditions of this process. This would be the case still more, as we actually see that at present the single beings which stand on a lower stage of existence no longer produce beings of a higher stage, although, according to that theory whose correctness we now assume hypothetically, the elements and factors for the production of those higher forms of existence are fully present in the lower ones. Inorganic matter no longer produces organisms; the lower species of plants or animals no longer develop higher ones; the animal no longer becomes man; and yet there were periods, lying widely apart, in which, according to that theory, such things took place. What else set free those active causes, at the right time and in the right place? What else closed again at the precise place and moment the valves of the proceeding development, and brought to rest again the inciting force of the rising development?—what else but the highest end-appointing intelligence and omnipotence?

Even the inherent qualities of the elements, and the products of all the higher forms of existence which in the future shall arise out of them, the whole striving toward an end of the processes in the world, would present itself to us much more vividly than now, where we are still in the dark as to all these questions. We should see in *atoms* the *real* inherent qualities of all things and processes which are to be developed out of them; in the inorganic the *real* inherent qualities for the organic and living; in that which has no consciousness and sensation the *real* inherent qualities for self-consciousness. Instead of being now obliged to recur to the ideal and metaphysical, we should see the threads of the world's plan uncovered before us in empirical reality; and far from bearing with it an impoverishment of our consciousness of God, all this would bring us only an immense enrichment of its contents; for with such an enlargement of our knowledge, we should only be permitted to take glances into the way and manner of divine creation and action— glances of a depth which at present we are far from being permitted to take.

Even very concrete parts of a theistic view of the world, as they present themselves to us—*e.g.*, in the Holy Scripture, from its most developed points of view—would now find only richer illustrations than heretofore. St. Paul, for instance, in Rom. viii, speaks of the earnest expectation of the creature that waiteth for the manifestation of the sons of God. As to the present state of our knowledge of nature, those who adopt this view are only entitled to see in the sensation of pain of the *animal world* a sensation of this longing, unconscious of the end; but as to all soulless and lifeless beings and elements in the world, they can see in these words of a sighing and longing creation only a strong figurative expression used because of its suitableness to denote suffering of the animal world, as well as of men,—for the destination of the world to another and higher existence in which the law of perishableness and suffering no longer governs. On the other hand, if, as we assume hypothetically, all higher forms of existence in the world could be explained out of the preceding lower ones, and if the before-mentioned theorem of a sensation of atoms should form a needed and correct link in that chain of explanation, those words of sighing and longing would have to be literally taken in a still more comprehensive sense than now and in their directly literal meaning would refer not only to the animal world but indeed to everything in the world.

Therefore, so long as attempts at explaining the different forms of existence in the world wholly from one another keep within their own limits, and do not of themselves undermine theism; and so long as there are men who on the one hand favor such a mode of explanation and on the other hand still adhere firmly to a faith in God, whether it be the deeper theism or the more shallow and superficial deism—so long religion has no reason for opposing those attempts at explanation. And there are such men; we need only to mention Huxley, whose position in reference to religion we have already discussed; or Oskar Peschel, who, in his "Völkerkunde" ("Ethnology"), says: "It is not quite clear how pious minds can be disturbed by this theory; for creation obtains more dignity and importance if it has in itself the power of renewal and development of the perfect." Even Herbert Spencer, with his idea of the imperceptibility of the super-personal, of the final cause of all things, is still a living proof of the fact that man can trace the mechanism of causality back to its last consequences and, as Spencer does, even derive consciousness and sensation from that which is without sensation, and yet not necessarily proceed so far as *negation* of a living God, even if he persists in his refusal to perceive in general the ultimate cause of things.

To meet those attempts, religion would have to take only two precautionary measures on two closely related points; and in doing this it would indeed make use of that before-mentioned right to defend freedom of investigation both in its own realm and in the border-territory.

One precaution would consist in the requirement of the acknowledgment that even in that purely immanent mode of explanation the *idea of value is fixed*, but that the value of the new appears only when the new itself really comes into existence; that we therefore do not call, *e.g.*, the inorganic *living*, because according to that mode of explanation life develops itself out of it; and that we do not ascribe to the animal the value of man, because according to that mode of explanation it also includes the causes of the development of man. Such a discrimination of ideas is indeed a *scientific postulate*, as we have had occasion to show at many points of our investigation; and we also complied with this requirement long ago in that realm of knowledge which is related to these questions as to the origin of things, but is more accessible and open to us, namely, in the realm of the development of the individual. We have spoken of this at length in § 3. But in the interest of *religion* also we have to request that the *differences of value* of things be retained, even when man thinks he is able to explain their origin merely out of one another. For without this, all things would finally merge simply into existences of like value; man would stand in no other relation to God than would any other creature, irrational or lifeless; and the quintessence of religious life—the relation of mutual personal love between God and man, the certainty of being a child of God—would be illusory when there should no longer be a difference of value between man and animal, animal and plant, plant and stone.

Many a reader thinks, perhaps, that with this precaution we make a restriction which is wholly a matter of course, and that nobody would think of denying these differences of value. Häckel, in his "Anthropogeny," repeatedly reproaches man with the "arrogant anthropocentric imagination" which leads him to look upon himself as the aim of earthly life and the centre of earthly nature; this, he says, is nothing but vanity and haughtiness. Several writers in the "Ausland" faithfully second him in this debasement of the value of man. Its editor ("Ausland," 1874, No. 48, p. 957), for instance, reproaches Ludwig Noiré, although he otherwise sympathizes with him, that in his book "Die Welt als Entwicklung des Geistes" ("The World as Development of Mind"),

Leipzig, Veit & Co., 1874, he still takes this anthropocentric standpoint and can say: "The anthropocentric view recognizes in man's mind the highest bloom of matter, which has attained to the possession of a soul." This, Häckel says, is nothing else but the former conception, not yet overcome, that man is the crown of creation. This pleasure in debasing the value of man is also a characteristic sign of the times. K. E. von Baer is right, when, in his "Studies" (page 463), he says: "In our days, men like to ridicule as arrogant the looking upon man as the end of the history of earth. But it is certainly not man's merit that he has the most highly developed organic form. He also must not overlook the fact that with this his task of developing more and more his spiritual gifts has only begun.... Is it not more worthy of man to think highly of himself and his destination, than, fixing his attention only upon the low, to acknowledge only the animalic basis in himself? I am sorry to say that the new doctrine is very much tainted in this direction of striving after the low. I should rather prefer to be haughty than base, and I well recollect the expression of Kant, 'Man cannot think highly enough of man.' By this expression the profound thinker especially meant that mankind has to set itself great tasks. But the modern views are more a palliation of all animal emotions in man."

The other precautionary measure referred to would be, that the *realm of mind*, and especially the *ethical realm*, is not dissolved into a *natural mechanism*. This precaution is also connected with the first one, the latter being its condition; for only where it is acknowledged that causes, so long as they are still latent, do not fall under the same category of value as their effects, when these are once realized, it can also be acknowledged that the realm of mind and morality, although it has grown out of the ground of the mechanism of nature, can still have brought something new and higher into the world. Besides, this precaution is also a postulate of anthropologic science. For spiritual and ethical facts have at least the same truth and reality as the material, and a still higher value, and can therefore not permit any injury to their full recognition. But religion also must require this acknowledgment. For if the specific *activity* of mind in man is endangered, we also lose his specific *value*, and thus get into the before-mentioned dilemma; and if the moral responsibility of man is endangered, the relation of man to God loses its ethical character. Of the consequences in reference to morality, we shall have to speak hereafter.

Moreover, religion does not require this acknowledgment without a rich compensation. For if that naturo-philosophic mode of explanation, whose correctness we hypothetically assume in this present section, prove to be right, and if the higher which comes anew into existence in the world, is to have the full cause of its origin in the preceding lower, such an admission, in accordance with the laws of logic, by which *causa æquat effectum*, is only possible when we either similarly, as above, invalidate all difference between higher and lower, all difference of value of creatures, and contest the possibility that that which appears anew can also follow new laws of existence and activity; or when, in the highest cause of all final causes in the world, we see the full abundance of all those possibilities present as real cause, which afterwards appear in succession in the world. This highest cause, then, lodges in material things the final causes of all which is to come, as still latent causes, waiting to be set free; and such a highest cause as the fullness of all that which is successively to be developed in the world, is offered to science by religion itself in the idea of a living God. We say expressly, that religion offers this idea to science, and not that science creates this idea; for the acknowledgment of God, as we have before had occasion to point out, is in the last instance not a result of science, but an ethical action of mind,— although from this acknowledgment the brightest light falls upon science and the whole series of its conclusions, and although science owes to precisely this idea of God the highest points of view to which it sees itself led and from which alone it is able to survey its entire realm.

§ 6. *Elimination of the Idea of Design or its Acknowledgment and Theism.*

In the whole preceding course of our investigation as to the position of religion and theism regarding the different scientific and naturo-philosophic theories, theism could quietly keep the position of a friendly and peaceful spectator. The degrees of our sympathy with the theories which have successively passed before our eyes, were on scientific grounds very unequal; but on religious grounds, and in the interest of a theistic view of the world, we found ourselves nowhere induced to take sides for or against a theory. But the position of religion and theism becomes quite different in reference to the assertion that the existence of ends and designs in nature is refuted by the evolution theory or by any other hypothetical or real results of science. With this assertion, the existence of a living and personal God, of a Creator and Lord of the world, is denied; and every religion which claims objective truth for its basis is eliminated. It is true, man can under this supposition still speak of a religion in the sense of subjective religiousness; but the life-nerve is also cut off from this subjective religiousness. We have repeatedly had occasion to prove this in our historical review, and also in the section in which we pointed out the plan of our own analysis.

But still, where we have had to represent this anti-teleological view of the world, we have happily convinced ourselves of the fact that an existence of ends and designs in nature is not only *reconcilable* with the conformity to law and the causal mechanism of its processes, but is also *postulated* by scientific contemplation of nature, as soon as the latter observes that in these processes, acting with lawful necessity, something in general is attained, and, moreover, when out of them comes forth something so infinitely rich and beautifully arranged, such a rising series of higher and higher developments, as the world. On the other hand, combatting the striving towards an end in nature leads to such scientific monstrosities, destroys so thoroughly the idea of God and also all ideas of value in the world, even all spiritual and ethical acquisitions of mankind, that we can explain the origin of such a doctrine only by the determined purpose of getting rid, at any cost, of the dependence on a living God: again a proof of the fact that faith, or want of faith, in its final causes, is not the product of reflecting intelligence, but an ethical action of that centre of human personality from which the spiritual process of life in the individual comes forth—an ethical action of mind.

Herewith the position of theism in reference to the elimination of the idea of design is also soon characterized: it is *the position of irreconcilable antagonism*. In rejecting the position of its opponent, theism perceives that it is in harmony not only with every correctly understood religious need, but equally so with every scientific interest—with the interest of a correct knowledge of nature, as well as with the interest of those sciences which have to take care of and try to understand the spiritual and ethical endowments of mankind.

If we now turn our attention to the *position of theism in reference to the idea of design in general*, theism on its part also gives an equally firm support to that intimate connection, proven by natural science, between causality and striving toward an end—between aetiology and teleology, as they are called in the language of the philosophical school. While a contemplation of nature perceives in nature a mechanism governed by laws and necessities, it finds results reached through this chain of causality in which it must acknowledge ends toward which the preceding has striven. Now, theism, on its part, proceeds from the highest end-appointing cause of things and processes, and finds that the reaching of these ends postulates a mechanism of natural conformity to law. In order to prove this, we certainly must take a course which is prohibited by many as anthropomorphism, *i.e.*, we must try to study the connection of ends and designs, and the possibility of such a connection where we are able to observe in general not only the *accomplishment* of purposes, but also the *forming* of purposes; and the only realm of this kind which we know of, is the realm of human action. He who, merely through fear of anthropomorphism, shrinks from this only possible comparison, may consider that for those who assume a highest end-appointing cause (and we, too, proceed from this standpoint) man also, who forms his designs and strives toward his ends, is a product of that highest end-appointing cause; and that, therefore, in the human striving toward an end, a certain analogue of the divine striving toward an end must occur. We are, indeed, not obliged on this account to identify the two, and to close our eyes against the immense differences which exist between them, and which, wholly of themselves, intrude upon our observation. What we mean by that analogy may thus be stated.

Man forms for himself designs and ends, and pursues and reaches them by using the objects and forces of nature as means. He can do this only because the forces in nature act from necessity, strictly conformable to law. Because, and so far as man knows the action of forces, conformable to law, and the inviolable necessity of the connection between certain causes and their effects, he can select and make use of such causes as means, by virtue of which he reaches those effects as designs intended by him. If he could not depend on this conformity to law, on this causal connection taking place according to simple necessities, he could not select, make, and use, with certainty, any tool, from the club with which he defends himself against his enemies or cracks the shells of fruit, up to the finest instruments of optics and chemistry, and even to the telegraph and steam engine. The conformity to law, with which the forces of nature act, far from being an impediment to his appointing and reaching his ends is much more the indispensable means by which he is enabled in general to reach them. Now, if we thus find, in the only action striving towards an end which we are able to observe to the extent of the appointing of ends and the selection of means—namely, man's end appointing action—such a strong dependence of finality on causality that the reaching of ends is not possible at all unless the means act of necessity conformably to law, then we are certainly obliged to draw the conclusion that the highest author of things has prepared the world so, that the reaching of ends requires the action of means, and that the category of finality and the category of causality are mutually prepared for each other. For, according to the theistic and teleological view of the world, the laws of nature, acting with causality and necessity, are certainly not laws which the Creator found in some way, and with which he had to calculate as with factors given to him from somewhere else, in order to make use of them, so far as he was permitted, for the accomplishment of his designs—this would be the way and manner of *human* teleological action, and transferring it to *divine* action would be an anthropomorphism which we should have to reject. On the contrary, these laws themselves are the work of the teleologically acting Creator—he, indeed, will have given to them such a quality that with them he is able to reach his ends as a whole and in detail. The inviolability of the laws of nature also results from this idea. For means which would have to be supplemented, sometimes set aside, occasionally replaced by others, would be less perfect than such means as by virtue of their quality are able with certainty to serve the designs which are to be reached by them. How theism can reconcile with this view the indispensable idea of divine freedom, we shall have occasion to show in Chap. II, § 4.

Among the writers who defend teleology, we can mention two who, starting from the analogy of human teleological action, have pointed out the idea that teleology itself requires a necessity, conformable to law, in the activity of the forces of nature. One of the two is K. E. von Baer, in his oft-quoted essays on striving towards end; and the other is the Duke of Argyll. At a time when the assault against teleology had just begun, this noble author perceived the whole importance and weight of these attacks, and most energetically defended teleology. The expression of the just-mentioned ideas, among others, forms one of the fundamentals of his work, "The Reign of Law" (London, Strahan & Co., first edition published in 1866, and since then in frequently repeated editions); a work which is well fitted to instruct us, in the most interesting manner, regarding the present state of the related questions as they are treated of in Great Britain.

CHAPTER II.

THE DARWINIAN THEORIES AND POSITIVE CHRISTIANITY.

§ 1. *The Creation of the World.*

Now that we have come to a clear understanding of the position of the Darwinian theories in reference to the basis of all religion and of all living religiousness, to theism in general, it remains to be seen what position those of the theories which are reconcilable with theism take in reference to the positive Christian view of the world.

We naturally omit all those objects and parts of Christian dogmatics which have no points of contact, or are very indirectly connected with the Darwinian ideas, or which—as, *e.g.*, their position in reference to the idea of God in general—have found their principal illustration in our investigation just finished. We shall nevertheless have now to take into consideration once more, although from another side, some objects which we have discussed in treating of the relation of the Darwinian ideas to theism, on account of the specific part which theism has in Christianity. This is especially the case with those Christian facts which belong to the first article of the Apostolic Creed, and immediately also with the doctrine of the creation of the world.

At first sight it seems that the evolution theory and Christianity are in no other place more sharply opposed to each other than in that of the history of creation. Darwinism claims for its theory immense periods of time; and geology seems to furnish them according to its demand. The Holy Scripture, on the other hand, teaches a creation of the world in six days.

With the attempt to find the right way to end this conflict, we enter upon that part of the border-land between theology and natural science, which, among all others, is most contested, and which has offered to the most luxuriant fancy the widest field of action and the one most profitably taken advantage of.

We confess at the outset that we sympathize with those who try to keep the peculiar realms of religion and natural science apart in such a way that a collision between the two is impossible. We quietly leave the investigation of the temporal succession in creation—especially the investigation of all that belongs in the finite causal connection of natural processes—to natural science; we also do not look to the source of our Christian religion, to the Holy Scripture, for a scientific manual, least of all for the communication of a knowledge of nature, supernaturally manifested and claiming divine authority, the acquisition of which is especially the task of scientific labor. But we bestow just as decidedly upon religion the specific task of showing man the way to communion with God, especially the way of salvation; a task in which it can as little permit itself to be hindered by natural science, as the latter in the pursuit of its peculiar tasks can allow an objection from any source. On the side of religion, the bond of unity which brings into harmony the two activities of the human mind—the religious and the investigating—in the realm of nature, and, in general, in the whole realm of exact science, consists in the fact that in all which exact science offers to religion as the result of its investigation, the latter perceives and shows the works and ways of God; and on the side of the exact sciences, the bond consists in the fact that they bring within the reach of their scientific, historical, literary, culturo-historical, and exegetical investigations all that which in the religious realm appears, or in the written word is fixed, as historical fact. Religion, therefore, concedes to exact sciences the full right of examining the biblical records as to all the relations of their historical and literary connections; it even makes these investigations a quite essential and, at present, very much favored branch of its own science of theology. On the other hand, religion reserves just as decidedly to itself the full right of drawing from them, of maintaining, and of realizing, the whole full *religious* basis and significance of those records.

We know very well that such a proposition is very simple in principle, but much more difficult in practice. For the quintessence of that which constitutes the basis of the Christian religion—namely, the leading back of mankind to communion with God by means of salvation—is not only a philosopheme, a theoretical or mystic doctrine, but a *fact*: it comes into the world as a series of divine *facts*; it is interwoven by innumerable threads into creation and the course of nature and history; and, as to this whole aspect of its appearance in the world of phenomena, it falls under the cognition of the exact sciences. But as soon as any given fact excites the interest of religion as well as that of exact science, collisions are possible from both sides. Some advocates of religion, through mistaken zeal for religious interests, may think it necessary to assert and to represent as indispensable to religion facts whose cognition as to reality belongs only to exact science and which are contested by exact science; as, *e.g.*, the creation of the world in six literal days, or the creation of the single elements of the world without the action of secondary causes. And some advocates of exact science, from reasons of a superficial analogy, may erroneously think it necessary to dispute the reality of facts, otherwise well attested, but wanting analogy, in which religion has a central interest; as, *e.g.*, the reality of the resurrection of Jesus Christ, or the reality of his miracles. Or they may unjustifiably try, from our experiences in this world, to forbid glances which religion permits us to throw beyond the present course of the world; *e.g.*, the eschatological hope of Christians is often enough contested, or as the laws of nature are called eternal in the absolute sense of the word, although natural science is only led to a recognition of the duration of the same, which is congruent with the circumstances and duration of this present course of the world.

We are perfectly aware of all these possibilities of a collision, and of all the difficulties of their prevention and reconciliation; but we nevertheless know of no other way for their avoidance than that simple principle of agreement which, on account of its simplicity and clearness, seems to us to be perfectly able to maintain the peace between the two parties interested, or where it is disturbed, to restore it.

Thus, we wholly agree that in the question of creation the investigation of the succession and of all modalities in the appearance of the single elements of the world, is entirely left to natural science, and that the biblical records should on the one hand be investigated wholly, and even to their remotest consequences, from a literary, historical, and exegetical point of view, and on the other hand be tested with equal fullness and completeness as to their religious contents. The literary and exegetical examination of the Mosaic account of creation will reveal that its conceptions of that which in the creation of the world belongs entirely to the natural process, do not go beyond that which otherwise belongs to the sphere of knowledge and views of antiquity, as well as of immediate perception of nature in general; and that we cannot expect any scientific explanation from it, because man really came last on the stage of earth, and is therefore not able to say anything, founded upon autopsy, about the origin of all the other creatures which preceded his appearance. Just as little could the first men possess and deliver to their offspring a remembrance of the first beginnings of their own existence. Moreover, the literary and exegetical interpretation of the Bible will also refer to other passages of the Holy Scripture which entirely differ from the succession of creations, as they are related in Genesis I; so, *e.g.*, besides Job XXXVIII, 4-11, the second account of creation in Genesis II, 4-25: again a proof that what we read in the Biblical record of creation about the succession in the appearance of creatures is not binding upon us. Religion can have nothing to say against these results; it will not reject the information of man as to the succession and the modalities in the appearance of the single elements of the world, which it receives from natural science, and will not expect it by means of a special supernatural manifestation; it will willingly accept it from natural science, and simply make use of it in such a way that in nature and its processes it also perceives a manifestation of God. Now, when it examines the different Biblical accounts of creation as *to their religious substance*, it will find in them such a pure and correct idea of divine nature and divine action— such a pure conception, equally satisfying to mind and to science, of the nature of man, of his position in nature, of the nature and destination of the two sexes, of the ethical nature and the ethical primitive history of man,—it will especially have to acknowledge in the Biblical account of creation, in spite of all points of collision with the cosmogonies of paganism, such an elevation above them, such an exemption from all *theogony*, with which heathen cosmogonies are always mixed up, that we are perfectly right in perceiving in these records the full and unmistakable elements of a pure and genuine stream of manifestation, which pours into mankind.

So far we find ourselves in full harmony with a theology which, in the manner indicated, reconciles the religious interest with the historical and critical interest. We find the points of view to which this perception leads, represented with special clearness and attractiveness in Dillmann's Revision of Knobel's "Commentar zur Genesis" ("Commentary on Genesis"), Leipzig, Hirzel, 1875.

But it seems to us that a readiness to be just to historical criticism and impartial exegesis has hindered theologians occupying this standpoint from being just also to *the religious element*, in its full meaning, in reference to a very important part of the Mosaic account of creation, in which the author of it shows quite a decided religious interest. We mean the *six days of creation*, together with the *seventh day*, the divine Sabbath. Theologians became too quickly satisfied with the exegetical perception of these seven days, as creative, earthly days, of twenty-four hours; and this hindered them from assigning to the religious meaning the full importance which these days have in that record. That the idea and the number of the days in that account have a high religious meaning to the author, is clear from the following: The account in Genesis I, 1-24, belongs to that series of parts of the Pentateuch which we call the original, and which has the Sinaitical Law as the centre of its belief. The division of the days into weeks, each having six working days and one day of rest, which possibly existed before, but which received obligatory importance to Israel first by the Sinaitical legislation, so far controls that account of the creation of the world that, next to the sublime perception of the dignity and position of man, it forms its very quintessence. The account makes that divine week of creation, with its six working days and its divine day of rest, the divine prototype and model for the human division of time; and the Decalogue also, in the conception which it has in Exodus xx, directly bases the commandment of the Sabbath on the divine week of creation. Now, if we suppose that the author took these days as earthly days of twenty-four hours, we are first of all obliged to reject as a child-like error the idea on which from *religious* reasons—not from reasons of a mystical idea of God, but from direct practical religious reasons—he puts great importance; an idea with which he establishes an institution of human life which has been preserved through many thousands of years and is still preserved as the exceedingly blissful basis of all social life. For that the creation of the world, from the beginning of things up to the appearance of man, demanded more than six times twenty-four hours, is beyond any doubt. Moreover, we should be obliged to reject the arguments of such a central religious custom as Sabbath-rest in a record in which we have to assign an absolute and lasting religious value to all other religious elements of it, as to the ideas of the unity, omnipotence, and wisdom of God, of his creation through the creative word, of the perfection of his works, of man bearing the image of God. We should even see that idea of God which presents itself to us out of all other characteristics of that record in such spotless purity and sublime magnitude, sink down to a decided insignificance through the identification of the divine days of creation with our earthly days of twenty-four hours. All this certainly brings near to us the question: do we make a correct exegesis, do we correctly *read* that record, when we think that the author, because he speaks of days, must necessarily have understood earthly days, such as we know now?

We readily perceive how interpreters have arrived at this view. The divine sections of creation in the Mosaic account show themselves too decidedly as days to make possible any other interpretation than to take them as days. Now from experience we do not know of any other days than of earthly days of twenty-four hours; and therefore the conclusion naturally follows, that the author also took the divine days of creation as such earthly days of twenty-four hours. A simple reference of the same to periods, so that we should again think of fixed periods of the earth or of the world, would especially pervert the literal sense—would entirely remove from the account the idea of "day" which is so essential to the author of the record, and thereby render obscure the archetype of the divine week of creation for the human divisions of time; and the looked-for harmony between the Biblical days and the geological periods of the earth would by no means be established by such an identification of the days of creation with the periods of the world: for the geological or even the cosmic and astronomical periods are nowhere in congruity with the Biblical days of creation.

But the question, however, is: are there not evidences in the Biblical account itself which show that the author did *not* take these days as creative earthly days of twenty-four hours? We have to answer this question decidedly in the affirmative.

In the first place, it is an established fact that these days of the week of creation were also, according to the meaning of the author, *days of God*. Now that such days of God, even with the most childish and simple worldly knowledge of that early period of mankind, so soon as such a pure *idea of*

God, as appears from the whole account, is at the bottom of the conception, can no longer be *identical* with the days of the creature, is to be inferred beforehand with the greatest probability from the purity of that idea of God, and is even expressly confirmed by special evidences in the record itself. We have to mention no less than four of them.

The days of creation present themselves *as days of God*, which as such *differ from the creative days of earth* by the fact that with them the *day* and the *work of the day* are absolutely identical. In the creative days, the day and the work of the day are always different from one another; the days come and go as temporal frames which include everything that happens during these days, whether we know it or not. Now we may turn our attention to and mention ever so many works of an earthly day: there always happen innumerable other things which also belong within the frame of that day and which are only not observed by us. It is quite another thing with those Biblical days of creation: here the day *begins* with the beginning of the day's work; it *exists* and *passes on* single and alone in the course of the work of the day, and it comes to an end when the day's work is completed, and the work of the following day begins: it comes to an end with "evening and morning."

We also lay some stress, though not very much, upon the fact that, in the account, that which makes and regulates the *earthly* day is created not before the fourth day of creation, Genesis I, 14: "And God said, Let there be lights in the firmament of the heaven *to divide the day from the night*; and let them be for signs and for seasons, and *for days* and years." We admit that if we were obliged for other reasons to suppose that the author of the account took the days of creation as common earthly days of twenty-four hours, we must and should find it possible that the author had been able to suppose the existence and the course of such earthly days even *before* the creation of sun, moon, and stars; for he certainly could not yet have the scientific perception that the sun with its light and the rotation of the earth were the only cause of an earthly day. But it is easier and more natural for us to bring that passage, Genesis I, 14, into accord with the conception that the days of creation are divine days which, as such, are different from creative days, and on one of which God also created that which originates creative days.

Another evidence in the account is of still greater importance for our conception of days. These days of creation in the Biblical record *have no night*. The account closes the work of each day with the words: "*And the evening and the morning were the first day*," "*the second day*," etc. Now, if we have to suppose that the author took these days as common earthly days, it would be quite impossible to understand why, after having mentioned at the close of the day's work that it now became evening, he omits the long night of twelve hours, and, although not having said anything of the night, makes the morning which follows the latter, the end of the preceding day; and why he does not say, "and it became evening" and "it became *night*, the first day," etc. We then could not avoid the question: what, according to the conception of the author, did God do in these six nights of his week of creation? But if we suppose that the author took the days as days of God, and therefore, in his conception of the days of creation, elevated the same above the common earthly days of the creature, and so represented them to himself as he alone, through his idea of God, thought he might venture to do, then that mode of expression, so exceedingly strange under all other suppositions, appears very simple and natural to us. For the author did not mention a night, because these days simply had no night; and they had none, because as days of God they *could* have none—because with God there is no night; because the rest of God, as the seventh day shows, is only a day of rest and not a night of rest. And the author saw the morning immediately following the evening of his divine day of creation, and recognized in this morning together with the evening immediately preceding it, the close of the day, because the accomplishment of the day's work (evening) already contained in itself the preparation of the following day's work, or at least pointed to the coming of the latter.

Finally, the fact that, according to the Biblical account, *the seventh day still has no end*, is just as decisive for us. The end of each of the six days is mentioned by the solemn repetition of the words: "And the evening and the morning were the first day," etc.; but it is not mentioned in regard to the seventh day. Now if, according to the meaning of the author, the seventh day had also had its end like any of the six preceding days, he would at the seventh and *last* day have had *double reason* for mentioning its end; and the omission of that concluding word would indeed be inconceivable. When Dillman says: "The formula 'and (it became) the evening' is wanting, because the account is here at an end, and is no longer to be carried over to another day, and because for that reason its designation as seventh day is presupposed in v. 2," we have to reply that, under the supposition of the days of creation having been common earthly days, a carrying over of the account to further days was certainly to be expected, even if from nothing else than the formula: "And the evening and the morning were the first day," etc. For then the human weeks could have followed the week of God, in which man, following the divine example, would have had to work six days and to rest one. The same commentator says (p. 24): "The author could not even have dared make a statement about the life-duration of the first men, if to him the day in which he was created had been an indefinitely long period of time." But, according to the conception of the Biblical author supposed by us, only the "day of

God," in which he was created, would have been an indefinitely long period of time (although we are not willing to identify the days of God with certain earthly periods of time); the earthly days and the earthly years, on the other hand, would have their existence after the fourth day of creation, and thus, according to that view, we could estimate and name the earthly years and days of all that which happened before the fourth day of creation, under the condition that we have, or believe we have, the means of estimating them. When Dillmann continues: "On the contrary, the author took these days as nothing else than days," we wholly agree with him; but add to it: "not days of the creature, but days of God."

By this long duration of the seventh day, we are obliged to draw still another conclusion; namely, that according to the conception of the author the six preceding days also must have far exceeded the duration of earthly days. This leads us to another Biblical analogy, whose direct power of demonstration for a long duration of the Biblical days of creation is, it is true, justly contested, but which, as soon as we have to assume for other reasons that according to the author the days of creation far exceed the earthly days as to duration, becomes a strong support of this view. For it is certainly not unimportant that in the 90th Psalm, the psalm of Moses, the mediator of the Sinaitical legislation, to the circle of ideas of which that account of the creation so entirely belongs, the thought is expressed which is also taken up in the second letter of St. Peter, with its developed cosmological conceptions: namely, the thought "that one day *is* with the Lord as a thousand years, and a thousand years as one day."

With that exegesis of the seventh day as one still remaining up to the present, we are in clear accord with the more developed theology of the New Testament, and with the interpretation which it itself gives of that divine day of rest. Jesus himself, in St. John, v. 17, puts aside a reproach of the Pharisees in reference to a healing on the Sabbath, with the words: "My father worketh hitherto, and I work." This answer only has a meaning in the sense: my father worketh hitherto, although, since the accomplishment of the days of creation, he enjoys the Sabbath-rest; and thus I also work on the Sabbath as on a workday. And the Letter to the Hebrews, in its fourth chapter, looks through the medium of the ninety-fifth Psalm back to this Sabbath of creation which, as a day of rest of God, exists to-day, and the entering into which is given and promised to the people of God.

By this whole conception of the Biblical week of creation, which appears to us *exegetically* much more natural and unconstrained than any other, we alone reach that conception which the author of that record *intends to* reach; namely, a conception really worthy of God, of his temporal relation to the world, and of the relation of human days to the divine days of creation; we get a foundation for the commandment to keep the Sabbath, the idea of which can be completed without disturbing the idea of God. The relation of God to the whole temporal course of this present world, from its beginning to its end, for the religious mode of contemplation of man who, as the image of God, looks to the creative activity of God for a prototype and an example for his own activity, can be comprised in one single, great, divine week, whose first six days last to the completion of the creation of man, and whose seventh day still lasts and will last to the completion of the course of the world—till the latter itself, and mankind with it, can enter into the divine rest.

From this religious interpretation, which we have to ascribe to that Biblical idea of the divine week of creation, it by no means follows that religion has to demand of natural science that it shall reach in its cosmogonic investigations the same succession in the appearance of things as we find in the Biblical account. This would be nothing else but an actual carrying of a pretended religious interest over beyond the limits of a realm in which the deciding vote belongs to natural science. However incomplete the cosmogonic knowledge of the latter may be, it nevertheless is at present established clearly enough to reject forever such a demand. Astronomy convinces us that it is entirely inconceivable that all which belongs to the work of the fourth Biblical day of creation, even the whole formation of stars and of our system of planets, *succeeded* the work of the third day, the formation of earthly continents and plants. And geology in its strata, which exhibit petrifactions, shows us that the relative Biblical days' works in reality did not succeed one another alternately in such a way that the one began where the other ceased, but that from the beginning of organic life the works of the third and the fifth days from the carboniferous period, also the works of the third, fifth, and sixth days, developed themselves perfectly by the side of each other. It would be an excess of refinement to identify any Biblical day of creation with any period or any complex of periods in the development of the earth or of the world.

On the other hand, for a Christianity founded upon the Holy Scripture, it is still not entirely without interest to compare *the results of natural science and the extent and succession of the Biblical days' works with one another.* For a declaration which undertakes to trace something which has so deep a hold on human life as the Sabbath-rest, back to the prototype of directly divine action, is certainly worthy of attention. Now if we wish to make such a comparison, we can only do it in exact analogy with the way and manner in which we compare the predictions of the prophetical word with their fulfilment. For in so far as the declarations of that Biblical record about the circumstances of creation have religious value of which we are to take notice, they as declarations concerning events of which man certainly cannot have historical knowledge of his own, come entirely under the point of view of the *prophetical word*; with the exception that they do not contain a forward- looking but a *backward-looking prophecy*. This is one of the most correct and fruitful thoughts which Johann Heinrich Kurz, in his "Bibel und Astronomie" ("Bible and Astronomy"), Berlin, Wohlgemuth, 1st edition, 1842, has expressed, but has fantastically misused, in that work, in general so prolific of indefensible positions; a fate which, as is well known, the forward-looking prophecy has had also often enough to undergo.

In the same manner as we have to explain the forward-looking prophecy from two factors—on the one hand, from the circumstances of time, the knowledge, the dispositions, and the characters of prophets; on the other, from the receptivity of their mind for the mind of God and the last purposes of his actions—we also have explained that record of creation from two factors: on the one hand, from the view and the knowledge of its time, and on the other from the receptivity of its author for a pure and living idea of God and of the religious relations of human life. And we shall also have to do likewise when interpreting it. For the interpretation of the forward-looking prophecy, we have behind us the experience of thousands of years, from which the following principles, of treatment and interpretation have resulted. As long as such a prophetic word is not yet fulfilled, so long, indeed, its meaning is and remains the object of Christian faith and Christian hope; but it is difficult and almost impossible to distinguish in it, what is lasting substance, and what is transient form. Perhaps many a thing is looked upon as substance, which in the fulfilment appears to be only an image and form; and perhaps many a thing as form, which in the fulfilment shows itself as a more concrete reality than we had supposed. And it would even be psychologically a violent assumption, if we should presuppose in the mind of the prophet a still greater knowledge of the future course of things, than that which he expresses; or if we should separate him in his worldly knowledge, and even in the form of his prophetic utterances, from the views and limits of his time. But by far the most fruitless effort of all would be to construct beforehand out of his words the particulars of the historical course of the future. Attempts of this kind have been defeated whenever they have been made. But if the fulfilment of such a prophetic word has once taken place, it is a joy and a strengthening of faith to all following generations, and even after the final fulfilment of all prophecy, it will still be a joy to the children of God in their perfection, to compare prophecy and fulfilment and to allow the prophecy to be illumined by the light of fulfilment, the fulfilment by that of prophecy.

All this finds its full application to the Biblical narrative of creation. That which in the forward-looking prophecy is the historical fulfilment, is in the backward-looking the scientific investigation. So long as the latter was not directed at all to the prehistoric history of the earth, it was an audacious undertaking to separate in the Biblical six days' work substance and form from one another; it was and is still an unpsychological violence to suppose in the human author of the narrative all possible knowledge of psychical and scientific secrets, and to lift him above the child-like views of his time concerning the things of this world. But it was by far the most fruitless undertaking to construct in detail from his words a picture of the real circumstances of the creation and development of the world. Attempts of this kind have been often made; but they have produced nothing but dreams. And certainly the attempt to control and correct natural investigation by means of such dreams would be like trying to correct well-established facts of history by the prophecies of a still earlier period, or even to prove them false. But from the time when natural science, as it is at present, began to pay attention to the prehistoric history of the earth and even of the universe, such a comparison has been possible.

It tells us, it is true, that the Biblical days' works did not follow each other in the course of earthly and cosmic developments in such a way, that the one began where the other ceased, but that they passed on in the long lines of their course, beside one another, and above one another. But looking upon their *meridian altitudes*, they nevertheless, where we are able to undertake certain geological comparisons, follow one another exactly in the same order in which the days follow one another in that Biblical record. The meridian altitude of the *third day* (for here the certainty of geological knowledge first begins for us) has to be looked for where the continents are formed and the vegetable life preponderates on earth: and that is the *carboniferous period*. The meridian altitude of the *fourth day* must have been reached where for the first time the covering of vapor and clouds of the earthly atmosphere permanently parted, and sun, moon, and stars became visible: and geology finds this time in the period which lies between the carboniferous period and the trias—in the *Permian period*, as it is called in England, in the *dyas* of the fossiliferous and of cupriferous slate and *Zechstein*, as we call it in Germany. The meridian altitude of the *fifth day* has to be looked for where ocean-life, with its sauria and innumerable animals, gave its impress to organic life on earth, and the air was filled with inhabitants: geology calls such a time the *secondary period* of trias, Iura, and chalk. That ocean-life preponderated in this period, is beyond any doubt; while in general geology gives us more meagre information about the inhabitants of the air than of the animals of the ocean and land. The flying sauria of Iura are still characteristic enough to leave at least the possibility that the winged world, which in value still stands below the mammalia, assisted in giving to that secondary period its proper type. Finally, the meridian altitude of the *sixth day* cannot be anywhere else than where the animals of the land became the most characteristic inhabitants of the globe, and where man appeared: and that is the tertiary period of geology, in which mammalia appeared in great numbers and variety, and at the end of which we find the first traces of the appearance of man.

We nevertheless do not assign special weight to the establishment of such a correspondence. The religious value of the idea of a divine week of creation is rendered perfectly certain to us, if we only find that it is reconcilable with a pure idea of God. That would not be the case, if we had to look upon the week of creation as an earthly week; but it is perfectly so, if the divine week stretches over the whole temporality of the course of the world. Therewith we can be satisfied. For we have neither theological nor philosophical nor scientific evidences enough to draw from these Biblical utterances any *metaphysical conclusions* in reference to the relations of God to the temporal development of the world. We should not dare to contest directly such metaphysical relations: for the human week, with its day of rest, is such an eminently fortunate and blissful invitation, the observance of this command is accompanied by such a striking prosperity in all life-relations of a people, its non-observance by such an evident curse, and, moreover, the idea of man bearing the image of God is such a fruitful idea, satisfying equally spirit and mind, that we have to remember the possibility that the institution of the human week, with its day of rest, is certainly founded on the real relations of the life-process of that creature which bears the image of God to the activity of its divine prototype upon the earth. But nevertheless, we just as little dare to attempt or to challenge the establishment of such metaphysical relations: for a theosophistic treatment of numbers seems to us no fruitful field for the promotion of religion—neither for the promotion of religious knowledge nor for that of religious life.

Still, however, the result of our comparison between Biblical and scientific interpretation seems to us worth mentioning for a special reason. It is true, we have found a succession of the *meridian altitudes* of the Biblical days in the same order in which, according to the Biblical relation, the days' works followed one another; but we have found in the *total course* of the Biblical days that their works in reality passed on in long lines contemporaneously with one another. Now, since that first part of our result—the succession of *meridian altitudes*—is the least we have to expect, if the counting of the days shall at all have an objectively real ground in the world's process, on the other hand, the second part of our result—the far-reaching contemporary existence of the different Biblical days—has an exact analogy with those prophecies whose partial or entire fulfilment permits us a more certain judgment of the character of prophecy and a more certain comparison between prophecy and fulfilment. Even the prophetic world knows of a divine day, which in the prophecies occupies an eminent and central position: it is the day of the Lord as the day of judgment and salvation. This day of the Lord also stands before the eye of the prophet, certainly not as a common earthly day of twenty-four hours, but as a day of God rising above earthly days and embracing an infinite number of them, although it also has its very distinct meaning which comes into the earthly temporality. But in the historic fulfilment, there happen along with it a thousand things which do not belong to it; for two-thirds of mankind that day did not dawn at all; and as to its temporal course, it had its dawn in the beginnings of mankind,—its sunrise took place eighteen hundred years ago, and its meridian altitude is still impending.

Finally, that even the piety of those who composed the Biblical records, and of all those who see in them the manifested evidences of their faith, assigns no religious weight to the succession of the days' works, becomes clear from the before-mentioned fact, that the second account of creation, which makes man and his ethical primitive history its centre, relates the creation of the inhabitants of the earth in quite a different order from the first one. We shall treat of this point again, and more in detail, for another reason, in the following section.

We still have to treat of the question as to what position the Holy Scripture and Biblical Christianity take regarding a *development in general*: and here also we have only to say that they are very favorable to such an idea. The works of the six days themselves are in their succession nothing else but a development, a permanent differentiation of that which was not separated before, a continuous unfolding of the more simple into the more complex, an always progressing preparation of the globe for newer and higher forms of existence, until finally man appeared. In the Biblical account of creation, the idea which forms the basis of every evolution theory, (namely, that the new which appears has its conditions and suppositions, its creative secondary reasons, in the preceding), is pronounced with special clearness. When it says: "Let the Earth bring forth grass and herb,… and the earth brought forth," etc.; "And God said: Let the waters bring forth abundantly the moving creature that hath life," etc.; "Let the earth bring forth the living creature; and it was so;" and "God made the beast of the earth,"—the creative causality also is mentioned in the clearest words by the side of and under the causality of the Creator, by means of which the latter had made creatures. The friendly relation between the Biblical account and the evolution theory even goes so far that the Holy Scripture, like that theory, does not permit animals to come forth from plants, although the latter represent the lower, the former the higher, and that, plants are a necessary condition for animals, but that even according to the Bible both kingdoms come forth from the inorganic of the earth. When treating of the creation of plants, it says, "Let the earth bring forth grass," etc.; and when treating of that of animals, it says, "Let the earth bring forth the living creature." At last, if science should once succeed in perceiving more clearly than now the origin of the organic from the inorganic, it would have in those words the means for a harmony with the Biblical conception.

Now, just as evidently as the Holy Scripture is favorable, in general and as a whole, to the idea of evolution, so certainly it seems to reject it precisely at that point where the whole interest of our question lies; namely, in reference to the origin of the single species. For here, when treating of the creation of plants as well us of animals, it is said in most distinct words: "*after his kind.*" But the contradiction is only apparent. As to the way and manner in which God created every species, whether he used secondary causes or not, nothing else is said than that God created every species, that the creatures exist in distinctly marked species, and that these species are not chance, but lie in the plan of God—that they are his work. This fact, that it was God who wished to create each species as species, and in reality created it, is just as firmly established, if the species came forth from one another and were developed in gradual transitions, as if they received their existence in some other way. As, in the fifth day's work, we find simply the words: "And God said, *Let the earth bring forth* the living creature: and it was so;" and "*God made* the beast of the earth,"—in precisely the same way God could indeed *create* single plants and animals *after their kind*, in such a way that one should come forth from another, that they should be developed from one another.

§ 2. *The Creation of Man.*

The most important facts which we have to mention, as bearing upon the position of the Christian doctrine of the creation of man in reference to the evolution theory, have been treated of in Chapter I, *A*. We have especially convinced ourselves of the fact, that the new, even if it has its secondary causes, and comes into existence in gradual development, is no less a creation of God, and has no less the full value of the new, than if it were created instantaneously. Likewise man also stands before us untouched in the full newness and dignity of his being, in the full qualitative and not simply quantitative superiority of the highest gifts of his mind, and especially of his personality, his ego, his liberty,—in one word, in his full image of God,— whether we have to look upon him as created in gradual development or as created suddenly.

There are two circumstances in the Biblical account from which we see that, although it is naturally silent as to the descent problem, it not only knows and acknowledges the connection of man with the lower creatures of the earth, but also expressly directs attention to it.

One of these circumstances is connecting man's creation with that of land-animals, in a single day's work. We do not lay more stress on this union than that of the Holy Scripture, although it emphasizes so strongly the dignity of man in his likeness to God and in his having entire supremacy over the whole earth, and although it could have found therein reasons enough for assigning a proper day to the creation of man, to which the whole preceding creation pointed, and whom the whole creation on earth should serve, yet in its account of the creation it evidently desires man to be looked upon in his connection as a creature with the animal world. Moreover, we should not overlook, in the Biblical account, that the benediction which God gives to the animals of the water and the air, at the end of the fifth day, is in the sixth day not pronounced over the land-animals—although they certainly are as much entitled to it as fish and birds—but over man. Of course, it is presupposed that the land-animals naturally partake of the benediction of man, so far as it can be due to them; the benediction, namely, of fertility and of increase. According to these indications and to the Biblical conception, man stands in still another and closer connection with the animal world than in that of mere supremacy over it.

The second circumstance to which we have to call attention, is the declaration (Genesis II, 7), that God created man out of earth; or rather, as the literal translation says: "*And the Lord God formed man (of) dust of the ground.*" It is of no importance whether the accusative "dust of the ground" is, as some say, a mere appositive, or, as others explain it, the accusative of matter. When the account calls man dust of the ground, or a being formed of dust, the difference is infinitely insignificant, whether the earthly matter out of which God formed man who is dust of the earth, was an animal organism or not; whether man was formed directly or indirectly out of the earth, and whether the forming demanded a longer or a shorter time. For that it did demand time, and that it was not an instantaneous creation, is implied in the expression "to form."

We call attention to this passage for still another reason. The second account of creation, as it begins Genesis II, 4, and goes on to the end of the third chapter, is strikingly different from the first account, Genesis I-Genesis II, 4. It has its origin in that author whose book is called that of the Jehovist, or, more lately, the judaico-prophetic book; and who, among all those that have contributed stones to the building of the Pentateuch, gives the deepest insight into the nature of sin and grace, and into the divine plan of salvation. Now in this book, from the religious point of view so extremely worthy of attention, the account of the creation is given quite differently. Man is the centre of the account; that which does not directly refer to him is entirely omitted. The order in which the inhabitants of the earth were created, is not only not divided into the six day's works of the first account, and in verse 4 is not only directly taken as the work of a single day, in the expression ביום (in the day, in which = when), without especial stress being put upon the expression "one day," for ביום has become a particle; but this order is entirely different from the other. In the second account, the succession is the following: "first, man; then, the paradise into which man is placed; next, the trees (the question at what time the rest of the vegetable world was created is left entirely without answer); then, the determination to create also an assistant to man; next, the creation of animals; finally, the creation of the woman out of a rib of man." Now, although it is wholly beyond doubt that the two accounts had different authors, the question will nevertheless arise, how it was possible that those who inserted these two accounts in the Holy Scripture, one after the other, could so harmlessly put side by side and read one after the other these two accounts, so entirely contradictory, without being obliged to think that the truth of the one would refute the other. They certainly must have had in some way the conviction that the one account was consistent with the other. But such an agreement between the two accounts is only possible when we either see in them only ideal truths, or when one of the two shall represent the actual reality of the circumstances of creation, and the other rather their ideal character. In case we should have to make such a distinction, it cannot be doubtful which of the two accounts has more of the real, and which more of the ideal character. In the first account nothing is related which does not give direct points of connection in the real process, as we can imagine it. In the second account, we find many points which hardly permit a direct literal conception, even on the part of the first readers of the account and of the editors of the canon of the Old Testament: for instance, besides the different order in which the first account is given, the creation of the woman out of the rib of man: this account, when ideally taken, is so inexpressibly comprehensive, pregnant, and deep—when taken really, so perfectly improbable. It will be likewise difficult to believe that even the old readers of the account—at least those of them who looked deeper and were more enlightened—took with extreme literalness the expression, that God breathed into the nostrils of man who is dust of the ground, the breath of life. The third chapter has still other features from which we have at least to assume that the author did not at all intend to give importance to an extremely literal conception of it. Now, if the second account is the more ideal one, the meaning of it is: that man, his being, his aim, his primitive history, is made the centre of the entire description, and around him all the rest is grouped; while in the first account he appears to be more the end of the whole creation

—as he presents himself to natural investigation in the real process of creation, as the last member in the chain, not as the centre in a circle or a star. Now if that is the case, if the second account of creation, having man as its centre, is the more ideal, then we certainly must not overlook the fact that in the ideal account man is called dust of the ground. Then the nature of dust also belongs, from the ideal point of view, so necessarily to the nature of man that the question, whether the connection of this man who is dust of the ground, with this ground, is brought about through the form of a preceding animal organism, or not, is no longer of importance. Therefore, if we oppose the animal ancestry of man for the general reasons that we do not wish to descend from something lower, that lower nevertheless is present as dust of the ground. And if we oppose such a pedigree on account of the ugliness and wickedness which exist in the animal world, we have to point to the fact that, on the one hand, mankind also has stains which are uglier than those which disfigure the wildest beast of prey, and that, on the other hand, the animal world shows features which are so noble that no man need be ashamed of them. It is certainly a right feeling to which Darwin, in his "Descent of Man," gives expression, when he says: "For my own part, I would as soon be descended from that heroic little monkey who braved his dreaded enemy in order to save the life of his keeper, or from that old baboon who, descending from the mountains, carried away in triumph his young comrade from a crowd of astonished dogs, as from a savage who delights to torture his enemies, offers up bloody sacrifices, practices infanticide without remorse, treats his wives like slaves, knows no decency, and is haunted by the grossest superstitions." We have but to add:—if only the coming forth from the creative hand of God, the creation in his own image, the communion with Him and being a child of His, are preserved. And that all this can be preserved, even when adopting descent and evolution, we have seen from repeated considerations.

But we have to draw still another conclusion from the difference between the two accounts of creation. If the succession, in which the inhabitants of the earth appear in the first account, is so entirely different from that in the second, as it evidently is, we have necessarily either to give up the historical reality of the one or of the other account, or of both, or to suppose that the creation of the inhabitants of the earth took place in a way and manner which makes it possible to perceive a *real* connection of the succession in the first account, *as well as* in that of the second, with the real processes of creation. Now we do not at all intend to argue with those who choose the first part of the dilemma; we ourselves join with them, and believe that salvation does not depend upon the objective reality of that succession, nor the possession of salvation on the faith of such reality. But we leave to the consideration of those who, in their religious convictions, think themselves bound to the objective reality of both accounts, the following thoughts: If not only ideal depth, but also a connection with the empirical and historical reality of the process of creation, is to be assigned to the succession of the first account as well as to that of the second, it is only possible by assuming a descent—namely, that man, *e.g.*, may be called in one sense the first of creatures, inasmuch as with the first organism that was already given which was afterwards developed into man, and inasmuch as all which was otherwise created and developed as aspecial species, was only present on account of that aim; and that man in another, in the merely empirico-historical sense, is still also the last of creatures. Thus, then, the advocates of descent would find themselves in the unaccustomed position, equally surprising to friend and foe, of being in a much more friendly relation to the Biblical belief in revealed religion than their opponents. We should see the apparent discords not only between Scripture and nature, but also between account and account, dissolved into harmony, and above the double relation of the two accounts we should see the morphological ideas of Oken and Göthe, the ideas of types of Cuvier, Agassiz, and Owen, the laws of development of K. E. von Baer, and finally the ideas of descent of Lamarck and Darwin, reach a friendly hand to one another. And even the old joys of a teleological view of nature, adorned indeed with queue and wig, but at present rejected with too much disdain, even if they are called ichthyo-teleological and insecto-teleological, would attain in this reconciliation their modest, subordinate place. Moreover, we should then have the satisfaction of seeing again that a religiousness which in its own realm gives absolutely free play to natural investigation, and does not find it beneath its dignity to learn from natural science, can on that account retain its own autonomy in its own realm much more uncontestedly; and that, as it seems to us in the present case, it can go much farther in the use which it makes of its autonomy and in the extension of the revealed character of its religious records to physical processes and circumstances, than is either necessary or safe, and that it nevertheless is rewarded for keeping peace with natural science by more rich, more living, and more correct glimpses into the harmony between the word of God and the work of God, than would be the case with a religiousness which, without regard to natural science, weaves its cosmogonies from the Holy Scripture alone.

§ 3. *The Primitive Condition of Man: Paradise, the Fall of Man, and Primitive History.*

After the Holy Scripture has narrated the creation of man in two accounts, the second of them gives us a continuation in the well-known account of Paradise and of the fall of man, with its consequences; and the further development, of the Biblical doctrine, as well as of Christian theology, has also taken the substance and quintessence of these narratives into its representation of the Christian truths of salvation.

We shall not throw any obstacles in the way of bringing about an understanding between the Darwinian views and the Biblical primitive history, by acknowledging the justice of the view that Christian piety might in some way contain in itself the demand that also the form in which the facts of truth in Genesis III are given to us, has historical reality. He who makes this demand has only his own short-sightedness and imprudence to blame, if he also loses the substance with the form, the figurative nature of which can be shown to him only too certainly. We acknowledge it as a real providence of God, which intends faithfully to guard believing man against a senseless and slavish adherence to the letter, and against grounding his means of salvation upon insecure foundations, that at the grand and venerable portal of Holy Scripture two accounts stand peacefully beside one another, which, if we penetrate through the form into their substance, complete one another in magnificent and profound harmony, but which, if we look upon the form as their substance, so diametrically contradict each other that we cannot do anything else but reject the one or the other, or, still more logically, both. We think that this hint is strong enough to be understood, and bears, like all bowing before truth and its power of conviction, rich fruit not only for our knowledge, but also for the purity, certainty, and richness of our religiousness. We shall not lose by this acknowledgment the character of revelation and the impression of the truth of these Biblical records, but shall be able through them, and through them alone, to gain and perceive it. It is true, the first account, and still more the second—the account of the creation and of the primitive history of man—has in its external form an exceedingly close relationship to the poetical myths of the ancient nations of the Orient; but its difference does not consist essentially in the form—although this too, being the form of a true and correct substance, shows differences enough from these heathen myths—but consists in the substance itself. These heathen myths certainly contain many beautiful, deep, and true factors, but always, besides, fundamental ideas which we have to reject as half-true or wholly erroneous: sometimes a dualistic conception of God and the world, sometimes a materialization of the divine, the spiritual, and the ethical, sometimes fatalistic and sometimes magic elements in great number. These Biblical representations, on the other hand, certainly appear to us still in a picturesque form which is analogous to that formation of myth; for it really seems to be the only form in which the mind of man, in his first epoch of life, was able to perceive and represent supernatural and ethical truth, as we are to-day able to represent the highest relations of our mind to the supernatural and the ethical only in pictures and parables; but the Biblical representations offer us, under this plastic covering, a substance which, in view of the most extensive criticism, of the deepest speculation, and of the most enlightened and practically most successful piety, is still established as the purest, the most correct, and the most fruitful representation of the nature of God, and of the ethical nature and the ethical history of man.

Moreover, we shall not make it difficult to bring about an understanding between the Darwinian theories and the Biblical doctrine, by supporting the other view taught by the Holy Scripture—that death came into the animal world first through the fall of man, and that the fall of man first brought the character of perishableness into the condition of the earth or even of the universe. There are essentially three Biblical passages to which those refer who think that they find such a view in the Holy Scripture; namely, Romans v, 12; Romans VIII, 19-23, and Genesis III; but they are wrong. That the Apostle Paul, in Romans v, 12, by the world, into which death came through sin, did not mean the universe or the globe, but mankind, is plain enough from the connection, and is only demanded by the difference of meaning which in the Greek, as well as in the German language, the word "world" has according to its connection. And in Romans VIII, 19-23, where he speaks of the subjection of the creature to vanity, he does not mention a certain time in which it happened, nor an historical occasion, as the fall of man, which should have given the impulse to this subjection; but he only says, in general, that it was God who "hath subjected the creature to vanity," and that he hath "subjected the same *in hope*." He who reads this passage without prepossession, can be led to no other idea than to this: that God has subjected the creature to the law of vanity from the very beginning of creation—not forever, but from the very beginning—with the intention that he shall also celebrate his transfiguration and deliverance from the yoke of perishableness, together with the perfection of mankind, and with the manifestation and transfiguration of the children of God. And even the curse of the ground (Genesis III, 17) is no cursing of the universe, or of the globe and its creatures, but only a cursing of *the ground*; and of this not on its own account, but only in its relation, as a means of subsistence, to man, and in opposition to the exemption from labor which his life hitherto had, and to the agreeableness of his means of support in paradise.

After having thus rejected these two perversions of the Biblical doctrine, there remains to us as an established substance of the latter, and as an essential part of Christian dogmatics, so far as it may come into contact with the *Darwinian* views, at least the following: Man was originally created by God, good and happy. To his goodness there also belonged the possibility of having a sinless development, as he ought to have had; and to his happiness there also belonged a life amid surroundings wholly corresponding to him, and the possibility of obtaining exemption from death and all evils by way of a self- controlling submission to God, which resists temptation. We purposely express ourselves thus. For the Biblical primitive history does not say that man was *created* with exemption from the law of death, but that the latter must have been *granted* to him as a reward for his submission: the tree of life stood *by the side of* the tree of the knowledge of good and evil, and only the eating of the fruit of the tree of life, by avoiding the eating of the forbidden fruit, should have given to man that immortality which he forfeited by disobedience. Man became disobedient, and, in consequence of it, subject to death; the harmony between man and his surroundings disappeared; the earth became to him a place of labor and of death; and now began for man his historical development as a web of guilt, of punishment, and of education and redeeming mercy.

Now, in the presence of this Biblical view, the question comes up first of all: is a view according to which man should have been able and obliged to take a sinless development, and, in case he had taken it, should have been exempt from the fate of death and of the ills preceding it, and endowed with immortality as to body and soul—is such a view in any way reconcilable with the Darwinian ideas of development, according to which man came forth from the series of lower organisms, subject to death?

We could avoid answering this question by a deduction similar to that which we drew in Chap. I, § 3, when treating of the question of the reconcilableness of the idea of evolution with theism, but of which we likewise made no use. We could show that in this question no other difficulties present themselves to the religious consciousness, than such as existed long before the appearance of the Darwinian theories and were overcome by pious consciousness and religious reasoning. For a difficulty entirely similar to that which here appears to us, when looking upon the whole human *species* and its origin, stood before us heretofore, when looking upon the human *individual* and his origin. From the standpoint of Biblical Christianity, we ascribe to the human individual an immortality of the soul and a coming resurrection of the body; but we do not to the human embryo at the beginning of its development in the womb. Now we know that the development of man from that embryo to perfect man is wholly gradual; that we cannot observe and predicate of any organ, of any quality, of any activity of body, soul, or mind, exactly the moment when it comes into existence; and that therefore we cannot give the moment when we could assume that something so decidedly great and new as the immortality of the soul and the prospect of a resurrection of the body, begins for the human individual. Although we know all this, nevertheless in all discussions of the question whether we have to hope for an immortality of the soul and a resurrection of the body, the gradual development has hardly ever been, so far as we know, a weight—in any case, never the decisive weight—in the balance *against* the supposition of an immortality. If we can look upon the idea of an immortality of the soul and of a resurrection of the body as reconcilable with the fact, that the human individual was only developed gradually out of something which was still soulless and perishable, we also have to look upon the other fact as reconcilable with the gradual development of the whole *species*; namely, that man, if he should have developed himself without sin, would have reached an immortality of body and soul. But we shall not enter this path which would lead us around the whole question. For the objection might be made, that the scientific and philosophic impossibility of assuming an eternal duration of an individual that originated in time, has, indeed, always been pointed out, and only the *assertion*, not the *proof*, of the contrary has been opposed to it; but that Darwinism puts this impossibility into new and full light. Therefore, if we wish to reach a certain basis for our conviction, nothing else remains to us but to enter upon that question wholly and exclusively from Darwinian premises.

Now these premises, indeed, indicate to us a *development* of things, but a development of such a kind that there appears to us something new, and always new in a rising line. The rising of this line of development consists in the fact that the spiritual comes forth from the natural in permanent progress and in always higher development: that mind vanquishes matter. The first new thing which meets us in the development of the globe, is the organic and life; the second, sensation and consciousness; the third, self-consciousness and free-will. Now let us once suppose imaginary human spectators of every first appearance of these phenomena. Would he who thus far had only known inorganic phenomena and processes, have dared, before the appearance of life, to utter the proposition: matter can also become living and live? And who would have dared to suggest the further doctrine: matter can also feel and get a consciousness of things? Finally, who would have dared even to say: matter can also become a self-conscious and free personality? To every person who would have pronounced such dreams of the future, there would have been opposed, apparently with full right, the inviolable mechanism of the inorganic world. But all this nevertheless took place. If something material can be led so far that a personality lives in it, that, with the assistance of this material basis, is able to perceive the ideas and the eternal, that can act in accordance with aims and designs and can set itself the highest aims, and that may even enter upon a loving and child-like relation to the highest primitive cause of all things, then we are no longer permitted to say that the material, of which the body of such a personality consists, could not have been subjected to the service of such a personality so far, that the latter could have vanquished the elements of the destruction of life in an eternal process of spontaneous renewal.

It is true, with such a concession alone we have not gained anything directly. For *in abstracto* everything is finally conceivable which does not contradict the logical laws of reasoning—even the basilisk and the mountain of diamonds in stories and fairy tales. But such an *abstract* conceivableness has not the least value for the knowledge of the *real*, nor even for the knowledge of the *really possible*. For in the world of being and becoming, everything in its last elements, forces, qualities, and laws, as well as in the last causes of its development, is something so absolutely *given*, that only afterward are we able to analyze that which is present, from our observations, or to follow from the given factors that which can be, or which under other conditions would have become different, and that we are not able to synthetically construct the one or the other in advance, independently from the factors of reality. If, therefore, that concession shall attain a scientific value, and if the conditional sentence: Man would not have been subject to death if he had not sinned, is to become an admitted and unassailable part of Christian theology, we have to look in the realm of phenomena, and in the course of that which took place, for *facts* which *prove* that man, if he had not committed sin, would not have died, and which thus change that merely abstract, possibility into a real one.

Now we have such a fact in the *resurrection of the Lord*. If it really took place, then it is the last earthly stage in the course of the Lord's work of Redemption, and then it permits us to draw conclusions backwards as to what would have become of man, if he had not been in need of this redemption, if he had had a sinless development instead of one with sin.

We know very well that in mentioning this fact we meet not only the opposition of those who contest a teleological, theistic, and especially a Christian view of the world, but also the natural doubts of those who defend with warm interest teleology and the ethical fundamentals and productive forces of Christianity, but who think it more advisable to pass over the whole question of the resurrection in cautious silence. The main consideration which hinders them from believing in the reality of the resurrection of Jesus Christ, is not the want of historical attestation, but rather the absolute want of any attested analogy in the other events which have taken place on the earth. What we commonly see and witness in the dead, is without exception precisely the opposite of that which is related about the further fate of Jesus crucified. Now we have repeatedly had occasion to point out that the want of analogy cannot at all be a proof of a fact's not having taken place, supposing it otherwise well established. Especially if a *development* of events follows aims, it lies in the nature of this development that in its course in all the places where we really and actually can speak of a development, of a process, things appear and must appear which were not present before, and which, even if they once appeared, nevertheless need not necessarily be repeated, except at certain times which correspond to the plan of development; namely, when "their time has come." All these are events which are wanting in analogy, but which cannot be doubted at all on that account. That was the case with the first appearance of organic life, also with the first appearance of beings having sensation and consciousness; moreover, it was the case with the first appearance of each of the thousands of species of organic beings: all these things, at the time when they first appeared, lacked every analogy in the past, and were perhaps repeated for some time, in primitive generations, perhaps not; at any rate, they have all ceased to have analogies within the memory of man. In an eminent degree does the first appearance of man want every analogy with what we observe elsewhere. We never see men appear on the stage of the earth, who were not originated by men; yet this event, so contrary to all analogy, did once take place, and stands without parallel and analogy in the midst of the series of events, so far as our knowledge can reach.

Thus the resurrection of the Lord must also necessarily want analogy, in case it is an event which really marks a station of progress in the development of earthly creatures and their history, and in case also its nature and its importance tend not to bring mankind, or at least those who believe in him who has been raised, at once under the influence of its physical consequences, but only so far to prepare the way for these consequences in intellectual and moral life-forces. And precisely such an event is the resurrection of Jesus, according to the announcement of the Lord as to himself and his work, and according to the development of this personal testimony in the minds of his first disciples, and also according to what Jesus actually became for mankind, and especially for Christianity. According to this testimony of Jesus and his apostles, and to this actual experience, Jesus is the Redeemer, whose work is to make amends for the destruction caused by sin, and thus to originate and establish a new creation in mankind which, from inner, mental, and spiritual beginnings, renews mankind, and becomes the leaven which, in long periods of labor, leads it to the goal of perfection; a perfection in which the whole creation shall participate—with which, indeed, mankind is inseparably connected on the whole natural side of its existence. But then it also lies in the nature of the resurrection of Jesus to be single in its kind, and without analogy, until that time shall have come in the development of mankind when the last enemy, death, shall be forever removed and overcome.

We quite fail to conceive how those who acknowledge design in the world, can avoid the acknowledgment of the resurrection of Jesus—supposing the fact to be historically established: whereof we shall have to speak hereafter. It is, indeed, quite impossible to speak of a goal of mankind, if annihilation—annihilation of single personalities as well as of mankind as a whole—is its certain destiny. Where and what is this end of mankind, if the last generation of the globe is to perish with the destruction of this globe, or languish and die even before that destruction, and if nothing will be left of mankind beyond the soulless material for new formations in their putrifying corpses and desolate homes and works of art? Where and what is this goal, if all which once set human minds and hearts in motion, and which stimulated the intellectual and moral work of the human races, simply ceases to exist, no longer finds anywhere even a place of remembrance, and nowhere has a fruit to exhibit, except perhaps in the mind of a God who once set the cruel play in motion, and now permits it to cease, in order to procure for himself a change in the entertainment? A mere immortality of human souls, without resurrection and without the perfection and transfiguration of the universe, is not afforded us by this goal, which we certainly need, if we are to think at all of a goal for mankind. For if all departing souls should be carried into another world whose only relation to the further course of the earthly history of mankind was in the fact, that the dead are always gathered in it; into another world whose only relation to the past of the earthly history of mankind should be in the fact, that it is divided into a heaven and a hell for those who reach it; if in this world everything should move on, without end, in eternal coming and going; and if nothing could be said of that other world than that everything there is different from ours—even that we should there have no possible points of contact with this world: then we should have nothing else but a gloomy dualism of the world for which neither our intellectual, nor our psychical, and least of all our physical, organization is in any way prepared, we should have in it no satisfaction of our noblest instincts, no goal to which we would be led by any of the guides who show us the paths which we have to follow on earth. Only a resurrection and transfiguration of the earth and the universe, as well as of a glorified mankind, show us such a goal. For this aim, for such a *real* continuation of life of the single personality, and of all mankind, after the long work of moral and intellectual development, all noble and worthy instincts of mankind are prepared—from the instinct of self- preservation up to the instinct of self-sacrifice for ideal purposes and the instinct of moral perfection and community with God. We find that in all the rest of creation, instincts and inherent powers are present to be satisfied. The naturalistic tendencies which at present control so many minds, are very much inclined to found their whole view of the world upon this correlation of instinct, function, and satisfaction. Should, then, the highest instincts of the highest creature on earth alone make an exception? Have they originated from illusions, and do they lead to illusions? We cannot refrain from quoting a word which Alb. Réville, of Rotterdam, has written in the first part of the October issue of the "Revue des Deux Mondes," 1874, on the occasion of a criticism of E. v. Hartmann's "Philosophy of the Unconscious"; though it was written only in defence of theism in general. We quote from a report of E. P., in the *Augsburger Allgem. Zeitung*, Oct. 27, 1874, which is all at present at our command: "When the young bird, fluttering its wings on the edge of its mother's nest, launches forth for the first time, it finds the air which carries it, while a passage is opened for it. Instinct deceived the bird just as little as it deceives the multitude of large and small beings which only live in following its incitations. And should man alone, whom spiritual perfection attracts—man whose characteristic instinct it is to raise himself mentally toward the real-ideal, the superiority of which he cannot sufficiently describe, should man, who obeys his nature, dash his head against the wall built of unhewn stones of unconscious, blind, and deaf force? Nature, indeed, has too much spirit—according to Hartmann himself—to indulge in such an absurdity; and the philosophy of the 'unconscious Unconscious' will never permit it." It is true, there is actually present in mankind, and in it alone, such a discord between instinct and satisfaction: man has in himself instincts which are opposed to sin and death, and nevertheless sin and death exist. But the redemption through Christ, and especially the knowledge of his resurrection, announces to us that this discord is removed.

Therefore, he who in general acknowledges that mankind in its development has had given to it goals which correspond to its gifts and instincts, has every reason to look about and see whether, in the course of human history, certain things have happened which point at such aims—indications which prophetically assure mankind, that it advances toward a spiritual and moral perfection, and toward an undiminished participation of all members of mankind in this perfection. Such an assurance is offered us in the resurrection of Jesus; and therefore, all who have not abandoned a teleological view of the world, have reason for *examining it with reference to the degree of its historical truth*. This degree is the highest which we can in general claim of any historical event.

In order to show this with such brevity as is necessary in the present book, and at the same time to guard ourselves against every danger of prejudice in the investigation, we shall for this occasion assume hypothetically that all, even the most extreme, assertions of Biblical criticism as to the authenticity and inauthenticity of the books of the New Testament, and as to the difference of their component parts and the time of their composition, are correct and proven; and see what then remains established. In the first place, it is an acknowledged fact, that Peter first, then the eleven apostles at different times, and between these more than five hundred "brethren" (*i.e.*, nearly or fully all who had preserved their attachment to the Lord till his death), saw the appearances of the risen one, a few days after his death; and, indeed, under the most different circumstances, and under mental conditions in which they did not at all expect any such second appearance. We have, in regard to this, the most authentic written evidence of the apostle Paul, in the fifteenth chapter of his first letter to the Corinthians: a letter whose authenticity no criticism has dared to doubt. This letter was written in the spring of 58: and Paul himself had already been changed from a persecutor into a believer in Christ in the year 36—*i.e.*, one year after the death of Jesus, which took place in 35; he went to Jerusalem in 39, and here everything was related to him by Peter, as we know from his letter (likewise not contested) to the Galatians. Thus the authentic information of the man, who in 58 collected the historical proofs of the reality of the resurrection of Jesus for his Corinthian Christians, goes back to four years after the death of Jesus, and to the personal witnesses of the appearances; as in that letter he also refers to the fact that "many of these five hundred brethren are still living." Moreover, it is an established fact, that the first written evidences of the evangelical history from which our canonical gospels subsequently originated, likewise contained accounts of the appearance of the risen one. Finally, it is an established fact that, from the very beginning, the whole meaning of evangelical preaching turned on the two facts of the death and of the resurrection of Jesus, as on the two cardinal points of all preaching of salvation; also that all the faith of those who embraced the Gospel was founded upon these two facts, as upon the historical fundamentals of the salvation which comes from Jesus; and that thus Christianity, with all its effects, which have unhinged the old world and diffused streams of blessing over mankind, has its historical basis in faith in the death of Jesus and his resurrection. This is our historical chain of proof. And that evidence which gives certainty to its most important link, on which everything depends—the *appearance* of the risen one—is the entire failure of all the attempts at explaining that appearance from a seeming death, from an intended deception, from a self-delusion, from a vision and an ecstasy, from a poetic myth; in short, from any other cause than, that the Lord really appeared to his disciples as the man who was dead, but who is risen and lives. We cannot follow Keim in all his methods of reconstructing the life of Jesus, and we believe that he is much too timid regarding the consequences which follow from an objective, real appearance of Jesus after his death; but we acknowledge it as a high merit of his christological works, that although he is willing to use criticism to the utmost, he has so thoroughly and strikingly shown the impossibility of explaining the appearance of Jesus after his death differently from the real manifestations of his still living person. It is well that Strauss, in his "The Old Faith and the New," declares the history of the resurrection of Jesus a *historical humbug*; for it may open the eyes of many, if the tendency, of which Strauss is leader, is no longer able to explain Christianity—the noblest, purest, and most successful religion which has come into existence in the whole history of mankind—otherwise than by calling it a humbug. With him who is pleased with this manner of explaining the most perfect blossom and fruit of the tree of mankind, we certainly can find no common ground of mutual understanding.

We have been led to all these discussions, by looking for something actual which should be able to throw its light back upon the earliest primitive history of mankind—a history which can no longer be historically investigated. We have found this reality in the resurrection of Jesus; and the light which it throws upon the primitive history of man, we have perceived in the conclusion to which it leads us: that man, if he had taken a sinless development, would also have been exempt from death.

The resurrection of Jesus throws its light upon still another side of the Biblical doctrine of the primitive condition of man: namely, upon that which is the religious quintessence of the Biblical doctrine of *Paradise*. As now the resurrection of the Lord is the beginning and the prophecy of a new creation on the basis of the old, and as we now hope, with St. Paul, that this beginning shall manifest its comprehensive cosmic effects, when the Lord shall manifest them in the resurrection of the "children of God:" so, in case of a sinless development of man, the beginning of this new and glorified stage of creation would certainly have been perceptible at the beginning of the history of mankind and in the relation of man to his earthly surroundings. But we are of course not permitted to make or to pursue such a suggestion at present, since a sinful development of mankind, with its consequences, actually took place.

We have no reason to enter into the discussion of another often and much debated question, which is connected with the primitive history of man; namely, *whether mankind is descended from one or more pairs of men.* We pass it by; because it has no connection whatever with the acceptance or rejection of the Darwinian ideas, and since it is not yet archæologically and scientifically solvable. There are Darwinians who think monogenetically, and others who think polygenetically; and there is still a third class—and they speak most correctly—who acknowledge that they know nothing about it. Besides, we can also pass by this question, for the reason that in spite of the important place which it occupies in the theological system of St. Paul, we have no right to assign to it, in the form in which we put it, the decisive dogmatic importance which it still occupies in many conceptions of Christian theology. For we cannot question the right of the natural sciences to enter into the discussion of this question, and to look for a solution of it. As soon as we make this concession, it necessarily and naturally follows from it, that we must no longer make the substance and truth of our religious possession, even in a subordinate manner, dependent on the results of exact investigations: for our religious possessions have too deep a basis of truth, to permit us to ground them on the results of investigations in a realm so dark for science and so far removed from religious interest. As to this question, we may hope for a future solution in the monogenetic sense: we may rejoice over the fact that, according to the present state of knowledge, the needle of the scale rather inclines in favor of a oneness of origin of mankind; but we must also be prepared to accept the possibility of a contrary result, without being afraid that in such a case we should have to abandon at once that religious factor for whose sake the advocates of a monogenetic descent might defend their view. This religious (and, we may add, quite as strong ethic) factor consists in the idea of the intimate unity and brotherhood of mankind. We must absolutely adhere to this idea; for it is in opposition to the particularism which, quite without exception, governed the entire old world, even its most highly developed nations, and which was only penetrated by some beams of hope and prediction in the prophecy of Israel— one of the most beautiful and blissful gifts of Christianity to mankind. This idea still contains, as ethical motive, one of the strongest, most indispensable, and most promising forces in the world. If this idea shall be a real and lastingly effective one, it certainly must also have its real basis in the history of the origin of mankind. But, we must ask, is the only conceivable reality of this basis a monogenetic pedigree, and do we lose this reality if science should once find that mankind came into existence not only in one single pair, but in several pairs, even in different places, and at different times? Even in such a case, the idea of the unity of mankind would only lose its real basis, if at the same time we were permitted to think also anti-teleologically—if we were permitted to suppose that that which came into existence, repeatedly, and in different places, had each time entirely different causes without a common aim and a common plan. If we think teleologically, we see the unity of mankind, also in case of a polygenetic origin, in the unity of the metaphysical and teleological cause which called mankind into existence; and to rational beings, endowed with mind, as men are, the metaphysical bond is certainly stronger than the physical. Precisely the Darwinian ideas of the origin of species through descent would show us in such a case the real bond which unites mankind. For then we should only have to go back from the different points on the stem-lines of the prehistoric generators of these primitive men, at which men originated otherwise than by generation, in order to arrive finally at a common root of all these stem-lines: the members of mankind would even then remain consanguineous among one another, not only in an ideal, but in a real sense.

Now that the idea of the unity of mankind was holy and important to St. Paul, is to be inferred in advance from such a universal mind. And when in Acts XVII, 26, he expresses this idea before the Athenians, so proud of their autochthony, with the words that "of one blood all nations of men dwell on all the face of the earth"; or when, in Romans V, and 1 Corinthians XV, he makes use of the idea in order to explain and to glorify the universal power of redemption of Christ by putting Adam and Christ in opposition to one another, as the first and the second Adam, so that he sees sin and death coming forth from Adam, grace and justice and life from Christ and extending over mankind; then we find this idea quite convincing and natural, and adhere firmly to the quintessence of these truths, even if we acknowledge neither in these passages, nor in Genesis I and II, the intention of God to give us a supernatural manifestation of the exterior process of the creation of man. Paul himself gives us a hint not to follow slavishly a literal interpretation, when he says, in Romans V, "as by one man sin entered into the world and death by sin," and calls this man Adam, although he knows that according to the Biblical relation, Eve was the one who was first seduced, and although he expressly points out and makes use of this priority of the sin of Eve in another connection, and for another reason.

Finally, we may here also take into consideration the contradictions which have come up by reason of more recent investigations, in reference to the *prehistoric conditions of man*, and which, especially in England, have been designated as the contradiction between the *elevation theory* and the *depravation theory*.

In general, this contradiction is looked upon as if a conception of the primitive history of man, remaining conformable to the Bible, could only be brought into harmony with a depravation theory, and not with an elevation theory; but certainly without reason.

The Biblical and Christian conception of the primitive history of man does not at all demand the conception of a gradual sinking down of mankind from a supernatural height—of a gradual depravation of our species—which many representations seem to assume. For, according to it, the fall of man had already taken place with the first pair of mankind; they were driven from Paradise, to long hard labor and development; and Paradise was taken from earth. Even the paradisaical condition, with its short duration, was deficient in all the various gifts of life which are a product of human inventive faculty and skill, and which can leave behind vestiges and remains. But what the Holy Scripture relates or indicates of the after-paradisaical primitive history of man, wholly corresponds to the idea of a gradual development out of the more simple and rough, which is demanded by the evolution theory in its application to history. That, even according to the Biblical conception, goodness and progress in outer culture, sin and intellectual stagnation, are not identical, we see from the fact, that by the Holy Scripture the most successful inventions of man are not assigned to the more pious Sethites, but to the Titan-like, rebellious Kainites. Likewise, the evolution theory does not at all require a constant, general, and exclusive progress of mankind in all its members. As in the realm of irrational organisms, so in the history of mankind; it has to assume the most various ramifications with progress, stand-still, and retrogradation. It is true, it sees in the nations of culture progress in an upward rising line; but besides, stand-still and retrogradations in great variety. It also sees in mankind in general a labor of upward rising development; but it also sees many hindrances of development, and many shavings which the work throws to one side. But exactly the same thing was also seen in every religious or profane contemplation of history, long before the evolution theory was born.

Therefore, the different views of the earliest primitive history of man, the theory of depravation and that of elevation, do not stand so opposed to one another—the former representing the Biblical and religious, the latter the anti-religious, view of the history—but the question as to the primitive history is not yet solved in that respect; the depravation theory, as well as the elevation theory, indicates rather the *directions* in which investigation has to put its questions to the archæological sources. Investigation, on the other hand, has free scope in both directions; and the primitive history of man shows itself to be a realm in which religious and scientific interest, opponents and advocates of the descent theory, can peacefully join hands for common labor. Up to the present, the investigations reach results which seem to fall now more into one, now more into the other, scale of the balance. On the one hand, the older the products of human skill are, the more simple they are; on the other hand, even the oldest remains show man in full possession of that which distinguishes him from the animal, and attests a spiritual life. The reader may think of the before mentioned sketches of the reindeer and mammoth (page 90). If we finally come down to historic times, and to the present, in order to try to draw conclusions from the comparisons of the remotest times of which we have historic knowledge, with the present, as to prehistoric times, we likewise find on the one side vestiges of the lowest barbarism in the past and present; but on the other side we find that the oldest written monuments afford a glance into a perfection of intellectual reflection and into a nobility of moral and religious views which permits us to draw the highest conclusions as to the intellectual worth of earliest mankind. The very oldest records of the Holy Scripture give evidence of this intellectual height; and even the royal programmes of Assyrian monarchs, which the wonderful diligence and ingenuity of recent investigators have deciphered from the cuneiform inscriptions, not only relatively correspond to the height of culture which we find in the ruins of Assyrian palaces, but even, when looked upon absolutely and aside from the morality of conquest which they indulge, are inspired by a nobility of mind, and permeated by a religiousness, which no potentate of recent times would need to be ashamed of. They have been made accessible to the public by the work of Eberhard Schrader: "Die Keilinschriften und das Alte Testament" ("Cuneiform Inscriptions and the Old Testament"), Giessen, 1872.

§ 4. *Providence, Hearing of Prayer, and Miracles.*

Before we enter into the special christological realm, we have yet to glance at the realm of the more common relations between God and the creature, as they have found, in faith in a divine providence, in hearing of prayer, and in divine miracles, their reflection in Christian consciousness.

It is true, we had to discuss the chief basis of an understanding in this matter when treating of the position of the Darwinian theories in reference to theism in general; but we have a double reason for entering again into the consideration of the concrete form which this faith has obtained in Christianity.

One reason is the fact, that faith in a special providence of God, in a hearing of prayer, and in a connection of the human history of salvation with miracles, forms a very essential part of the Christian view of the world and of Christian religiousness. All Holy Scripture is interwoven with assurances of a providence of God, going even into details; with the most distinct and solemn promises of the hearing of our prayers; and with the most emphatic reference to the miracles which it relates. The Lord himself not only found all these doctrines, and left them untouched, but he developed them in the most pregnant way, and brought them into the most intimate connection with the quintessence and centre of his doctrine. According to his teaching, "a sparrow shall not fall to the ground without the will of your heavenly Father; but the very hairs of your head are all numbered." He encourages us to pray, with the words: "Verily, verily, I say unto you, Whatsoever ye shall ask the Father in my name, he will give it you;" and he proves himself to be the Redeemer, through signs and wonders, and refers to the greatest sign which was to be manifested in him—the sign of the resurrection.

The other reason for entering upon the discussion of these questions, lies in the incredible thoughtlessness with which a great part of modern educated people, even of such men as do not at all wish to abandon faith in a living God, permit themselves to be governed by the leaders of religious infidelity, and to be defiled and robbed of everything, which belongs to the nature of a living God. By many, it is considered as good taste, and as an indispensable sign of deep scientific learning and high education, and it forms a seldom contested part of correspondence in newspapers, which have for their public a wide circle of educated people, that in referring to the inviolableness of the laws of nature they declare faith in a special providence of God to be a view long ago rejected, and which is only consistent with half-civilized individuals; that they look down with a compassionate and self-conscious smile upon the egoistic implicit faith of congregations who still pray for good harvest- weather, and see in the damage done by a hailstorm a divine affliction; that they criticise it as a sad token of ecclesiastical darkness, when even church- authorities order such prayers in case of wide-spread calamities; that they fall into a passion over the narrowness and the dulling influence of pedagogues who see in the histories which they relate to their pupils or put into their hands for reading, the government of an ethical order of the world which goes a little farther than the rule that he who deceives injures his good name, and he who gets intoxicated injures his health; that they give a man who still believes in the resurrection of Jesus, to understand that he has not yet learned the first elements of the theory of putrefaction and perishableness. That the adversaries of faith in a God thus express themselves, and try to conquer as much ground as possible for their frosty doctrine, is certainly quite natural; but that even advocates of theism should permit such stuff to be presented to them, and can keep silent in regard to it—nay, that even preachers offer it to their congregations as ordinary Sabbath edification, and that their hearers can gratefully accept it—is certainly a suggestive and alarming evidence of the rapidity with which, in many men who still do not wish consciously and certainly to be thought godless (*i.e.*, to be separated from God), their connection with the source of light and life is decreasing, and of how strongly the fear that they may be looked upon as unscientific and imperfectly educated, overbalances the fear of losing the living God and Father, and therewith the support of both mind and life.

Now, that this faith in a *special providence*, in a *hearing of prayer*, and in *divine miracles*, forms an essential part of Christian religiousness, we do not need to show more in detail; it is an established historical fact, and an object of direct Christian knowledge. On the other hand, we have still to say a word concerning that which, on the part of those just described, is so strongly contested; namely, about the scientific worth of such a faith, and also about its reconcilableness with the Darwinism theories.

In the first place, as to the faith in a *special providence of God*, and, in connection with it, as to the possibility of *a hearing of human prayer*, such a faith is by itself the inevitable consequence of all theism; nay, it is precisely identical with theism; it is that which makes theism *theism*, and distinguishes it from mere deism—*i.e.*, from an idea of God, which merely makes God the author of the world, and lets the world, after it was once created, go its own way. Now, the theistic idea of God, which sees the Creator in an uninterrupted connection with his creation, is in itself the more scientific one: for a God who, although the author of the world, would not know how to find, nor intend to find, a way of communication with his creation, would certainly be an idea theologically inconceivable. We should, therefore, still have to adhere to the idea of a special providence of God, even if in our discursive reasoning and exact investigation of the processes in the world we should not find a single guide referring us to the scientific possibility of such a direct and uninterrupted dependence of the world on its author. We should then have simply to declare a conviction of the providence of God to be a postulate of our reasoning, which is given with the idea of God itself; and would just as little call this conviction unscientific on account of the fact, that we are not able to show the modalities of divine providence, as in reference to the exact sciences we should contest the character of their scientific value on account of the fact that they are no longer able to give us an answer exactly where our questions become most important and interesting.

But the ways in which we are able to realize scientifically the idea of a divine providence are, indeed, not entirely closed for us. We have several of them; one starts from the idea of God, others from the empiric created world.

It belongs to the *idea of God*, that we have to think of the sublimity of God over time and space, of his eternity and omnipresence, in such a way that God, in his being, life, and activity, does not stand *in* time nor within any limits or differences of space, but absolutely above time and above all limits and differences of space; that he is *present* in his world everywhere and at any time. He who objects to this, can only do it with weapons to which we have to oppose the objection which the adversaries of the Christian idea of God so often raise against it—namely, the objection of a rejectable *anthropomorphism*. In contesting the possibility of the idea of an uninterrupted presence of a personal and living God in the entire realm of the universe, the adversaries seem to permit themselves to be daunted by the difficulty which is offered to man in controlling the realms of his own activity. The greater such a realm, the more difficult becomes a comprehensive survey, the more the human influence has to restrict itself to the greater and more common and to neglect the little and single. The more removed is the past which helps to constitute the circumstances of the present, the greater is the human ignorance and oblivion; the more removed is the future, the greater is the human incapability of influencing it decisively. Such measures ought to disappear, even in their last traces, when we reflect on God and divine activity. If once the idea is established for us of a living God, who is always present in the world created by him, and in whose "sight a thousand years are but as yesterday when it is past, and as a watch in the night," the final causal chain of causes and effects may be ever so long, and stretching over this course of the world from its beginning to its end; the single phenomena may be woven together of ever so many thousands and thousands of millions of different causal chains: we nevertheless see above them all the regulating hand of God from whom they all come, and who not only surveys and controls their texture in all its threads, but who himself arranged, wove, and made it. Such a view is not only more satisfactory to the religious need of man, but it also seems to us more scientific, than a view which traces everything back to a blind and dead cause, or even to no ultimate cause at all, and thinks it has entirely removed the last veil, if it pronounces the great word "causal law."

Now, while our *idea of God* thus tells us that God has in his hand all causal chains in the world, and its million-threaded web in constant omni-surveying presence and in all-controlling omnipotence, our reflection on the *world* and its substance and course also leads us from the *a posteriori* starting-point of analytical investigation precisely to the same result; it even leads us to a still more concrete conception of this idea—namely, to the result, that not only the *causal chains, in their totality and in their web*, but also *all single links* of these chains, have their force and existence only by virtue of a transcendental, or what is the same, of a *metaphysical*, cause.

For if we analyze the single phenomena in the world, we certainly observe in the activity of their qualities and forces such a conformity to law, that, in our reflection on these phenomena, we can go from one phenomenon to the necessity of another as its cause or its effect, and thus form those particular causal chains and causal nets in whose arranged representation natural science consists. But that those qualities and forces exist and act precisely thus, and not otherwise, and why, we are no longer able to explain. We can only say: the material and the apparent is no longer their cause, but their effect; therefore, the cause of that which comes into existence lies beyond the phenomenon— *i.e.*, in the transcendental, in the metaphysical.

This becomes evident in the *inorganic world* and in those qualities which are common to all matter. Such common qualities of the latter are, for instance, cohesion and gravitation. That all matter has the quality of cohesion, we can only say because we observe it; but that it must be so, and why, we are not able to say. This becomes still more evident in gravitation. Gravitation is so decidedly an action in space, that it appears to us, together with cohesion, as precisely the bond which binds the entire material world together. Each single material atom is subject to its force; but how and why, and especially how and why matter acts upon the matter *in space*, physics can no longer tell us, but refers us to a metaphysical cause.

This dependence of each single being, and of all its qualities and forces, on a transcendental and metaphysical cause of its existence, becomes most clear to us in the world of the *organic*, and especially in the transmission and development of organisms. *That* individuals originate new individuals of their species; *that* the fecundated germs, if the necessary conditions are present, develop themselves out of the first germ and egg-cell in continually progressive and distinct differentiations, each after its kind, into the full- grown condition, so that individuals endowed with a soul and intellectual life are also developed out of such beginnings;—these are facts which are continually repeated before our eyes, and men of science have not yet reached the end in pursuing the actual in these processes into its finest ramifications. But how it is that individuals *must* transmit themselves—that the seeds and eggs *must* have this force of germination and development—they have not yet been able to explain, and will never be able to do so. The word "inheritance," which is to solve the problem, is only a *name* for the *fact* which we observe, and for the regularity of its repetition; but for this fact of inheritance itself, we seek in vain a *physical* explanation: we are referred to a *metaphysical* cause. Thus, not only the *first* origin of life on earth is an enigma to us (as we have seen in Part I, Book II, Chapter I, § 3), but organic life itself, in its whole existence and course, is a process which, at every step, and in every place of its course, remains to us in its last causes physically unexplained, and refers us to metaphysical causes.

If we finally see in all these inorganic and organic processes a striving towards ends—and we must see it, as soon as we in general observe order, the category of higher and lower, and the appearance of the higher on the basis of the lower—we are, with all our teleological observations, again referred to the metaphysical, and still more decidedly to the goal-setting metaphysical; and a metaphysical which sets and reaches goals is nothing else than that in philosophic language which in the language of religion we call a living *Creator* and *Ruler of the world* and the activity of his *providence*.

From still another side, the knowledge of the world, even in a scientific way, leads us to the acknowledgment of a divine providence which controls with absolute freedom every process in every place and in every moment of the world's course. We see continually, in the midst of nature, and in its causal course conformable to law, something supernatural, transcendental, and metaphysical, acting decisively upon the course of nature; and that is the *free activity of man*. Every man carries in the freedom of the determinations of his will something transcendental and metaphysical in himself, which we can call natural only when we mean by nature the summary of all that which exists, but which we have to call supernatural when we mean by nature the summary of that which belongs to the world of phenomena in its traceable causes as well as in its traceable effects. The scale of life-activities, from the lowest arbitrary motions, from the impulses and instincts of the animal up to the highest moral action of the will of man, shows us in indistinct transitions all stages which lead from the natural to the supernatural, until, in the ethical and religious motives of man, we arrive at superphysical (*i.e.*, supernatural) motives which daily and hourly invade the natural, and in this invasion consciously and unconsciously use the forces of nature and their activity, conformable to law, and in spite of their metaphysical and transcendental origin, from the moment of their activity, join the natural causal connection of the world's course. This observation of an invasion of the physical by the supernatural, as it continually takes place in the free action of man, leads us in a triple way to the acknowledgment of an action of divine providence upon the course of the world.

In the first place, this observation shows us, in a very direct way, points where the free disposition of God acts determinatingly upon the course of things, and where this action becomes accessible to our observation. These points are the human personalities, in so far and inasmuch as they permit themselves to be influenced and determined by the will of God in the ethical and religious motives of their action, and, when these motives become actions, determinately act upon the course of things.

In the second place, this observation further leads, by way of two conclusions, to the acknowledgment of a divine providence.

One conclusion is the following: If there exist in the world free and intelligent beings which, through their free determinations, guided by reflection, decisively act upon the course of nature, and if these beings, on account of these very qualities of freedom and intelligence, occupy the highest stage among the creatures which we know, the last metaphysical cause of their existence must also have qualities which are able to produce such free and intelligent beings—at least the qualities of freedom and intelligence in the highest degree. And this highest metaphysical cause which produces free and intelligent personalities in the world, can at least be no more dependent upon the entire world, whose author it is, than those personalities are dependent upon that realm in the world in which they have their existence. We call such a metaphysical cause, to which we have to ascribe freedom and intelligence in the highest degree, God; and we call its free position in reference to the world, the government of the world, or providence.

The other conclusion leads us to the acknowledgment of a connection of providence with conformability to law in the actions of all forces and qualities in the world. It is the same conclusion to which we had to refer in Chap. I, § 6, but which now, as we draw from theism the conclusion of the acknowledgment of a special divine providence, falls with increased weight into the scale. It is the following: On the one hand, we observe in the processes of the world a striving towards ends; on the other, we know in the world itself only one single creature which acts according to aims, which sets itself its ends and reaches them with freely chosen means. This one creature is man. Now man can, as we pointed out in Chap. I, § 6, choose and use the means with which he wishes to reach his ends, only because he can rely on the conformity to the end in view and the regularity in the effect of all the qualities and forces of things. If he could not rely on them, he certainly could set himself ends; but the reaching of them he would have to leave to the play of chance. Now if we see, on the one side, that the only creature known to us which sets itself ends is able to reach these ends by virtue of inviolable conformity to law in the forces and effects of its means, and if we see, on the other, that in the course of the world ends are also reached, and that at the same time all secondary causes which lead to these ends act with a necessity conformable to law, we certainly are right in drawing the conclusion that the highest metaphysical cause of all things—we now say, the living God—has so prepared the whole universe that his free but regular and systematic goal-setting and end-reaching action upon the course of all things rests, as a whole as well as in detail, directly upon the conformity to law of all forces and their effects.

The observation of a free action of the human personality upon the course of things, once more leads us back to a reflection on the *idea of God*. For if we have reason to acknowledge a *freedom* of the determinations of human will—and the consciousness of ethical responsibility will be a proof of this freedom which cannot be invalidated by any contrary reflection—the question comes up: *how is this freedom of a creature reconcilable with the idea of God?* Far be it from us to claim to have found a solution of these last and most important problems of the human mind. For all meditations on them but lead to antinomies in the presence of which we dare not churn to remove all difficulties of reflection still less to solve the difficulties by pursuing only one chain of reasoning and ignoring the other. The way of science leads rather to mere *compromises*, and these compromises consist in the fact, that on every side of our observations or arguments we look for and adhere to that which results for us in incontestable fact or indispensable postulate, and that we adhere to all results or postulates thus found even when we are no longer able to trace their unity and harmony back to their last sources. Now if, on the one hand, our idea of God is established as a self-testimony of God to our ethical consciousness and as a result of our teleological reasoning, and if, on the other, is established the fact of the world and of its processes going on conformably to law, and likewise the fact of human freedom and its actions upon the course of things, and finally the fact of the admission of the human will and action into a higher teleology which is superior to human will, and which, in the history of mankind, of individuals, and nations, reaches its higher ends, now by affirming, now by denying, human will; then we have simply to account for all these facts as mere *facts*, and the scientific attempt at pursuing them into their inner connection is nothing else but a more or less successful compromise. We have to be satisfied with these indications, for the further discussion of them would lead us far beyond the task of the present publication. We shall only point out the fact, that precisely the knowledge of the image of God in man shows us the way to the knowledge of how it is conceivable that God can create personalities through whose freedom of will he relatively limits the absoluteness of his own will.

In all our discussions hitherto, the scientific basis of a faith in the possibility of an *answer to prayer* has been evident. All reasons for a divine providence, also speak with the same force of persuasion for the hearing of our prayers, as soon as the *idea of being a child of God* has become an integral part of our idea of God. And this idea—the idea of God as the father, and of a relationship of love between the divine and the human personalities—is so much a part of the Christian idea of God, that it belongs to its very essence. Only one consideration might offer scientific difficulties to our faith in the hearing of prayer: namely, if God hears the prayers of his children, in the course of time new motives for his action present themselves to him; now, is it reconcilable with the idea of God, that God makes himself in any such way dependent on that which first appeared in time, and on the changing moods of the creature? But this difficulty is precisely the same which we met, when acknowledging human freedom and its reconcilableness with a divine providence; and we have tried to indicate above the path which leads to its solution.

It is the principal idea which penetrates all our reasoning about the relation of God and the world—namely, the idea of a *teleology in the world*—which is to lead us to a correct conception of the *miracles* and their reconcilableness with a mechanism of nature and with the Darwinistic ideas of development. In the much discussed contest about the problem of miracles, clearer results would certainly have been attained, if one had questioned more closely what the record of the Christian religion means by miracles, and what position, according to it, these miracles have to take in the order of the world and in the divine plan of salvation; and after having satisfied himself as to this position, had further asked what position they take in reference to our exact science and our theistic view of the world. Instead of doing this, we have often enough seen friend and foe of the idea of miracles, as soon as the question was even touched upon, at once set to work with the insufficient conceptions of old rationalism and supernaturalism, and thus raising objections and attempting solutions which could satisfy nobody. Especially every inadequate idea which was put forth by the advocates of faith in miracles, was gladly accepted by its adversaries; for thereby they were furnished with a caricature of the idea of miracles, the tearing to pieces of which was an easy and agreeable sport to them.

The very ideas of the *natural* and the *supernatural* are a category which is to be treated with caution. When discussing the question of divine providence, we have seen that, with every free act of the will of man springing from an ethical motive, something supernatural invades the natural, so that in every normal human life we always see supernatural and natural by the side of and in one another.

The distinction between the *direct* and the *indirect action or invasion of God* is also to be used with great caution and restriction. For where we are no longer able to find secondary causes, who can assert that God no longer uses any? Where the realm of visible causes ceases and that of the invisible begins, who can exclude secondary causes? And on the other hand, where God acts directly, who can deny the concurrence of his direct presence and his direct action, or reduce the value of that which was indirectly produced?

Moreover, the often-returning conceptions of a *breaking of the laws of nature*, or the compromises which were made between a breaking and a non-breaking of the laws of nature by assuming a "supernatural acceleration of the process of nature," were still more misleading. In the whole world, infinitely many higher and lower forces act according to laws and order. In every process, a part of the forces which in the single case surround it, become active, and thereby hinder another part from its activity. But the laws of this other part of forces are not thereby invalidated or broken. When a man acts with moral freedom, from mere moral motives, the highest of the conceivable forces over which we have control comes into direct action upon the natural. But therewith those forces, with their laws, which would have been active if another motive had determined him, are not yet overcome, but only hindered from their activity in exactly the same way as one part of forces can be active and another not, where mere mechanical actions take place. Thus, in miracles, no law of nature is overcome, but only a force which otherwise would have been active according to the law of its activity, is for the time hindered from action by another force becoming active. Moreover, through the conscious and unconscious connection of the idea of irregularity and lack of plan with the idea of miracles, not only the idea of a God who works miracles, but also that of a personal Creator and Ruler of the world, in general, has come into discredit. For that reason, Häckel, for instance, when he attacks the Christian idea of creation, never fails to speak of the "capricious arbitrariness" of the Creator; and Oskar Schmidt also speaks of the "caprice" of the God of Christians.

With these criticisms, which we have made in reference to the treatment of the question of miracles, we certainly have undertaken only to characterize the superficial skirmishing which took place between the two opposing views of the world, but not the labors of more recent theological science. But that skirmish has made, like all superficiality, the most noise in the world; and since the adversaries of the faith in miracles endeavored almost exclusively to reflect in this manner, and almost ignored the deeper deductions of theological science, they succeeded in making the idea of miracles almost the most dreaded object of antipathy to modern education, and many of those who feel that the conceptions of traditional dogmatics are in need of revision, and religion and science of a reconciliation, endeavor to find that revision and reconciliation especially in the fact, that religion gives up miracles. On the other hand, *theology as science*, in its main advocates, long ago gave up these insufficient and misleading categories and conceptions, and established a conception of miracles which can easily be received into the science of the processes of nature, as well as into our reasoning about God and the divine. The first who adopted this mode of treatment, is one of the pioneers of more recent positive theology, and of a theology still uninfluenced by science— Karl Immanuel Nitzsch. It is certainly interesting to read what this man, as early as 1829, said, in the first edition of his "System der Christlichen Lehre" ("System of Christian Doctrine"), and also in the succeeding edition printed without alteration. He says, on page 64: "The miracles of revelation are, in spite of all objective supernaturalness, derived from their central origin, *something really conformable to law*: partly in relation to the higher order of things to which they belong and which is also a world, a nature in its kind, and acts upon the lower in its way; partly in reference to the similarity to common nature which they retain in any way; partly on account of their teleological perfection; and they must not only be expected as the homogeneous phenomenon from the inner miracle of redemption, from the standpoint of perfect Christian faith, but also by virtue of the union between spirit and nature, be looked upon *as the natural in its kind*." In these words we find the fruitful germs of a sound dogmatic development which the idea of miracles has found on the part of more recent theology.

Let us, in the first place, try to keep free from all preconceived, correct or incorrect, opinions, and ask how the miracles appear to us, when they present themselves with a claim to acknowledgment as integral parts of a divine revelation of salvation, namely, in the religion of redemption and its record. In regard to their name, they appear to us in the Holy Scriptures as amazing bright processes, as great deeds and signs; and in regard to their nature, as signs which are destined to call the attention of man to the government in grace and in judgment of a living God, to the salvation of redemption which God gives to man, and to the human instruments which he uses for that purpose. Now, in a view of the world which, like the Biblical, so decidedly sees a revelation of God in all that which takes place, in a view of the world to which everything natural has also, as a work of God, its supernatural cause, and everything supernatural, at present, or in the future, is transposed again into nature and history, not only all those above rejected conceptions of miracles lose their significance, but all remaining conceptions with which one otherwise tries to distinguish the miracles from all that is not miraculous, or to classify the different species of miracles, also diminish in importance, as do also all those distinctions of direct and indirect actions of God—the distinctions of relative and absolute, of subjective and objective miracles: and there remains hut a single inviolable kernel and central point of the Biblical conception of miracles, and that is the above mentioned *teleological character* of miracles. Indeed, we are not willing to reject all these logical distinctions and investigations as worthless: they have helped to render clear our conceptions and ideas, and they still help. But a deeper investigation of the idea of miracles and its relation to a scientific knowledge of the world may perhaps finally lead our more developed reflection back to the fact that we find the quintessence and the nature of miracles only where the pious people of the Bible found it. And this quintessence of miracles consists precisely in their *teleological nature*, and not at all in the fact that they cannot be explained physically: it consists in the fact that miracles are *signs* through which God manifests himself and his government over man, and actually shows the latter that *he* wishes to bring him to the pursuit of perfection by the way of redemption. Ritschl, in an essay which appeared in the "Jahrbücher für Deutsche Theologie," as early as 1861, pointed out this decidedly teleological character of Biblical miracles and the indifference shown by pious men in the Bible as to the question whether these deeds and signs can be explained naturally or not.

The profit which we derive from this reverting to the Biblical conception of the idea of miracles is by no means small.

In the first place, we help to establish the full recognition of that direct religious consciousness and sensation which is not only characteristic of the pious men of Scripture, but which yet characterizes all genuine religiousness; and this consists in the fact that the religious man sees *miracles of God in all that turns his attention to God's government*,—in the sea of stars, in rock and bush, in sunshine and storm, in flower and worm, just as certainly as in the guidance of his own life and in the facts and processes of the history of salvation and of the kingdom of the Lord. In this idea of miracles, the essential thing is not that the phenomena and processes are inconceivable to him—although certainly in all that comes into appearance there is still an incomprehensible and uncomprehended remainder. For a form of nature, *e.g.*, which turns his attention to a creator, is of course a miracle, even if he is able to look upon it with none other eye than that of the unlearned: but it even then remains a miracle,—nay, it is increased to a still greater miracle, if he has learned to contemplate and investigate it with all the auxiliary means of science. A hearing of his prayers remains a miracle, whether or not he is able to perceive the natural connection of the process in which he sees his prayers answered, or even to trace it back to the remotest times which preceded his prayers. The events and facts of the history of salvation remain miracles to him, whether the history of nature and the world offers to him auxiliary means of explaining them or not. The pious man, therefore, does not find the essential characteristic of miracles in their relative inconceivableness, but in the fact that they refer him to a living God who stands above this process, whether perceived or unperceived in its relative causal connection, and unites it with the course of things in order to reach his ends and to manifest himself to man. Now, in our attempt at a scientific reproduction of the idea of miracles, if we return to that Biblical conception, we see no longer in this just mentioned religious conception of miracles a pious sophistry which avoids the difficulty of the idea, or a child-like *naïveté* worthy of being partly envied and partly pitied, which does not at all see the difficulties and remains on the child-stage of Biblical conceptions; but we only perceive in it a confirmation and fulfilment of that profound and beneficent word of our Lord: "Verily I say unto you, Whosoever shall not receive the kingdom of God as a little child, he shall not enter therein." Of course, piety as well as science makes *distinctions* among miracles. The former separates the *mere products and processes of nature* which, through what is explicable as well as what is inexplicable in their qualities and processes, point to an almighty and all-wise Creator, and thereby become miracles to the religious view of the world, from the *historical events* which, by their newness and uniqueness, and by their pointing toward divine ends, manifest God and his teleological government to man, and calls them miracles in a still more specific sense than science does. And among historical events, piety as well as science assigns the name miracle, in the most pregnant sense, to those events which belong to the *history of salvation*, and, by their newness and uniqueness, introduce new stages into it, render legitimate its new instruments, or bring new features of redemption to our knowledge. Our religiousness has the greatest and deepest interest in this history: for it is the history of the leading back of man into communion with God by the way of redemption; and therefore the events of this history are precisely those miracles upon which our deepest religious interest is concentrated. But in spite of all these distinctions in degree, that natural relationship and that common character of the miraculous between the miracles of nature, the miracles of the history of man, and the miracles of the history of salvation, remain established; and we render a service to religious consciousness, as well as to the scientific conception of the idea of miracles, if by returning to the Biblical idea of miracles, as we propose, we make a more comprehensive definition of miracles possible.

Another advantage which we derive from returning to the Biblical idea of miracles consists in the fact that it preserves us from the *magical* and necromantic in our conceptions of miracles; that it allows us a *grouping of miracles according to value*, which corresponds with the idea of God and of the divine government as well as with the idea of miracles itself; and that in the presence of all single relations of miracles it summons us to *criticise* and *investigate the real state of the case*. For the nature of miracles does not consist in the inconceivable—at least not in the planless and arbitrary,—but in the fact that they call the attention of man to God and his government; and this leads to the reverse of all that is magical and necromantic, because the magical is unworthy of the idea of God and contradicts all the other self-testimony of God. Now if the nature of miracles consists in the fact that they call my attention to God and his government, an event will become a miracle to me, and increase its value, in the degree in which it refers me to God and his government, and especially in the degree in which it refers me to that government of God which is the most important to me—namely, to the action of God in me and mankind, with which he is bringing about his ends in salvation; but in the degree in which an event loses this character, it becomes to me an event without miraculous or religious significance. This gives a quite definite grouping of miracles according to value, from those which belong to the central manifestations of the divine plan of salvation and way of redemption, to those which lie in the extreme periphery of religious interest. It is a grouping which corresponds with the idea of God just as much as with the idea of miracles; while all other divisions or groupings of miracles according to value, which might take their principle of division and their weight from the greater or smaller conceivableness of the causal connection, from the greater or smaller difference of a miraculous event from all other events, are indifferent in reference to the idea of God, and change the centre of gravity in the idea of miracles. Besides, if these miracles are to be real signs to me which refer me to God, his government, and his ways of salvation, they must, in the first place, in order to secure my conviction, be real events and facts and not mere falsifications and fictions; and this point leads us to the duty and right of criticising and investigating actual circumstances. In presence of all Biblical and non-Biblical miracles, we have the full right and the full duty of using criticism in reference to the confirmation of actual circumstances, and where the latter cannot be established with certainty, the question is in order whether the related event is really of such a character as to legitimate itself as a sign of God and his government. In the preceding section, we have had occasion to use this principle in reference to the investigation of that event which, next to the coming of the Redeemer, offers itself to us as the central miracle of the history of salvation and redemption: namely, in reference to the history of the resurrection of the Lord.

We have by no means the wish to avoid *difficulties* which meet us, when trying to bring miracles, and especially the specific and pregnant miracles of the history of salvation, into harmony with our scientific knowledge of the world: only we can no longer admit that these difficulties consist in the inconceivableness or in the supernaturalism of miracles. For to the religious view of the world—which traces equally the explicable as well as the inexplicable back to God, which even derives the natural from the supernatural causality of God—neither the occasional inexplicability nor the supposed supernaturalness of an event can be that which makes the event a miracle. But an event in the history of salvation becomes a miracle from the fact that something *extraordinary*, something *new*, happens in it, which by its newness and its extraordinary character presents itself to man as the manifestation of certain divine *ends in salvation*, and can be explained *at first sight*, but only at first sight, from nothing else than from the service which it renders to the plan of redemption. Whether afterwards these extraordinary and new features can or cannot be perceived in their natural connection, or explained out of it, does not at all change anything in the miraculous character of the event, as soon as it has *once* had the before-mentioned effect. The only task and the only difficulty which meets us in the question of miracles, is to show that such extraordinary and new things really happen, and to bring the reality and possibility of such new things into our perception of the causal connection of the course of the world, conformable to law. But it ceases to be a difficulty, so soon as we acknowledge a teleology in the course of the world and a teleology in the history of mankind, and especially as soon as we acknowledge that teleology in the history of mankind which, by the way of the divine means of redemption, leads man back to God. Where there are no ends, nothing can happen which calls the attention of men to these ends; nor, indeed, can anything new happen; for nothing prevails in more absolute sovereignty to all eternity than the maxims *causa æquat effectum* and *effectus æquat causam*. But where ends are appointed and reached, something new also happens; and every new thing refers to its end. For each step leading nearer such an end is something new, and refers, as soon as we compare it with preceding steps, to the end towards which it strives. All ends to which the course of things refers us, are to the religious view of the world ends which are appointed by God; all means which serve to reach the ends, are means which God created and chose; and every phenomenon and every event which manifests this teleological government of God to our mind, is a miracle to us. Now this whole course of the world is interwoven with such new things, in events which manifest to us, now more clearly, now more dimly, the striving of the course of the world towards an end, because the latter is really striving towards an end. Even prehistoric times show us new things which, from a scientific and historical point of view, we have to place in the line of the course of the world; and from a religious point of view, in the line of miracles. The first appearance of organic life on earth was new, and indicated new ends; the first appearance of each single species of animals and plants was new; new, also, and indicating the highest end of creative life, was the first appearance of man. All these things we call *miracles* of creation; and we especially place the creative miracle of the appearance of man on a level with the greatest miracles of which we have knowledge, and use the name miracle for all before mentioned newly appearing formations, whether or not we are able to explain those originations from the preceding connection of the course of nature and its forces. Now, in the history of mankind, where the intellectual and ethical motives of that which happens become active, where also the greatest ends which come up for consideration are spiritual and ethical ends, where man himself acts freely according to ends, and where, therefore, human and divine teleology come alternately into play, the manifestation of a striving toward an end, in which religious consciousness immediately sees also ends and means of God, is repeated in an eminent degree. Every event which brings about a progress in the history of mankind as well as of individuals, is as to this side something new, extraordinary, teleological: *i.e.*, a miracle to the religious mode of contemplation; and this miracle is the greater as is more important the end under consideration, and the greater and the more decisive the step towards this end which the event accomplishes. Now, if we recognize the return of mankind into a communion with God as the highest goal of the general and individual history of mankind, and if we find in the latter facts which lead to this goal, then these facts are the great central miracles of history. As such, the facts of redemption present themselves with all that for which it once prepared the way; and, now that it has come, leads to full and complete perfection—and among them all, the coming, the person, and the history of Jesus Christ, stands as central fact and central miracle in the midst of all events in the history of salvation, and forms the central point of all religious interest. We see how unjust it is when one urges, as an objection to a belief in miracles, that it assigns to God arbitrary and capricious actions. We call the manifestations of divine teleology miracles. But striving towards an end and conformity to a regular plan is not arbitrariness or caprice, but the contrary; and the greater our estimate of the highest cause of all things, the greater will appear to us the conformity to a plan and to law of all which presents itself as miracles in the course of events. There is perhaps one objection which is about as equally unjust as the objection of caprice; and that is the objection that faith in miracles, in teaching a belief in supernatural things, lends to introduce into the course of events something which is against nature. But since miracles, as a sign of divine teleology, manifest ends for which nature also is prepared, and through which the fallen nature of man, fallen by sin, is again restored; and since to the religious view of the world all natural phenomena and processes expressly rank among miracles, the faith in miracles teaches the contrary of an opposition to nature. It is incontestible— and will become still clearer and more certain to us through all farther investigation of the subject—that the acknowledgment of the idea of miracles as a necessary and a justified part of religiousness stands and falls with the acknowledgment of a teleological view of the world.

We certainly do not indulge in the foolish hope that with the deductions of this section we should be able suddenly to win over any of the decided adversaries of faith in providence and miracles. For, as we have had occasion to remind the reader, the acknowledgment or the non-acknowledgment of God and his living government in the world is not the result of this or that reflection and chain of conclusions, but rather an ethical action of the centre of human personality in which God discovers himself in his self- manifestation. Now, if this centre, in the freedom of its decision, has once denied the acknowledgment of God and his government, then the intellectual actions of the soul offer themselves to this atheistic and anti-theistic standpoint, and build up atheistic systems in which the ideas of providence and miracles naturally find no place. Thus system is opposed to system, although the one is not able to overcome the other. For the last and deepest power of conviction lies, neither for one nor the other system, in its chains of conclusions, in its superstructure, but in its foundation, its standpoint, and its principles; and the choosing of one or the other standpoint, the theistic or atheistic, is an ethical action which precedes methodical reasoning—or if it takes place at the same time or precedes it, has still deeper motives than those of more or less clear forms of mere reasoning. But we believe, and we wish and hope in our modest way to have shown by our present investigation, that the standpoint of faith also has its logical and justified science, and that it is able to appreciate the world of the real more universally and candidly, and offers to logical reasoning fewer and less important difficulties, than the systems of atheism.

We have now discussed all the essential and direct points of contacts between Christianity and the theory of evolution. But a remaining part, still more closely related to the centre of the Christian view of the world, yet offers some indirect points of contact which demand treatment.

§ 5. *The Redeemer and the Redemption. The Kingdom of God and the Acceptance of Salvation.*

As soon as it is once an established fact that an evolution theory of the origin of man as a merely scientific theory permits all the valuable qualities of man, when they have once come into existence, to show themselves undiminished in their entire greatness and importance, and must so permit them, then the whole Christian view of the world, of the Redeemer, his person, his course of redemption, and his work, remains entirely untouched by all these scientific theories of evolution. Yet the Biblical representation, the orthodox perception, and the actual history of the Redeemer and his work, present us with some evidences which are rather in sympathy than in antipathy with these scientific theories. First, the long preparation for his birth, which began immediately after the fall of man and stretched over at least four thousand years, perhaps over a much longer period, the special preparation of his human genealogy, the selection, separation, and guidance of the ancestor and of the people of Israel, of the tribe, the family, and finally of the mother of Jesus—all these are manifestly just as favorable to the idea of evolution as they would have been to the idea of a sudden creation of man out of nothing, if Christ, the second Adam, had come into existence by a sudden creation. Moreover, the Redeemer himself was wholly subject to the ordinary laws of development of the human individual, and was, from his annunciation and conception, developed entirely like man in the long process of evolution from the egg and its still absolutely indifferent spiritual worth through all the imperceptible stages of development before and after the birth up to the full age of man. Likewise the result of his course of salvation, redemption, and entrance into the kingdom of God, underwent the same process of gradual development. It began with a few disciples, and was slowly propagated; it has to-day reached but a small part of mankind, and even where it took root, it sees infinitely many things by its side which it has not yet been able to penetrate with its leaven:—facts which have much more elective affinity with the scientific ideas of development than with those of sudden creations.

Finally, precisely the same analogy forces itself upon us in the Christian doctrine of the way of salvation. The work of the Holy Spirit in the human individual is nothing less than a new birth; its aim is the revival of the entire man, in mind, soul, and body. In most men, this work takes place by a slow process, advancing step by step. This gradual course is even the rule in Christianized nations; although a decisive change of mind often enough, though by no means always, takes place in marked epochs of the inner history of life. And in all Christians—even in those whose conversion takes place by a sudden awakening, like that of Paul—the transformation of the entire man into the similarity of Christ, and the full restoration of the image of God, is certainly a process of development, and must await its completion in the resurrection. This view is also confirmed by the Lord's parable of the seed, growing up imperceptibly.

Every believing Christian knows these facts, and judges and acts according to them: therefore, when in the realm of nature, which God certainly submitted to the free investigation of the human mind, he meets similar views, what right has he to protest against them as being hostile to religion?

§ 6. *Eschatology.*

In our discussion of the preceding questions, we have seen that an entirely neutral, not to say friendly, relationship is taking place between religion and the theories of development, which will continue so long as the latter keep within the limits of their proper realm, the perception of nature; and that a hostile relation takes place, and anti-religious attacks are to be guarded against, only when a disbelieving system of metaphysics, which has grown on other ground, in an uncalled-for way, tries to connect itself closely with the theory of descent. This is in an eminent degree the case with the great eschatological hopes of Christianity. The evolution theory so exclusively contents itself with the attempts at perceiving the causal circumstances of organisms in the *present* world, that it does not at all wish to, and cannot, express itself concerning the *end* and *goal* of the world and the laws and circumstances which may reign in a *future æon*, and that it gives free scope to every perception of the ultimate which might come from another source.

On the other hand, Christian eschatology is alone able to do most essential service to the evolution theory, in case it should be verified, by giving an answer to questions to which the evolution theory tends more decidedly than any other scientific theory—namely, to the questions as to *the end of the world and mankind*, with such distinctions as no philosophy which treats of the doctrines of nature, is able to give, although natural science itself demands the answer to these questions the more peremptorily, the higher the points of view are to which it leads us.

The world shows to every investigating eye a development, whether we have to take this development as descent or as successive new creation; and therefore we shall take, in the following discussion, the idea of development in this broad sense which comprises all conceivable attempts at explanation. All nature—its most comprehensive cosmic realms as well as the realms of its smallest organisms—together with the corporeal, psychical, and spiritual nature of man, shows a *harmony*, a *conformity to the end in view*, and a *striving toward an end* of its development, the denial of which will certainly not add to the laurels which transmit the scientific fame of our present generation to posterity. Now, what is this end? The answer which we receive from those who reject Christian eschatology, may be given by two scientific antipodes: by Strauss and Eduard von Hartmann. Strauss takes sides with those who reject all striving toward an end in nature; and his answer to the question (which still asserts itself in his system of the world), is: eternal circular motion of the universe, death of all individuals and of all complexes of individuals, even of mankind. Eduard von Hartmann, on the other hand, is filled by the knowledge of the teleological, but he rejects the hope of Christians and the end which offers itself to him in the place of the rejected end of Christian hope, is destruction—destruction of all individuals and destruction of the world. In view of such ends, is not the Christian's hope *the* answer which not only satisfies the deepest ethical and religious need, but also all heights and depths of the most faithful, most devoted, and most enlightened investigation of nature?

Finally, we have still another eschatological conclusion to mention and reject; a conclusion which is drawn from this theory by the advocates of the evolution theory. It opens the perspective into a future development of still higher beings out of man. *In abstracto*, we can naturally make no objection to the possibility of such a development, as soon as we once accept the evolution theory; but we have to object to the supposition of such a process *in infinitum*. For such a process would certainly be interrupted by the final destruction of the globe; and in case the mechanico-naturalistic view of the world should be right, this destruction would be only the more cruel as would be more highly organized the beings which should find their destruction in this inevitable catastrophe. Moreover, as we have repeatedly seen, a development *in infinitum* suffers from a self-contradiction: for development involves an end, and this end must certainly have been once reached. Now, if we have reason to assume that this end has been reached in the development of the inhabitants of the globe, by the creature being in the image of God and his child, and that it is also reached in fallen man through redemption and its perfection, then the idea of development, it is true, allows and postulates a relative development of mankind, so long as this takes place within the limits of the now valid laws of the universe,—a development towards the perfection of this likeness to God and filial relationship; but that idea of development has no longer an influence that would lead to the production of new beings which should be more than man.

With the foregoing, we believe that we have discussed all essential points of the relation between religion and Darwinism; and we now proceed to the last part of our investigation.

B. THE DARWINIAN THEORIES AND MORALITY.

CHAPTER III.

DARWINISM AND MORAL PRINCIPLES.

§ 1. *Darwinistic Naturalism and Moral Principles.*

If we consider the ethical consequences of a view of the world which, proceeding from Darwinism, permits the universe, man included, to be taken up into a mechanism of atoms—a mechanism in which everything, even the ethical action of man, finds its sufficient explanation—we certainly cannot perceive how such a view of the world is able to arrive at firm moral principles. If man, even in his spiritual life and moral action, is a mere product of nature, originated through descent, and if his whole spiritual life is fully consumed by these merely mechanical factors, then all moral principles are also nothing else than inherited customs founded upon those instincts which in the struggle for existence have proven to be the most beneficial to man. Then their influence is subject to continual change, always corresponding to the existing state of human development. As these moral instincts have displaced the former instincts of the animal predecessors of man—say, *e.g.*, of sharks, of marsupialia, of lemurides—so they must also expect it any time to be displaced in turn by new and still more useful instincts. And even in the same period of the development of mankind, the moral or immoral principles which have actual authority in each nation or tribe, have their full right of existence as long as they are not displaced by still more advantageous instincts. Moral principles in which infanticide, prostitution, and cannibalism have a place, are inferior to the highest form of Christian morality only so far as they do not hold their own in the struggle for existence, when nations having those low views come into collision with nations of higher moral culture; but in themselves they have full value and full right, so long as they attain the end of all instincts, and so far as we can speak of ends at all; in such naturalism, apart from human activity, the end consists only in the preservation of the individual and the species in the struggle for existence.

Under these suppositions, moral principles not only lose their objective and solid consistency in the mass of mankind, but they also become irrevocably subject to the arbitrariness of the single individual. An individual who either has not, or asserts that he has not, a determined moral instinct, or who allows it to be smothered by some other instinct which in a normal individual is subordinate, but in him stronger, is fully justified in his immoral action so long as he is successful with it. Every individual is entirely his own master and his own judge. If man is morally good, it may be the consequence of an especially happy individual disposition, or of an especially clear perception, or of happy circumstances and influences; but it is not the consequence of a free subordination under the authority of a moral law; for there is neither freedom nor an objective moral authority. The single man is but the product of a certain sum and mixture of powers of nature, acting of necessity, which may with him turn out fortunately or unfortunately. If, on the other hand, man is morally perverted, society may defend itself against his perversity; wisdom may try to convince him of the bad consequences of his perversity for himself and society; the effect of his perversity may make him sensible of the bad consequences of his actions: but there is no other objectively valid corrective of his perversity. If he is successful in his immoral action, and if he silences his conscience, this voice of the unobserved higher instinct in favor of the preferred lower—which unfortunately, as is well known, succeeds oftenest and most easily in the case of those whose perversity has become the most habitual, and in whom another grouping of instincts would be most desirable

—then the whole affair is settled, and he is absolved. Let us be understood correctly. We do not say that all advocates of mechanical or monistic ethics draw these conclusions in reality; we know very well that many a man is better than his system; but it seems to us inevitable that the logical pursuit of that naturalistic principle leads to this dissolution of all solid fundamentals of moral principles, and that it is but an inconsequence, certainly worthy of honor and of notice, if all the advocates of naturalism do not profess this dissolution of all moral principles with the same cynic frankness that is shown by many of their partisans.

We do not say too much, when we charge ethical naturalism with dissolution of *all* moral principles. Let us examine them, for a moment, according to the old but still fundamental division into duty, virtue, and highest good.

According to the principles of that ethical naturalism, there can be no *duty* at all, no objective moral law, binding absolutely and in general. The motives of action are either the strongest and most durable instincts, or, in case of high culture, conventional agreement of that which benefits society. In the one as well as in the other case, when the duty is neglected, the appeal is not made to something absolutely objective and binding, but either to the highest instinct (and to this every individual has the right to answer with a *Quod nego*), or to agreement and custom; and as to this, every individual has the right to make his reformatory or revolutionary attempt at change—of course only upon the condition that his attempt is successful, and that it stands proof.

Relatively it is easiest for ethical naturalism to establish a principle of *virtue*, inasmuch as we have to look upon virtue as the principle of individual perfection, and inasmuch as even naturalism, by means of the indestructible impulse of man to attain moral ideas, can postulate an ideal of human action. But on closer examination even the naturalistic idea of virtue vanishes under our hands. Virtue, as individual morality, is constituted of the factors of duty and of the highest good, which form the motives of virtuous action. Now a system of morality which, as we have seen, is entirely wanting in an objective solid principle of duty as the motive of action, and which likewise, as we shall see immediately, is wanting in an objectively established highest good as the end of action, cannot possibly produce any other idea of virtue than an abstract formal one. In ethical naturalism, even this form is subject to change. For, according to this system, not only the motive and end but also the form of moral action depend on that which in every circle of society and at every time proves to be the most successful form. It is the proof of success or failure which gives this form a certain traditional authority and a relative solidity— but only a relative one, and only until it is displaced by a still more successful form.

That, finally, ethical naturalism is also wanting in an objective end of moral action, in the idea and meaning of the *highest good*, is indeed not denied by naturalism itself. It is true it speaks with predilection of the idea of species, which man is to represent and to realize, and in that respect we can say that the highest good of naturalistic ethologists is the species or the idea of species.[11] But the idea of species is only the empty vessel which first becomes valuable by reason of its contents. Now, if we ask ethical naturalism the properties with which that idea of species is to be endowed, it certainly mentions properties, but those which are too rich; namely, it mentions the idea of all that is good in human life and the forms of human life, *in concreto*, the whole sum of all the conditions and acquisitions of the culture of mankind, art, nature, and science: the comprehensive idea of these acquisitions, the enjoyment of them, the work at them, is the highest good. Now, since no human individual can enjoy them all and work at them all at the same time, every individual, as to disposition, inclination, and circumstances, has to enjoy a part of them, to work at a part of them, and to renounce a part of them. And since each single one of these good things, however valuable to the individual, may be refused to or taken away from him, he has again to learn to be satisfied with that idea of species, however little it is able to offer him, when separated from the empiric possessions of this earthly life. Thus with naturalism the highest good is either mentioned in an abstraction which does not offer us anything, or which, if we ask the meaning of that abstraction, is instantly drawn down into the low sphere and the varied multiformity of empirical and individual life, left to the chance of individual taste, and confounded with that which is connected with the highest good only in the second line and in a derived manner—namely, with the formations and actions of life which strive at and serve the realization of the highest good. Ethical naturalism is not able to produce out of itself an objective highest good which is for each individual alike attractive, rich, and comprehensive.

Moreover, since ethical naturalism proves itself insufficient for the principles of any and all morality, it is but a natural conclusion that it is still less able to produce those principles which are characteristic of the highest representation of human morality known to mankind, namely: *Christian morality*. Ethical monism has no room for three ethical fundamental views, whose full possession morality owes to Christianity, and which gives to Christian morality its highest motive power. One of these is a deeper conception of evil as a sin, as a positive rebellion against the good; another is faith in a future absolute realization of the highest good in an end sometime to be reached by mankind and the individual and by means of a moral order of the world; and the third is the acknowledgment of the full worth of personality. Evil—to which of course no objective valid moral law, but only one conventionally established, stands opposed—is to ethical naturalism nothing but the action of an instinct which in this given case is not beneficial to man in his struggle for existence; the category of good and evil is entirely replaced by the category of the useful and detrimental. With the disappearance of the idea of sin as a transgression of the divine law, the correlated idea of holiness also disappears from the system of ethical naturalism. Besides, blessedness, complete harmony of the outer and inner man with the ideal in the state of mankind as well as of every individual, complete realization of the highest good for the whole as well as for the single through the means of moral work and perfection on the part of man and of holy and loving guidance and endowment on the part of God, is an aim which naturalism is not able to acknowledge, since, according to it, mankind and individuals continue in the ever-flowing stream of earthly incompletion until both reach their destiny in annihilation. A moral order of the world is an impossibility to it, since no holy and loving Ruler and Governor of the world, but only a blind mechanism, causes the course of things. Finally, the personality of man can be only perceived in its worth and in its full importance, when, in the first place, it is in the possession of freedom, of full moral responsibility; and when, in the second place, it lives beyond the span of its short earthly existence and may hope for a full realization of all its ideals of virtue and the highest good for itself as well as for mankind. Both these points must be contested by monism and naturalism. The place of freedom is taken by absolute determinism; even man is only a natural product, the highest which naturalism knows, but still no more than a product of nature; his personality and his life, bound to the material body, cease with the death of this body, and therefore never reach the ideal of either morality or blessedness. All ideals are and must forever remain objective illusions which came forth out of the power of the corresponding noble impulse, imaginative objective conceptions of the moral impulses.

§ 2. *Scientific Darwinism and Moral Principles.*

Whilst Darwinistic naturalism surely injures the moral principles, the Darwinistic theories are friendly to them, if they, as mere scientific theories, restrain themselves within the limits of natural science. But in no other point of the entire realm of contact between the natural and intellectual sciences is it more difficult to observe the boundary-line than in reflecting upon the moral self-determination of man; here natural science is always in danger of going beyond its limits.

In the question as to the relation of the evolution theories to religion, the boundary-line can everywhere be easily drawn in theory and easily observed in practice. For it is entirely natural for man to look upon the phenomena of the visible world on the one hand, with a religious mind, as works and actions of an almighty Creator and Ruler of the world, on the other, with his observing and reflecting mind, as products of natural causes. With this double view, man by no means feels himself dragged hither and thither between two conflicting views; he is able in his logical contemplation of the world scientifically to establish and arrange each for itself and both in their harmony, and has the full consciousness that the one, like the other, has subjective as well as objective truth. Or, if a single individual does not have this consciousness, he must at least admit that it is not Darwinism primarily which created the difficulty of this combined view of the world, but that the latter existed for man in the past as well as in the present.

But the relation of the *Darwinian* theories to ethical problems is quite a different thing. Here, in the first place, it is not the same process which is to be explained as well in regard to its natural conditions as to its moral cause. It is true that this double view deserves attention in so far as we can look upon every action which results from a moral determination also in reference to its natural side. If I have to raise my arm in consequence of a moral determination, then physiology and mechanism can demonstrate with it the whole theory of the motion of members. But this is not the question, when we treat of the relation between the natural and the ethical. In this example, the moralist examines the motives of my action, the scientist describes and explains the activity of the nerves and muscles of my arm, and as long as the scientist is not guilty of going beyond the boundary to which he is tempted, and which even now we are endeavoring to make clear, as long as he does not include the ethical motives in his physiological attempts at explanation, the one keeps himself neutral with reference to the other; each of them knows that he is operating in a field which at first has nothing in common with that of the other. In a moral action, *as such*, the question is no longer as to a process which is to be explained as well in regard to its natural conditions as to its ethical cause, but of a process which *either* has its ethical cause, and then in its ethical value *no* natural cause, *or* which even in its ethical motives belongs to the causal connection of empirical nature with its indestructible chain of natural causes and natural effects. Now at this point the scientist, as such, is always exposed to the danger of denying the first part of our dilemma and affirming the second. For, in moral action, something which is elevated above nature and its causal connection always makes its way into this causal connection of nature, and with its action and the effects of this action wholly enters into this connection: and natural science which has to deal particularly with this causal connection of nature and with it alone, is on that account nevertheless always tempted to explain everything that it sees coming into this connection, in *all* its causes (even in those which no longer belong to this natural causal connection), out of it. It is therefore always tempted to trace even ethical action which, with its deeds, makes its way and enters into this causal connection, but which with its motives stands above it, as to its motives, back to a natural causal connection; and thus to contest the independence of ethical motives and their principles—which independence is not dependent on nature, but, on the contrary, frequently contradicts it. Ethics must adhere to the fact that the ethical determination of the will has its origin not in a natural condition, but in the ethical centre of personality; although all the conditions under which the ethical motive originates and acts, belong completely to the causal connection of natural life, in which man himself stands as to the whole natural part of his being. The ethical realm stands above the natural realm, and shows its superiority partly by the category of moral demands whose imperativeness cannot have grown out of the mechanical necessity of the natural law, because it often enough contradicts the latter and carries out its demands in opposition to it, partly by the consciousness of individual responsibility which cannot be got rid of even by him who mentally establishes a system of determinism that denies responsibility, partly by the voice of the injured conscience which cannot merely be the dislike of a dissatisfied higher natural impulse, when it can speak of the same action for years, even for an entire human life, and even, where man has counterbalanced that once felt dissatisfaction of the higher impulse, by an oft-repeated satisfaction of it. In Book I, Chapter V, § 1, we tried to show that even Darwin seems not to have entirely avoided this danger of explaining the moral from physical causes; while at the same time we acknowledge that he otherwise esteems the realm of the moral, and that he even finds the lofty position of man above the animal world still more decidedly expressed in his moral than in his intellectual qualities.

But such an intrusion of the physical into the ethical is by no means a necessary consequence of scientific Darwinism—only an ever-present temptation of it. He who once admits that even by means of development something new can originate, that even under the full influence of the evolution theory there appeared in the series of creation entirely new phenomena with the appearance of life and the organic, and of sensation and consciousness, and still more with the appearance of self-consciousness and freedom, which phenomena no evolution theory is able to explain; and he who takes into consideration the weight of that other obvious fact that, in the origin and the growth of each single man, a time in which he acts with moral responsibility follows in gradual development a time in which he had but the value and the life of a cell,—such an one can explain the whole origin of mankind according to the evolution theory, and yet see something absolutely new coming forth with the appearance of moral determination. All conditions of the moral determinations of the will may be and are naturally conditioned, as, indeed, in this world the entire spiritual life of man is certainly bound to the conditions of his corporeal life; all preliminary stages of moral types which preceded the temporal appearance of moral beings, and which surround us still, those stages which appear in the animal world, may have preceded and prepared the way for the introduction of morally responsible beings into the world: the moral determination of the will itself nevertheless remains something new and independent—something which transcends nature.

If this fact is once admitted, then ethics also has free play to establish independently and render valid its principles. And then we have no longer any reason to treat of the relation of the different ethical principles to naturo-historical Darwinism; for this relation is that of absolute mutual peace.

CHAPTER IV.

DARWINISM AND MORAL LIFE.

§ 1. *Darwinistic Naturalism and Moral Life.*

Precisely the same relationship between Darwinism and morality, which we found in treating of moral principles, presents itself when we ask about the relationship of Darwinistic ideas and moral life in its concrete reality. He who builds a system of monistic naturalism upon his Darwinism, if he is logical, and not better than his system, comes into inevitable collision with concrete moral life; while he who limits his Darwinism to the realm of natural science, remains in concrete life in peace with morality.

That Darwinistic ethical naturalism also comes into conflict with concrete moral life, becomes evident from the joy with which the advocates of subversion and negation greet the new principle of the "struggle for existence," and make it the principle of their own actions and social theories. This is not chance sympathy, but is founded upon the nature of ethical naturalism. Of him who learns to look upon himself only as a product of nature, though highly ennobled, we cannot expect any other principle than that of following his nature: not, indeed, the ideal nature of man—for this is an abstraction which man reaches only by means of a long process of reflection—but his own empirical nature, as he finds it present in himself; for this is indeed that natural product as which man has to consider himself according to that theory. Where this leads to, everybody knows who knows human nature. If these consequences are not to be found in all ethical naturalists, and if they are perhaps the least evident in the system and life of the very ones who otherwise teach naturalism the most logically (Strauss, for example), we again most cheerfully admit that many men are better than their systems, and that in making objection to a system, even an ethical system, we in the first place do not say anything at all about the advocates of this system and their moral value. Often enough some noble and fruitful truth has been advocated by men who are personally contemptible, and often enough some dangerous error is propagated by men who are personally very amiable and moral, although the damage which such an error carries with it, must become evident in their lives, on closer observation. Besides, we must not overlook the fact, that what in a perverse system is still relatively true, and the thing which gives it a relative vitality, is borrowed from truth and from the correct system; and that all those who oppose the present fundamentals of morality, and especially of Christian morality, in a thousand ways live upon and consume the possessions which they owe to the same influences against which they contend.

But to whatever relative height the moral nobility of single advocates of ethical naturalism may rise, it is not able, at least not from its own principles, to produce thoroughly moral and truly cultivated characters; such are only produced where that which forms the character, flows out of a spring of life whose origin is *above* nature and its series of causes.

From this we see that for the most part a very low idea of personality, a very low derivation of the motives of human action, is found in the works of Darwinistic moralists—as, *e.g.*, we have seen in the works of Häckel that to him the idea of a personality of God is inseparably connected with the idea of capricious arbitrariness, and that he derives all actions of all men from the motives of egoism.

But we also see, from still more common evidences, the fact that some of the very highest blossoms and noblest fruits of human virtue, as they ripen on the ground of Christian morality, are not even acknowledged, much less required, by ethical naturalism. We think particularly of the virtues of *love*, of *self-denial*, and of *humility*. Certainly, we do not deny that men who are inclined toward naturalism can and do possess love to a certain degree, but the highest exemplification of love, the love of enemies in the fullest sense of the word—not only compassion on the battle-field, but the full, forgiving, blessing love which renders good for evil, and even intercedes for a personal enemy, although he may be the intentional and successful destroyer of our whole earthly happiness—such a love may perhaps be demanded and admired by a naturalistic moralist under the imposing influence of the presence of such a love and in unconscious dependence on the motives of Christianity which surround him; but he will never be able to show from what point of his system it is to be deduced. On the other hand, it is easy to show him more than one point of his system which, far from requiring such love, stigmatizes it as simple foolishness. Such a fruit only ripens under the care of him who gave his life for us while we still were enemies, and under the influence of the remission of our sin by our Heavenly Father.

Moreover, an ethical naturalist can also accomplish much in *self-denial*: he can make many great sacrifices, if he can thereby reach a desirable end that cannot be reached without acts of self-denial; he can show great strength and patience in a resigned endurance of the inevitable; and if we take into consideration the possibility of its being logically at variance with his system, he may perform all that which the highest morality requires. But a renunciation which is more than silent resignation, and which under certain circumstances can also become a joyful renunciation of all that was beloved and dear to man on earth, does not grow out of the soil of naturalism, and is possible only there where man carries in himself a possession which would render him still more fortunate and happy than the idea of species, and where he knows the cross of Jesus, and understands the word of the Lord: "He that loveth his life shall lose it; and he that loseth his life for my sake, shall find it." Strauss is a striking proof that naturalism is not able to estimate the tasks of self-denial at their full importance. In his "The Old Faith and the New," although he speaks with great earnestness of moral demands, yet he deeply degrades that which is connected with a Christian renunciation of self and the world, when he reproaches Christianity with "a thorough cult of poverty and *mendicity*" (!) and, regarding its demand for self-denial, he denies that it has any comprehension of the tasks of industry, of the virtues of home and family life, of patriotism and civil virtue.

Finally, we may make a similar statement in regard to *humility*. There certainly are ethical naturalists also who are modest. But when the prophets of ethical naturalism again and again announce that the great aim of all the discoveries of the evolution theory is to show us how far mankind has fortunately progressed; when their spirit of devotion is nourished by Göthe's Promethean word: "Hast thou not thyself accomplished all, thou holy glowing heart?"—and even when Häckel prints as the leading motto of his "Anthropogeny" Göthe's poem "Prometheus"; when the struggle of selection is also elevated to a moral principle, and the life-task of an individual is limited to creating elbow-room for himself: then humility, indeed, is a virtue which a naturalist may acquire, not through his naturalism, but in spite of it; and the great *naïveté* with which, in books of that tendency, haughtiness and passion for glory are treated as something necessarily understood, and their own ego is glorified, is a much more logical result. "We are proud of having so immensely out-stripped our lower animal ancestors, and derive from it the consoling assurance that in future also, mankind, as a whole, will follow the *glorious* career of progressive development, and attain a still higher degree of mental perfection." (Häckel, "Hist. of Creat.") This is the theme which is repeated in many variations in all books of similar tendency. In the same book already referred to, we read: "Each free and highly developed individual, each *original* person, has his own religion, his own God; *so it is certainly not arrogance* when we also claim the right of forming our own idea of God." Or, "The recognition of the theory of development and the monistic philosophy based upon it forms the best criterion for the degree of man's mental development." L. Büchner, in his collection of essays, "Aus Natur und Welt" ("From Nature and the World"), dedicates a long chapter to self-glorification, and finds confirmed in himself the word of the poet, "Great destinies are always preceded by spirit messengers"; and he, still living, prefaces his own biography in the latest edition of "Kraft und Stoff" ("Force and Matter"), and on the first page of the same publishes the testimonial which he received, when leaving the gymnasium: "The bearer of this testimonial excelled in the thorough study of literature, philosophy, and poetry, and as regards style in his productions showed an excellent talent." In view of these things, we certainly do no injustice to this tendency when we deny to it the conception of the idea and the practice of humility.

§ 2. *Scientific Darwinism and Moral Life.*

It is evident from the peace-relation between mere scientific Darwinism and moral principles, that naturo-historical Darwinism also remains in peace with moral life. We therefore have no longer to treat of any question of competency in the realm of concrete moral life, but only to mention the points of contact in which both realms, fully acknowledging their mutual independence, yet in an inferior way exercise some beneficial influence upon each other.

Moral life influences Darwinism in so far as, by its mere existence, it cautions the advocate of the scientific evolution theory against effacing the differences between the moral and the natural, and against degrading man to the level of animals on account of his connection with the animal world. The naturo-historical idea of evolution, in case it should turn out to be correct, would exercise an influence upon moral life in a three-fold direction: First, it would add to all the motives of the humane treatment of the animal world—which certainly without it already has moral demands—a new one, and establish them all more firmly. Man would then recognize in the animal world which surrounds him branches of his own natural pedigree, and exercise his right of mastery only in the sense which Alex. Braun expresses, when he says: "Man consents to the idea of being appointed master of animals; but then he must also acknowledge that he is not placed over his subjects as a stranger, but proceeded from the people itself, whose master he wishes to be." A second service which the idea of evolution would have to render to the forming of moral life, would consist in the fact that it would favor all those ethical modes of contemplation and those maxims which regard the gradual process of development and the growth of character as the relative power of influences and conditions, and that it would give them hints for the perception of moral growth, in like manner as, in the before-mentioned parable, the Lord illustrates the imperceptible and continual growth of the kingdom of God with the growth of a plant. A third service which the evolution theory might be able to render to moral life, would consist in the fact that it would give to the motive of perfection and progress, which is always and everywhere a moral lever, a new illustration and a new weight by pointing at the progress which development has to show in the life of nature.

CONCLUSION.

If now, having reached our goal, we look back upon the way which we have traversed, we find a justification of the regret expressed at the beginning, that a scientific treatment of religion and morality is compelled to take a position in regard to theories which are not yet established. We found the most different problems—scientific, naturo-philosophical, metaphysical, religious and ethical—inextricably mixed, and were obliged, as one of our first tasks, to make an attempt at finding the clew and at examining and testing each single problem, together with attempts at its solution, separately, although keeping constantly in mind its connection with all other problems and their attempts at solution. We found ourselves led into the presence of a series of the most interesting problems, but not a single solution finished. That very attempt at solution which brought up this whole question, and which was repeatedly announced as the infallible key to the solution of all scientific problems—the selection theory—we found a decided failure, at least in the direction of the extension and importance which was given to this theory. And yet in spite of the hypothetical nature of all attempts at solution, we see investigators in all the realms of natural science strongly attracted by the very promising character of these problems and busily engaged in making attempts at solution; and we see even philosophy strongly attracted by its interest in these works. Such a diligent work can certainly not be without gain; but wherein will this gain consist? Will it, as its antagonists prophecy, be like that which in former times alchemy brought to science, which, indeed, enriched chemistry by an entire series of new discoveries, but did not find what it sought, the one fundamental element from which all the rest are derived, which only confirmed, with a power acknowledged even to-day, the old doctrine of the elementary difference of the elements? Will the Darwinian investigations thus also make all possible discoveries *by the way*, but in place of that which they look for, in place of a common pedigree or of a few pedigrees for all organisms, finally only give additional strength to the permanence of species and the unapproachableness of the secret of their origin? Or can we derive from the reasons which the investigators urge in favor of the idea of an origin of species through descent and evolution, the hope that that mysterious darkness of prehistoric times upon which the works of our century have shed so much light, will still be illuminated even to the sources from which organic species came, and from which mankind also originated? We must leave the decision of these questions to the future and to scientists.

But we have to note *one* gain, which is so great that on its account, we willingly cease our regret in regard to the unfinished condition of these theories; for we owe the full enjoyment of this gain to that very unfinished condition. It is the gain which *religion and morality* get from these investigations, and which consists in the new and comprehensive confirmation of the conviction, which, indeed, was established before, that religion and morality—Christian religion and Christian morality—rest on foundations which can no longer be shaken by any result of exact investigation.

The triumph with which the Darwinian theories were greeted by many as the new sun before whose rising all that mankind had thus far called light and sun turns pale, and the antipathy with which, on that very account, many to whom their religious and ethical acquisitions are a sacred sanctuary, turn away from these theories, urged us to investigate their position in reference to religion and morality. Now, if these theories had produced a certain undoubted result, we should unquestionably have been satisfied with the examination of the position of religion and morality in reference to this certain result. But since not a single result of those investigations is really established, we have found ourselves obliged to give our investigation a much greater extension and to discuss even all imaginable *possibilities*. The beneficial result of this comparison was, that religion and morality not only remain at peace with all imaginable possibilities of *scientific* theories, but can also, in the realm of the *philosophy of the doctrines of nature*, be passive spectators of all investigations and attempts, even of all possible excursions into the realm of fancy, without being obliged to interfere. It is in the realm of *mere metaphysics* that we first perceive an antagonist whose victory would indeed be fatal to the religious and ethical acquisitions of mankind: this antagonist is called elimination from nature of the idea of design. Fortunately, this metaphysical idea is in such striking opposition not only to the whole world of facts but also to all logical reasoning, it has everywhere, where man perceives organization and a difference between lower and higher, especially in the contemplation of the world, of this *cosmos* of wonderful order and beauty, so decidedly all philosophical as well as all exact sciences as its adversaries, it lays its hands so rudely and so destructively not only upon the religious and ethical acquisitions but also upon all ideal remaining acquisitions of mankind, that religion and morality know, when fighting this adversary, they are in firm accord with all the spiritual interests of mankind.

This, in its most essential features, is the pleasing result of our critical examination; and such a demonstration of the immovably solid foundation, secure from all the change of opinions and all the progress of discoveries on which morality and religion rest, has still an entire series of further pleasing consequences in its train.

In the first place, it is a living and actual proof of the fact that religion and morality give to all sciences *the full freedom of investigation*. The religious and ethical interest itself not only gives, but even *requires*, this freedom of investigation. It requires it in consequence of that *impulse of truth* which religion has in common with every impulse of knowledge, and which in itself is an ethical impulse. In consequence of this impulse, religion must found its possession on nothing else than subjective and objective truth, and can look upon all the paths which lead through even the remotest realm of knowledge to the establishment of truth, only with sympathetic interest. Precisely those who see in religion more than a mere expression of emotion, and all those who require that their religious life and the object of their religious faith shall possess truth, subjective and objective, cannot commit any greater folly than treating search for truth in any other realm with suspicion, or even ignoring it. They only injure that which they meant to defend, by rendering the purity of their own religious interest suspected, and by establishing more firmly the breach between religious life and faith and the other acquisitions of culture and interests of their time, of which neither religion nor science, but only a misguided tendency of their minds and hearts, is guilty. How much unfriendly and unjust judgment has already found utterance by means of the pen and voice, in reference to honest and meritorious workers, on the part of religious zealots who fail to recognize that close relationship of the religious with the scientific impulse of truth! How often and how much does such a judgment gain great consideration from a public of which but a few are able to form an independent opinion of the men and works which are thus abused before their eyes and ears, and how much of the aversion to the form in which the religious life of the present offers itself, on the part of those men who are thus suspected, is in the last instance to be attributed neither to be irreligiousness of these men nor to the deficiency of the present form of our religious life, but to the repelling effect of that unjust treatment!

Another gain of our discussion, correlated to that just mentioned, consists in the proof *that religion and morality have their autonomous principle and realm* which is not at all obliged to borrow the proof of its truth from the present condition and degree of our knowledge, but carries it in itself, although it stands in fruitful reciprocal action with all the other realms of knowledge and life. Just as decidedly as we had to caution the advocates of religion against keeping themselves indifferent, suspicious, or even hostile, regarding the advances into the realm of secular knowledge, so decidedly do we like to see the workers in the realm of the knowledge of nature cautioned against confusing points of view, in thinking that they can through their scientific knowledge purify and reform the religious and ethical realms. They may purify and reform as much as they please, but only in their own realm. The only thing they are able to reform is our knowledge of nature, and in our religious and ethical life and perception only that which belongs to this natural part; but this is only the outer part of religious and ethical life: the source of our religion and morality springs from quite another ground than that which they cultivate.

A third gain from our discussion is the actual proof of *the harmony between faith and knowledge, between the religious and the scientific views of the world.* In our investigation we had no occasion for psychological or theoretical investigations as to faith and knowledge and their mutual relation; but if our discussion is not an entire failure, perhaps the actual exposition of a standpoint on which faith and knowledge may live at peace with one another, which is not bought by a sacrifice on either side, and which does not consist in a compromise of the two, but which has its reason in the deepest and most active interest of the one, in the full and unconstrained freedom of the other, a stronger proof for the intimate relationship of these brothers, between whom the present generation wishes too often to sow discord, than if we had undertaken long religio-philosophical and theoretical investigations.

Finally, the results of our analysis have given us still another gain: they have led us beyond Lessing's "Nathan" and his parable of the "Three Rings." We call this a gain, without the least intention of discrediting by it the motives of tolerance and the points of view for the judgment of the character and religiousness of human individuals, which lay in that parable, or suspecting the motives of so many of our contemporaries whose religio-philosophical judgment is entirely expressed in that parable. We saw ourselves compelled to make a choice either of accepting or of rejecting ends in the world, and found that the world resolves itself into a senseless game at dice, and that the phenomena become more unintelligible the more important they are, if we ignore or even reject teleology. The acknowledgment of the latter prevented us from seeing in the world and its events merely the eternal stream of planless coming and going; it prevented us from accepting such an endless stream of appearance and disappearance, and therefore also an endless stream of the appearance and disappearance of new forms of religion in that creature for whose appearance we see all other creatures are only a preparation, and are even obliged to look upon them as a preparation in accordance with no other theory more than that of evolution. It also urged us to inquire as to the ends and designs of mankind, and we found this end in the disposition of man for a communion with God, for the state of bearing his image and of being his child. Now we have fully to acknowledge that Christianity, like all religions which claim truth and universal acceptance, is to be analyzed with the very same means of science as all phenomena in the world of facts, and that therefore it is especially subject to all investigations of religio-philosophical, religio-historical, and historical criticism, to its fullest extent. But precisely such an analysis of Christianity leads us to a result which elevates Christian religion high above all other forms. It also confirms by means of science what, indeed, is established to a Christian mind as certainty from his own direct experience, that the quintessence of that which Christianity offers us, is truth and gives full satisfaction to soul and mind. For that analysis establishes, in the first place, that Christianity shows us the idea of God and the nature and destiny of man in a purity such as no other religion does, and in such a life-creating power that it is able to satisfy most completely all the nobler desires and impulses of soul and mind, and to overcome most successfully all ignoble ones. Furthermore, it shows us that these gifts of Christianity offered themselves, and still offer themselves, not only in philosophemes and doctrines, in parables and myths, in postulates and prophecies, but what, indeed, is not the case in any other religion, in an arranged course of deeds and facts which, in everything that is necessary and essential for the acquisition of that idea of God and for the realization of that ideal of mankind, legitimate themselves to criticism as historical facts, and which legitimate themselves as actions of divine manifestation by the fact, that they and their consequences also are really able to fulfill what they promise, and to bring mankind nearer to the accomplishment of that goal which they set up for it. Finally, it shows us, when it reviews and compares the development of culture among all mankind, that the Christian nations have really borne the richest blossom and fruit which has appeared hitherto on the tree of mankind, and that Christianity, for the life of nations, has not only, like other religions, powers of preservation, but also powers of renovation and renewal which other religions are wanting. Even all the errors of superstition and immorality, of intolerance and lust of power, of so many of its advocates and confessors, at which the adversaries of the Christian view of the world so willingly point, are but a confirmation of its value. For they show us how divine and heavenly the gift must be, if even such errors were not able to smother its fruits. If we do not wish to suppose that mankind has foundations and ends which up to the present it is not yet allowed to know, we certainly must look for these foundations and ends where we find the best which has so far been given to mankind and which has been accomplished by it.

This acknowledgment of Christianity as the only true and only really universal religion leads us beyond another sentiment of Lessing, which has found an equally strong or perhaps still stronger echo in the mind. We mean the expression that, if he had to choose, he would prefer the continual search for truth to the possession of truth itself. We emphatically acknowledge the holy right and the high nobility of this impulse of investigation and activity, but we need not buy its acknowledgment and satisfaction at the price of being obliged to renounce a consciousness or the hope of a consciousness which is equally indispensable to our inner happiness as that impulse of investigation, and which first gives to this impulse its overwhelming power—namely, the consciousness and the hope of really possessing the truth. For, in fact, we are not required to make this choice. There is a possession of truth which does not exclude, but requires, the search for truth: that is the possession of truth in the answer to the questions as to the starting point and the goal of our life, the possession of truth in the fundamentals of our religious view of the world. It is the certainty about the starting-point and goal of our life, which lastingly and effectively invites us also to look for and perceive all the ways which, in theory as well as in practice, lead from a firm starting-point to a certain end, and only the possession of truth in the fundamentals of our religious view of the world gives value and satisfaction to investigation in a world which, without this possession, contains for us only transitory and fleeting, and therefore only unsatisfactory, things, but which stands before us as the work and the theatre of revelation of a God and Father, and therefore gives to investigation inexhaustible joy and satisfaction when we look upon it from those stand-points.

In like manner as, at the outset of our investigation, we perceived in organic species creations of God, and in spite of this, or rather on account of it, looked upon the attempts at exploring their origin with so much deeper interest, we also see ourselves, in the still more direct religious realm, not at all condemned to stagnation when we acknowledge Christianity as absolute religion. This very acknowledgment alone makes a real progress possible for us. For every progress, in order to be a real progress, needs a firm starting- point and a certain goal; hence that which is shown and offered to mankind in Christianity. From this starting-point and toward this end there are tasks enough for religious progress. The ever more definite investigation of the facts and doctrines of Christianity, the improvement and ever more complete reproduction of the scientific image in which these facts and doctrines are reflected in the mind of man the progressing adaptation of ecclesiastical life in divine service, and organization to the substance and the need of Christian religiousness, the harmonizing of our possession of faith with all other elements of culture of each period, the working up of that which is given to us in Christianity into the spiritual and ethical acquisition of a single personality and its ever more complete representation and realization in the individual and the common life, the progressing penetration of generations by the transfiguring light of religion and morality, and the progressive overcoming of the likewise progressingly developing kingdom of evil—in short, all that which the language of religion calls the growth of the kingdom of God, is work and progress enough, but certainly work and progress on the ground of a certain basis as the starting-point given to us by God, and work and progress toward a certain goal set for us by God.

It is only from this basis of a possession of truth as it is offered to us by Christian theism, and by the facts of redemption and of a reconciliation of man with God, that the breach between faith and knowledge, between religion and the life of culture, which at present takes place in so many a heart and mind, can be healed; and, far from seeking to cripple or hinder those who stand on this basis, it alone gives to their theoretical and practical activity its joyous strength and certain end, to their sphere of knowledge its universal breadth. The Apostle Paul, at the end of 1 Corinthians, xv, when he takes a comprehensive view from the highest points of Christian hope to which he found himself led from those fundamentals, knows of no fitter words to conclude with and to give it a practical application than these: "Wherefore, my beloved brethren, be ye steadfast, unmoveable, always abounding in the work of the Lord, forasmuch as ye know that your labour is not vain in the Lord."

Notes

[1] "The International Scientific Series." No. xiii.
[2] "Evolution of Man."
[3] It was only when the manuscript of this work was nearly finished and the first part of it had gone to the press, that the author received the second part of K. E. von Baer's *"Studien aus dem Gebiete der Naturwissenschaften"* (Studies in the Realm of Natural Sciences). It contains another essay on teleology, *"Ueber Zielstrebigkeit in den organischen Körpern insbesondere,"* and a treatise on Darwin's doctrine, *"Ueber Darwin's Lehre,"* which Baer had promised long ago and which the public had anxiously awaited. It is no little satisfaction to find that I, from my modest premises, reached results regarding the naturo-philosophical problems and their weight in the religious realm which so fully harmonize with the views of this first authority in the realm of the history of development. I shall still have occasion here and there to avail myself of a study of this latest and most important publication upon the question of Darwinism, and shall confine myself here to the remark that von Baer, although he rejects the selection theory and the superficial treatment of the principle of evolution on the part of materialists, is by no means disinclined to the idea of the origin of species through descent, whether in gradual development or in leaps; and that in this respect he could no longer be counted among the advocates of the group above referred to, but among those which we mention farther on, had he not repeatedly and forcibly confessed, with a modesty worthy of acknowledgment, his total ignorance concerning the manner in which certain forms of life, especially the higher ones, originated. The origin of higher species without the supposition of a descent is to him unexplainable, because the individuals of these species are, in their first development of life, so dependent on the mother. Furthermore, he points out the fact that in early periods of the earth the organic forming power which ruled, must have been a higher one than it is at the present time; in like manner as the first period in the embryonic development of individuals is to-day the most productive. This higher power of organization, he says, could consist in a higher power of changing organisms into new species, as well as in a higher power of producing new species through primitive generation; or it could consist in both. In general, there is no reason to suppose that primitive generations which took place at the first origination of life on earth, could not have been repeated

later and oftener. The nearer a generation was to these individuals originated through primitive generation, the greater was undoubtedly its flexibility and changeableness; the farther, the greater the fixity of type.

[4] After the completion this manuscript, the author found that K. E. von Baer, in his treatise upon Darwin's doctrine, pays especial attention to the change of generation and also to the metamorphosis of plants and animals in exactly the same sense and reaches the same conclusion.

[5] Compare Max Müller, "Lectures on the Science of Language," 6th ed., London, 1871, vol. I, p. 403.

[6] Compare v. Baer, "Studies, etc.," p. 294 ff.

[7] Darwin says, on page 146, Eng. Ed., of his "Descent of Man": "In the earlier editions of my 'Origin of Species', I perhaps attributed too much to the action of natural selection or the survival of the fittest.... I did not formerly sufficiently consider the existence of structures which, as far as we can at present judge, are neither beneficial nor injurious; and this I believe to be one of the greatest oversights as yet detected in my work.... An unexplained residuum of change, perhaps a large one, must be left to the assumed uniform action of those unknown agencies, which occasionally induce strongly-marked and abrupt deviations of structure in our domestic productions."

[8] This word, which is of recent coinage in Germany, has been found so incapable of being rendered by an exact English equivalent, that it has been thought best to retain it and to give the author's own explanation of the meaning which he desired it to express. He says, in a note to the translator: "I was led to this idea [of *Auslosung*] in a small essay of Robert von Mayer ("Ueber Auslösung," 1876). Afterwards Mayer personally stated to me that he heartily approved the emphasis I had given to this idea, and said that he had only thought of the fact that psychical processes, like the action of the will, *losen aus* (release) physiological processes, like the action of the muscles, and that I had carried the idea farther, in saying that psychical processes are *ausgelost* (released) by physiological processes, and that this is a very important step farther on the way of investigation. Mayer himself thought it would be necessary to call the attention to this, when he further developed the ideas he had given in the before-mentioned essay; his intention to do so was prevented by his death.

"*Auslosung* is a word originated by modern mechanical science, and means: (1.) Slight mechanical operations of detaching and the like, by which another and more important action, whose forces were heretofore restrained, can be set into activity: *e.g.*, the pressure which sets in motion a machine, previously at rest, is *Auslosung*; the pressure on the trigger of a gun is *Auslosung*; the friction of a match which is the beginning of a great fire is *Auslosung*. (2.) This idea may now be applied to chemical processes: *e.g.*, a glass of sugar-water will remain sweet unless some foreign element is introduced into it, but the moment it receives a fermenting substance either by chance, from the air, or with intention, then the sugar water is brought into a process of chemical decomposition, and from this there results *Auslosung;* but the introduction of the fermenting agent into the sugar-water is *Auslosung*. (3.) Von Mayer applies this idea to psycho-physical relations of life, and says: when the will acting through the agency of the motor nerves sets in motion the muscles, this is *Auslosung*."—[Trans.]

[9] For the use of readers who do not understand Greek, we may state that the word *teleology* is derived from the Greek word *telos*, Gen. *teleos*: end, purpose, aim; and means the "doctrine of design or a conformity to the end in view," or, as K. E. von Baer prefers and wishes to have introduced into scientific language, "the doctrine of the striving toward an end" (*Zielstrebigkeit*). It seems to be quite a superficial treatment of an idea on whose reception or rejection no less a thing than an entire view of the world with all its most important and deepest questions depends, when Dr. G. Seidlitz, in an essay on the success of Darwinism ("Ausland," 1874, No. 37), states incidentally that teleology is derived from the Greek τέλεος *perfect*. It is true that the Greek adjective for perfect is also derived from that noun, τέλος, which has the same root as the German word *Ziel*, and there is even an Ionic form for that adjective
which is τέλεος, but the Attic form is τέλειος; and since modern languages, when a choice is allowed, do not derive their Greek foreign words from the Ionic, but from the Attic dialect, that word —were it really derived from that adjective and did it express "doctrine of perfection"—would have to be teleiology, or, in Latinized form, teliology. As far as we know, the word, since it was introduced into scientific language, has never been derived from any other root than from τέλος, Gen. τέλεος, *end*, and has never been used in any other sense than to express the doctrine of a purpose and end in the world.

[10] Compare "History, Essays, and Orations of the 6th General Conference of the Evangelical Alliance," New York, Harper Bros., 1874, p. 264-271.

[11] Compare D. F. Strauss, the most celebrated moral philosopher of Monism, in § 74 of his "The Old Faith and the New."

www.ingramcontent.com/pod-product-compliance
Lightning Source LLC
Chambersburg PA
CBHW051220300426
44116CB00006B/653